NUMBER SEVEN

n+1

FALL 2008

n+1

CORRECTION

THE INTELLECTUAL SITUATION

POLITICS

NUMBER SEVEN
FALL 2008

BLOOD SAUSAGE

HOME AND AWAY

REVIEWS

LETTERS

n+1

n+1 is published twice a year by n+1 Foundation, Inc., 68 Jay Street #405, Brooklyn, NY 11201. Single issues are available for $11.95. Subscriptions for $20 (two issues); in Canada, $25; other international, $30 (surface), $40 (airmail). Subscriptions and correspondence to the Editors, 68 Jay Street #405, Brooklyn, NY 11201. Manuscripts will not be returned. Please correspond before submitting. *n+1* is distributed by Ingram, Ubiquity, and Emma Marian and Disticor in Canada.

To place an ad in *n+1* contact ads@nplusonemag.com. *n+1*, Number Seven
 ISSN 1549-0033. ISBN 0-9760503-6-6.

WWW.NPLUSONEMAG.COM

THE INTELLECTUAL SITUATION

A Diary

PRESIDENT OBAMA! WE SALUTE YOU. WE salute you here in mid-October, though we've been hurt before. In 2000 we had "GO-RE" tattooed across our chest, and had to turn it into "GO REDS" and move to Cincinnati. (Eventually we put a shirt on and came back to New York.) Still: *President Obama!* If this is a dream, then we'll stay in it. Forget reality! Lately we find ourselves shouting in our sleep: President Obama!

"What?!" says our old friend, shaking us out of the trance. "It's me. It's *Michael*. Jesus, you see a black man and all of a sudden you're shouting 'Obama!'"

His wife is up. "Let's all just go get breakfast," she says. We've been staying with them for a couple weeks, just between jobs.

"He thinks we all look like Obama," Michael says. "That's incorrect."

Forgive us. We've got to go to the shrink. A 10 AM appointment.

"You ought to go. You could use some help. You've got to make a correction."

We get up off the couch and pull on our skinny jeans.

"You know who looks the same?" Michael says. "It's you hipsters."

CORRECTION

IN ISSUE SIX, WE PUBLISHED A POEM, "Literature Will Be Tested," which was included in an untranslated essay by the Russian poet Kirill Medvedev who, because of his principled opposition to all literary institutions, refuses either to give or deny anyone the right to publish him. This superb Medvedev poem, we later discovered, was written by Bertolt Brecht.

We now publish another Brecht poem, "For Future Generations," produced by the same method of translation from German to Russian to English.

For Future Generations

We live in a dark time.
When to speak without anger is only to
  reveal that you're a fool.
When a forehead without wrinkles
Is testament to your heartlessness. When
  he who laughs
Has simply not yet heard
The terrible news.

What sort of time is this, when
To speak of the trees seems a crime,
Since it means you're keeping silent about
  violence?
He who steps calmly down the street
Must be deaf to the sufferings and sorrows
Of his friends.

We can still earn enough to live on,
But believe us: That's an accident. Nothing
We do gives us the right
To eat our fill.
We've survived by accident.
(If they notice our success, we're finished.)

They say to us: "Eat and drink! Be glad at
least you're not hungry!"
But how can we eat and drink if
We're taking food away from the starving, if
The glass of water we drink is what a
thirsty man needs?
And yet we eat and drink.

We'd like to be wise men.
The ancient books tell us what wisdom is.
It means to put aside the battles of the world
and live one's life
Knowing no fear.
To abjure violence.
To answer evil with kindness.
Not to get one's wishes, but to forget them.
This is considered wisdom.
And we're incapable of it.

We live in a dark time.

CORRECTION

THE PUBLISHING HOUSE SOFT SKULL, IN A recent catalog, announced that its new book *Coming of Age at the End of History*, by the young Frenchman Camille de Toledo, had been excerpted in *n+1*. Unfortunately, it hadn't been. To fix the historical record, we here excerpt the book.

> I ask you, and try to use your imagination, do you think growing up is easy when your mother is a cemetery? Was Fukuyama right? That's a question for philosophers, not for me. But take the phrase "We're at the end of History." Try to listen to that with the ears of a child at bedtime. Try to hear what those words sound like as the book closes and voices are hushed, as the lights are turned out and the dim figures of the people who put us to sleep slip away with a phrase gentle and disturbing at the same time: Sleep tight.
>
> . . . The crisis was past. We were the happy campers. There was nothing left to do but live happily ever after and sleep tight. We are the children of that funeral elegy. It would have been easy to believe it. To believe that any attempt at creating something is in vain, that writing is just a form of masturbation, that resistance is futile. The various causes that might have given us a reason to keep going were either retro or obsolete, check the right box. Independence? Retro. Alienation? Obsolete. Punk Rock? Retro. Rock and Roll? Obsolete. Unionism? Obsolete. Communism? Retro. Modernity? Outmoded.

CORRECTION

IN ISSUE THREE, WE VOICED SKEPTICISM toward the rhetoric of the "reading crisis" that uses the grim statistics—the declining numbers of serious readers—to cover up shoddy literature and literary practices. We deplored the protective argument that anything that encourages reading is good, and that all writing encourages reading, especially writing that's not hard to read, even when it's written by people who themselves don't read.

We were right about the bogus crisis but we missed the real story. We have a *writing crisis* on our hands. Everybody in the country is writing books but only a fraction of that number is interested in reading them; while the Chinese *work*, we workshop. There's no bigger folly than writing instruction displacing "literature" in college English, though this seems to be what's happening—not because you can't teach writing, but because there's no point in teaching writing when you haven't reproduced the art of reading. The best you can hope to do is create an artificial market of people who will have to purchase the current round of books, whatever they may be, because they weren't given the skills to read the books that came before. It's like those Hollywood remakes that trade on the fact that modern viewers *can't* watch black and white, or Technicolor, or even actors with bygone accents and uptight hairdos.

CORRECTION

WE HAVE KEPT UP A CONSTANT CRITIQUE OF hipsterism as a new politics of identity adopted by a subset of the bourgeoisie at the end of the 20th century—a particular manifestation of class privilege in the West. (Cf. in particular Christian Lorentzen's work at nplusonemag.com.) Our failure was not to look into the future: What will happen to the hipster in the age of American decline? In New York already we can see the forces ranged against each other in the next century. On the Lower East Side, Chinatown has fought Hipsterville to a standstill. It is the forces of immigrant dynamism against the forces of "native" capital. The hipsters expand southward; the Chinese northward. Right now the hipsters control the area from Grand up to 14th Street, the Chinese from Delancey down to City Hall. That Chinatown will now expand southward to take over the canyons of the abandoned financial district is beyond a doubt, but who will rule the battle zone between Delancey and Grand? If the hipsters once had, through the good graces of their wealthy suburban parents, a serious economic edge to counter the superior numbers in Chinatown, that disappears with the collapse of the credit bubble.

Our analysis will be continued in an upcoming Research Series pamphlet, "What Was the Hipster?," sponsored by the State Department.

CORRECTION

SINCE OUR FIRST ISSUE WE HAVE MAINtained a steadfast policy against the overvaluation of the dead and gone. Until the current issue, we have not published works by dead authors or artists, nor devoted articles to the long dead, nor reviewed the ubiquitous reprints of dead people's publications—not because dead authors aren't the best (they are), but because we believe in the necessity of a contemporary and progressive American literature, fed by and in dialogue with the foreign and the dead, and the foreign dead, but facing forward. Really, the dead have too many publishing opportunities already. Since they don't need to eat, they don't need to be paid: a favorite situation of publishers. Plus they've already turned in their manuscripts.

We believe in the idea of a magazine devoted to the best unpublishable and unpublished work of our own time, working toward a new culture to rival any in the past. But confidence is harder to muster these days. Maybe it's the economy. Maybe it's the writing crisis. Anyway, we're publishing work by dead people, just in this issue—lucky number 7. We'll be carting the corpses back into the tomb for Issue Eight.

WE WENT BACK TO SLEEP in our jeans as soon as Michael and Mary went out to breakfast. All these weird dreams again. Maybe it's the Ambien; it's been months now that we've been taking it, ever since the summer. Lately we wake shouting the poll numbers; we see the swing states hovering, blurring, merging. Or maybe it's just that, as the poll numbers improved, we started to relax, swaddled under the promise of an American patchwork quilt turning blue in the dawn.

Now we sleep enough to dream, and this one's a doozy. We're in a familiar—an unfamiliar place. Smells of boiled cabbage . . . the tang of unwashed bodies . . . signs along the walls, in an alphabet we can't read. We're in a crowd of people, faces tired and greenish under flickering fluorescent bulbs, the young in tracksuits, the old in winter coats, a group of drunks in desert fatigues against a wall, two of them missing legs. The tottering soldiers come toward us, waving bottles, and one of them, a white-haired veteran with the face of John McCain, grabs us by the lapels with his working arm. "You!" he exhales. "You will be the third!" Then the metro roars into the station, the Cyrillic letters assemble a language, and, in the header of a fluttering newspaper scrap, we learn where we are: Moscow, November 5, 1988. How on earth—?

AMERICAN GORBACHEV

THE AMERICA OUR NEW PRESIDENT INHERits bears an uncanny resemblance to our old enemy, the Soviet Union—right before it went under. Our country's paranoia and stubbornness have secured us indifferent allies and intractable commitments. Not only is there Afghanistan—still Afghanistan—where we fight the same enemy we once created to bleed the Russians, but just to show that we can do everything twice as much, twice as well, as anybody else, we've added Iraq. And as we export our defective version of democracy to the Middle East, in Latin America, our own "near abroad," our efforts have raised resistance to American influence to new levels. The Chileans, the Argentines, the Bolivians—they were pioneers, they privatized everything, and look at them now. Our satellites are dropping from their orbits! But what is to be done? As Colin Powell once said: "We do deserts, we don't do mountains."

Late-imperial malaise prevails on the home front too. Our new President presides over a recession (if not worse), a dilapidated infrastructure, an aging population, and more numerous environmental catastrophes: wildfires and drought in the Southwest, a longer and more brutal hurricane season along the Gulf Coast and Eastern seaboard, harbingers of greater, unknown changes to come. We didn't have a Chernobyl, but we had Katrina. (Or was it *Katarina*?)

There's also the problem of the government itself. It wasn't discussed much in the campaign. No anchorperson asked the candidates: What will the next President do to restore trust in American government and democracy? People may not like George Bush, but they have been liking Congress even less. They think the politicians are in it for themselves, or care more for party than for country, or are too tightly intertwined with the heads of industry: *nomenklatura*, in short. It may not matter that, like the Soviets did, we have a lovely Constitution.

What happened to us? In the earlier days of the cold war, America's struggle with the Soviet Union was supposed to be the struggle of democracy against totalitarianism. (Never mind that half the guys we overthrew—from Arbenz and Mossadegh onward—had been democratically elected.) Then, in the '80s, following Reagan and his party, America's gradual defeat of the Soviet Union was set down to the inevitable triumph of capitalism over communism. This story, which also became the Democratic Party's narrative, and, for much of the last two decades, the whole world's fairy tale, did America the disservice of recasting it in the image made for us by our former adversaries: that of the capitalist imperialist. With our invasion of Iraq, we at last fully embraced the caricature. (The Bush people, in drawing up new laws allowing 100 percent foreign ownership of Iraqi banks, mines, and factories, and permitting the repatriation of 100 percent of profits, revealed what they thought a *really* lovely constitution looked like.) By throwing Marx into the dustbin, we accidentally dusted off and polished his view of history as the history of class struggle. Meanwhile, the self-evident truth of free-market thought has in recent months come to resemble the statist gospel of the Soviets. Who believes in it now?

WE TELL OUR SHRINK—an NYU student shrink, really it's as cheap as beauty school haircuts—that we don't really think America will turn into a latter-day Soviet Russia.

"Are you trying to convince me or yourself?" the shrink replies.

But aren't all dreams wish fulfillments of a kind?

"Who's the Freudian here?"

Well, *do* we secretly hate America? *Do* we want it to fail? Is that what our dream was telling us? No, what we really want, our actual heart's desire—

"Now we're getting somewhere."

—we want a President who will end the cold war!

"Hmn?"

Don't you see? Gorbachev tried to end the war—and did, only things got out of hand—and we want a President with the courage to abandon the false ideological struggle between capitalism and everything else. Let the members of our old bloc go their own way—let them be Bolivarians if they want. We won't intervene. We also believe in *glasnost*: at home, we need a new intellectual openness to wriggle free of the intolerant "old thinking." Abroad, we need to stop staring into people's eyes to see their souls, and start reminding them of American sanity and civility. And we want electoral reform while we're at it—proportional representation, instant run-off voting, public financing of campaigns, all that stuff—because the way the *nomenklatura* currently acquire their posts has them flattering ideologues and servicing lobbyists. And we want *perestroika*, because without some economic restructuring we're sunk. You can't hold down wages while increasing consumer spending forever. You can't run an economy on petroleum, debt, and accounting tricks!

We want our new President to be an American Gorbachev—to preserve the country by changing it—if only it's not too late for him to avoid Gorbachev's fate.

BACK AT HOME BASE, our hosts are entertaining bespectacled, curly-haired Josh, their friend from interfaith Kwanzaa-Hanukah celebrations. In fact, Michael and Mary aren't so big on Kwanzaa but Josh has somehow latched onto it, designating a special menorah and encouraging them to pour libations to African ancestors. We're always a little put off by the comparative victimology that seems to be the basis of their friendship, but maybe that's just because we don't exactly have "roots" of our own.

"Six million!" Josh is crowing. "Six million!"

"Oh yeah?" says Michael. "How about sixty million? How do you like that?"

"But not killed in death factories, specially built!"

Still, the middle passage can't have been fun, we point out.

Mary is holding her head.

"*This* one," Michael says, pointing at us, "he's always on about Obama. It's Negrophilia to the utmost. It's getting on my nerves."

"Yeah, you guys had a big year, with Obama!" Josh protests. "What have we had, the sixtieth birthday of the State of Israel? *Meh.*"

"You get every year!" says Michael. "You had Amy Winehouse get a Grammy, stealing my people's shit!"

"You had Lil Wayne at number one. And that new Kanye album! Kanye dominated the Grammys!"

"You've got, like, the whole *New York Times* editorial page, and you're complaining? Not to mention the whole newsstand. You know those magazines they're pushing now?"

"*Vey iz mir,*" Josh moans. "Not the magazines. *The magazines.* Oh, I know."

THE PEOPLE OF THE MAGAZINE

THE NEW JEWISH MAGAZINES CAME ALL AT once in the first years of this decade. September 11 formed their background more than it informed their contents; further back and more explicit was the breakdown of the peace talks at Camp David in the summer of 2000 and the start of the Second Intifada that September.

A certain period of confidence for American Jews began in 1967 with the Six-Day War, as people watched on television the reuniting of Jerusalem and thousands of Israelis streaming for the first time to the Western Wall. (Those television-watchers ignored the acquisition of the West Bank and Gaza.) The period of confidence ended in three stages: July 2000, when Arafat and Barak could not reach a settlement at Camp David; September 2000, when Sharon walked atop the Temple Mount; and September 2001, when Islamic terrorists attacked the United States. The proximity of the Intifada to the terrorist attacks made something clear, finally, to younger American Jews. Israel was not a metaphysical abstraction. It was a country with a particular politics (which happened to be a bad politics). It was not the only place where Jews lived, and it was not the only place where Jews could die. The attacks meant that the Holocaust was suddenly toppled from its status as the national trauma par excellence. Almost immediately the production of Holocaust literature ceased. It was as if American Jewry had been called into history once again, not as a successful group looking backward to a historical catastrophe and sideways to a troubled distant country, but as contemporary actual living Jews. And what was our response? A restructuring of secular young Jewish life around religion was no longer an option for an urban and suburban middle class one or even two generations removed from orthodoxy. So we got the rise of JDate, the triumph of Birthright, and a group of lavishly funded Jewish magazines.

Heeb is the most professionally produced of these publications, with the highest circulation, and the most aggressive sense of its mission, which is to insult, desecrate, and otherwise trample the feelings of religiously observant or just simply liberal Jewry—while always insisting on the possession of an essential Jewish identity. The old-style Jewish magazines carry ads with photos of attractive young Jews on their Birthright tours of Israel. *Heeb*, with its photos of even more attractive young Jews, argues that you can find them here at home. The old Jewish magazines carry long essays on the fate of the Jews, Israel, and anti-Semitism in Europe. *Heeb* profiles Joan Rivers. The old Jewish magazines are written by octogenarians. For *Heeb*, no one over 40 exists, and no one over 30 gets to be photographed naked.

Heeb's natural progression seemed like it would lead into the field of Jewish pornography. The most notable advertisement in the spring 2008 issue was for the Israeli porn site Assreal.com. In summer 2008 they put out a swimsuit calendar, or half of one, with six glossy photos of blondes in bikinis. The injunction had once been to marry Jews. Now it is merely to masturbate to them. Or is it *also* to masturbate to them—so that even your sins are Jewish sins, forever circumscribed, and underwritten, by this unalterable essence? *Heeb*—and this is why older Jews, and advertisers, tolerate it—is conservative as only the truly self-satisfied can be, pretending to be victims while giving up none of the prerogatives of the dominant. To those who want to encourage the young toward "Jewish continuity," which is to say, not marrying shiksas and shaygetses, the *Heeb* writers are useful idiots. *Eventually they will grow up*, the old can safely presume, and "*return to Judaism*," which for them will mean donating to a reform synagogue and sending exactly the same party photos they now print in their magazine to the Temple Brotherhood newsletter.

Guilt and Pleasure, a publication of Reboot, an energetic group that organizes desert retreats for successful young American Jews to discuss their cultural Jewishness (explicitly defined to exclude religion), arranges its issues according to theme. There is the Fight Issue, the Health Issue, the Magic Issue. At the front of each issue we get neat factoids about Great Jews: "Great Jewish Boxers"; "Greatest Yiddish Insults." (These straight out of the Hebrew School Chanukah gift catalogue.) The essays follow a pattern—identify a problem, subject it to stereotypical Jewish analysis, overcome the stereotype. The stereotype to be overcome in the Health Issue is that Jews are unhealthy, neurotic hypochondriacs. And yet *Guilt and Pleasure*, like *Heeb*, includes photos of its contributors at the front of the magazine, and every single author looks attractive, fit, and healthy. In the Fight Issue, devoted to the exploits of tough boxing Jews and Harry Houdini (a Jew of great fortitude), some actually wounded people—with limbs missing—suddenly make their appearance in a photo essay about the Israeli-Palestinian conflict. These photos are brutal. Equally brutal is the photo of the beautiful Israeli photographer who took them. You think of the line from the Health Issue, in an essay about being diagnosed with a brain tumor: "As luck would have it," writes the author, "my cousin was the head of neurology at Sinai." *As luck would have it*—ha! The position of *G&P* is that it's the fate of the Jews to think of themselves as slouchy and neurotic, however glamorous they really are; occasionally they will "luck into" a post as the head of neurology at a New York hospital, as if this were not the achievement of generations of striving. In a publication that commands such resources; that attracts some real talent; that photographs the sufferings of maimed Israelis and Palestinians and can't figure out what to say about them, this represents a refusal to take responsibility for the talent, perseverance, and courage of the Jews—who once had to build our own hospitals so as to employ our own doctors, who in times of trouble in the Pale of Settlement organized our own militias against the pogroms, and who built, both for better and for worse, the state of Israel. In 1969, in *Portnoy's Complaint*, such suburbanized forgetting and refusal of the "world of our fathers" represented confusion, exhilaration, pain, and freedom. In 2008 it's straight-up bad faith.

Nextbook.org, a web magazine about books, is an online resource for Jewish book lovers—like a more serious, more engaged version of Jbooks.com. It runs a very successful Jewish-themed reading series in various cities in the US. It publishes substantial essays about writers of the Jewish past and sometimes of the Jewish present. But the magazine has a basic identity problem.

Highly conservative Jewish funders handed a mandate to highly liberal Jewish editors, courtesy of several million dollars from Keren Keshet–The Rainbow Foundation. The editors could run essays as excellently written and brilliantly conceived as they wanted, *as long as they were only about Jews.* The articles could be by anyone the editors liked—Jews and non-Jews alike—as long as the products *pretended that only Jews have contributed to Jewish thought.* But Jewish intellectual life since the fall of the Second Temple has not taken place in a vacuum. To create a venue that pretends it ever could have is to betray intellectual conscience. The money is a golden straightjacket.

At the opposite end of the spectrum from *Heeb, Zeek* is the only other new Jewish magazine without an identity crisis. Cheaply produced, terribly laid out, *Zeek* is straightforwardly a (grad) student literary magazine filled with essays on Jewish themes. Many of these are straightforwardly boring; some are very good. In fact it seems that by allowing itself to be dull, nonprescriptive, and nondescript, *Zeek* opens itself to the possibility of being lively, controversial, and intelligent. (It is also the only one of these magazines to take religion seriously.) A recent Music Issue highlighted some of the problems of the other new Jewish magazines—is one supposed to care what is on Sasha Baron-Cohen's iPod because he's a celebrity, or because he's a Jew?—but also had an interesting discussion of the Eurovision scandal surrounding the Israeli rock band Teapot. One of the two essays on Teapot was by an Israeli artist who took a moment to look into the national situation: "Openly or secretly," he wrote, "fears of an Iranian nuclear holocaust have seeped into the Israeli psyche. Last summer's failed war in Lebanon shamed us, and the continued missile attacks from evacuated Gaza have frustrated and confused us, but the Iranian threat is something else." You would be hard-pressed to find these sentiments in the hyper-self-conscious pages of any of the other new Jewish magazines—or, for that matter, in the old Jewish magazines. "Shame" is not a word they allow themselves to associate with Israel. But the artist went further still. "Israel," he wrote, "is a country whose true European roots are not in song contests, but in the Holocaust. The Holocaust, not Herzel, offers us the real founding narrative of Israel. . . . In Israel 'Never Again' is not a rally slogan, but military policy." This, too, you would not read in *Heeb*, or *Guilt and Pleasure.* In Nextbook.org it would have to hide in a book review.

Compared to the Jewish magazines of previous generations—*Commentary*, founded in 1945 and now a stalwart of the neoconservative movement, or *Tikkun*, founded in 1986 and still a stalwart of Jewish progressivism—all these magazines are either silly or unfocused and confused. Compared to the very Jewish-inflected but non-identitarian magazines—Irving Howe's and then Michael Walzer's *Dissent*, Martin Peretz's (and Leon Wieseltier's) *New Republic*, Robert Silvers's and Barbara Epstein's *New York Review of Books*, William Kristol's *Weekly Standard*, and even, for God's sake, David Remnick's *New Yorker*—they are just provincial.

And we began this essay with the intention of denouncing them. But to read them all through is to sense that even if their proximate cause is the easy availability of gobs of money from wealthy men who decided, in their declining years, to do something for the Jews after betraying *tikkun olam* for their whole working careers, they are nonetheless associated with a real historical situation, and a generational one: that of a group of young people raised on simplistic fairy tales about the Holocaust as the core of Judaism and then suddenly placed into a real world for which the Holocaust is no longer a useful analytical tool. It's interesting to note that the one political intervention carried out by the website Jewcy.com (founded in 2006) has been not on behalf of Jews, but Armenians. When Abraham Foxman of the Anti-Discrimination League *fired* an employee for saying publicly that the Armenian genocide (by unrepentant Turkey) should be acknowledged by the Jewish organization, Jewcy.com organized a protest in New York. For years, some Jewish charities and even some Jewish intellectuals have said two incompatible things simultaneously about the historical position of the Holocaust—on the one hand, the Holocaust must be studied and taught in American schools because it was a tragedy with a universal character; on the other, it was an utterly unique event, to which no other mass murder should ever be compared. The campaign by Jewcy.com was not really directed against the conservative hysteria of the ADL, or of a Holocaust/Israel lobby more generally; it simply asked that the lessons taught in Hebrew school be given their logical, moral application. If you say "We must not forget" for one mass murder of a people, why is it fair to forget another one? It was an extremely effective point to make.

Likewise the pornography of a *Heeb*, the feeble "conversationalism" of *Guilt and Pleasure*, the bookish earnestness of Nextbook.org—all represent the laying bare of previously buried contradictions in the mind of the young American Jewish community. "Here is your Birthright tour—to Assreal!" says *Heeb*. "Here is the watered-down third generation of your victimization," says *G&P*. "Here is how you hobble yourself when you look at intellectual history from an exclusively Jewish perspective," says Nextbook.org.

The result of all of the money poured into Jewish "cultural" programs is a stifling, undeniable *sterility*. A people does not reproduce itself from such bad faith. "The greatness of this people was once that it believed in God, and believed in Him in such a way that its trust and love toward him was greater than its fear," Hannah Arendt once wrote in her reply to Gershom Scholem over the Eichmann affair, during which Scholem had accused the great philosopher of lacking *ahavat yisrael*, a love for the Jews. "And now this people believes only in itself? What good can come out of that?"

No good can come of it, but maybe this: That our nationalism—racism, even—finally allowed unfettered expression on these American shores, will burn itself out as its contradictions become clearer. No one can look at *Heeb*, or the "Superjew" and "Yo Semite" T-shirts, without feeling ashamed—even if that magazine and those T-shirts are themselves products of that feeling of shame and are meant as a rebuke to it. The greatness of this people was *also* that it once believed its experience of oppression to be a universal one, and its fortunes tied to all those who are oppressed. There are many ways back to that belief, including through ethnic particularism, if one wants to find that way. Otherwise secular Jews deserve to become like people of Scottish descent: to wear yarmulkes twice a year like kilts, and toot shofars like bagpipes, calling no one back to righteousness.

"I KNOW WHERE you're coming from. Think of this, though. You still can't find a serious black magazine that isn't about music, or news, or lifestyle. Not even an asinine journal that pretended no one had ever contributed to intellectual culture but black people.

As a matter of fact, that's just the journal we need! All of American culture was made by us anyway. Meanwhile, the media thinks our opinions are wholly determined. Why, during the election, every time I'd turn on a McCain rally and there'd be a crazy brother up there shaking his hand—saying 'You don't know what hell this costs me at home'; or even when ABC would show a black undecided voter—I'd get a thrill, you know, much as I hated the Republicans. As if everything's done racially, by stupid racial fellow-feeling. Men and women have ideas, they have beliefs!"

"But black people *should* vote for Obama," Josh protests.

"Would you vote for Joe Lieberman?"

Josh pretends to spit over his shoulder. "'He should grow like an onion, with his head in the ground.'"

"You know what Ralph Ellison said to his Jewish friends?" Michael says. He goes to find the book on the shelf. "Ahem. 'Many Negroes, like myself, make a positive distinction between 'whites' and 'Jews.' Speaking personally . . . I would like to see the more positive distinctions between whites and Jewish Americans maintained.'"

"Ellison," Josh says admiringly. "Yup, we blew it. If there were a good secular Jewish magazine, it would have to be a 'minority' magazine. And you can't have a minority magazine if you want everything the majority has, *plus* something special of your own."

We're starting to feel a little weird in this company—having been raised Satanist. Not orthodox Satanist, though. Reform Satanist. We worshipped our Dark Lord through folk songs.

CORRECTION

IN MID-2007, THE MIGHTY NEW DIRECTIONS intended to send *n+1* a copy of Roberto Bolaño's *Nazi Literature in the Americas*, for possible excerpting in the magazine. Unfortunately, the book was accidentally mailed to *Harper's*, which published an excerpt. We apologize for any inconvenience this may have caused.

ON BOLAÑO

JUST AS THE '90S WITNESSED THE AMERICAN canonization of one important foreign writer—W. G. Sebald—the current decade has seen the same happen to the wandering novelist and poet Roberto Bolaño, who spent his boyhood in Chile, his youth mostly in Mexico, and who died in Spain in 2003, at the age of 50, after a decade of Stakhanovite productivity. His massive novel *2666*, unrevised at his death, is only now appearing in translation, earlier books like the monologue *By Night in Chile*, the tragic mockumentary *The Savage Detectives*, and that vicious counterfactual lark *Nazi Literature in the Americas* having already secured the highest praise. Bolaño's canonization has taken place so rapidly and completely, and with so little demurral, that one can only reluctantly pile aboard the bandwagon. But Bolaño is the real thing, as urgent, various, imaginative, and new as any writer active in the last decade. The question is: why *not* canonize anyone else? Why reserve for him the once-in-a-decade beatification?

In the '90s, it didn't matter to most American readers that Sebald had taken the hoariest tropes of German romanticism (the solitary wandering, the unnamable sorrow) and renovated a totally discredited literary tradition by employing it to honor the victims of that variety of German romanticism known as Nazism. What mattered was simply that these were literary books about the Holocaust. Bolaño, of course, was not Jewish or German, and was released from Pinochet's prisons after a few days. He returned to Mexico to read books and smoke weed. (Later on, he took heroin.) Nevertheless, if you can only take your serious literature with a lump of state terror, eventually you run out of authentic Nazis and have to make do with the next best thing: South American generals of the '70s. Foreign writers are like our own candidates for President: it helps to have been a prisoner of war or at least to have grown up poor. (Poor Mario Vargas Llosa, preppy and smooth with excellent hair, is the John Kerry of Latin American letters.)

Fortunately, it's possible to appreciate books for better reasons than we know. Back-story carries you only so far as a reader, and if you've made it through *The Savage Detectives* or *2666* it must be because this writer is doing something to you that the mere mention of Pinochet or heroin can't. As with Sebald, Bolaño is always referred to in terms of his singularity or strangeness; people who think he's a big deal, including professional critics, mostly can't say why. Still, an attempt may as well be made.

Bolaño's reputation among Spanish speakers is secure, but his significance to us can't be what it is to them. The same goes for Borges, the model Bolaño most often invoked. For Spanish speakers the importance of Borges is not confined to the black metaphysical jokes purveyed in his mind-bending fables. Hispanophone readers often describe a sense of their language as dripping with high-flown inclinations; literary Spanish tends to become humid with rhetoric and profuse with metaphors, something easy to see in modern poetry from Lorca onward. So Borges in his own language counts as a champion dessicator; he pushes Spanish toward the hard, cold, and dry. Even so, he strikes us as rhetorical enough. It fell to writers like Bolaño to complete the drying-out of literary prose already accomplished in other languages by writers like Hemingway and Camus. Bolaño can write page after page without indulging in a single metaphor, or adding a dab of rhetorical color to the account of a dinner party or a murder. Of course you can find perfect sentences in Bolaño, and crazy metaphors too, but for the most part he proceeds as if literature were too desperate an enterprise to bother with being well written. The rationale for his anti-eloquence belongs to the internal dynamic of any modern language: an idiom encrusted with poeticisms needs a solvent bath. But for Latin Americans of Bolaño's generation there may also be political grounds for preferring writing degree zero to purple haze. One more disgusting feature of the Argentine junta (it is Argentines who predominate in Bolaño's gallery of imaginary Nazi writers) was the generals' magniloquence.

Our problem in America is hardly that our worst politicians speak too well, or that we lack for plain stylists. What is our problem, then—to which Bolaño seems a solution? American critics and regular readers alike usually don't care for sweeping literary-historical arguments. And yet in recent years we have been celebrating Sebald and Bolaño as if we really do believe in some big metanarrative about the novel—one that proclaims that, even post postmodernism, the form remains in crisis. Sure, Sebald and Bolaño deal with fascism, and both died at the height of their powers. More decisive is that *neither fiction writer writes as if he believes in fiction*. Our canonization of these writers implies a sense, even a conviction, that you can't be a really important novelist anymore unless you can't really *write novels*.

Both writers are striking for the documentary or testimonial, as opposed to fictional, feel of their productions. Sebald assembled his material from interviews (especially in *The Emigrants*) and library-burrowing (*The Rings of Saturn*), and from his own life. He also interlards his texts with snapshots, ticket stubs, archival photographs: documentary proof. He makes no effort to write convincing scenes or dialogue: a character stands silent and motionless as an old Victrola, then the needle drops and the aria commences. Sebald's fiction consists of facts and reworked testimony, and constantly points to their opposite: what we'll never know about what really happened. Whereas ordinary novels, epistemologically unruffled for two centuries, have mostly delivered unimpeachable accounts of events that never took place.

The case of Bolaño is more complex. Where Sebald perfected a single deep and narrow mode, Bolaño was an experimenter. The impression you get from the short stories is that nothing at all has been made up, and nothing comprehended. There is a virtually Seinfeldian ban on moral growth or learning. These stories' conclusions are by no means the poetic or pregnant endings we know from magazine fiction; they are the flat conclusions we know better from life: *Then he died.* Or: *We lost touch.* Or: *That's all I know.* And yet Bolaño boasts tremendous powers of invention; especially in his longer novels, truly fictional characters, with no originals in life, proliferate alongside the personages à clef. Curiously, he treats the pure inventions as he does the lightly fictionalized acquaintances. Some facts are known about them, most not. Some literary work of dubious merit may have been left behind. There is rarely any pretense to psychological insight (though this begins to change in *2666*), or characterological summing-up. Bolaño behaves toward his characters as if he were a court stenographer or deputized witness rather than a profiler or portraitist. He and his heroes care only for literature—but can't seem to produce it in any way we recognize (except by reading Bolaño). Opaque fictional persons replace transparent fictional characters, and, instead of plots, you get one damn thing after another.

Why then, you begin to wonder, are you reading these books? What for, if they are each going to eschew psychology, characterization, pretty language, and neat conclusions, and if the narratives are all to devolve into shaggy-dog Iditarods mushing after some fugitive poet or novelist about whom—even if he ever turns up—we learn next to nothing? Why read and write at all if these empty Chinese boxes constitute the only goods ultimately in receipt?

In Bolaño, literature is a helpless, undignified, and not especially pleasant compulsion, like smoking. At one point you started and now you can't stop; it's become a habit and an identity. Nothing is so consistent across Bolaño's work as the suspicion that literature is chiefly bullshit, rationalizing the misery, delusions, and/or narcissism of various careerists, flakes, and losers. Yet Bolaño somehow also treats literature as his and his characters' sole excuse for existing. This basic Bolaño aporia—literature is all that matters, literature doesn't matter at all—can be a glib paradox for others. He seems to have meant it sincerely, even desperately, something one would feel without knowing the first thing about his life.

Bolaño's incoherence—books mean everything and nothing; the writer is hero and jerk—has come to seem one of the few plausible literary attitudes these days. Considered simply as a job, writing is erratically paid but with flexible hours: potentially not so bad, especially with the hedge funds laying everybody off. But as a vocation? Look around, and all you see is literature and publishing faltering in tandem. People read less and less; worse yet, they're right to. It's clear that, besides the occasional small or large check, most writers—ourselves included—write out of vanity and compulsion. One believes in being a writer more, it seems, than in writing. What is it, again, you once had to say? And who, supposedly, wanted to hear it? Still, Bolaño-like, you can't conceive any redemption for you and your friends except through the production of masterpieces. Masterpieces, however, are always unlikely, and redemption impossible.

The whole thing's hopeless and pathetic, not less so for being a reason to live. And this, finally, must be what literary people like so much about Bolaño: his career illustrates for the novel Gramsci's famous slogan: *Pessimism of the intellect, optimism of the will.*

We have pressed our barbarous Spanish into service to translate one of Bolaño's poems. (It is not by Bertolt Brecht.)

Los Neochilenos

The trip began one happy November day
But in some way the trip was already over
When we set out.
All times live at once, said Pancho Ferri,
Our singer. Or flow to the same place,
Who knows.
The prologues, in any case,
Were simple:
With resigned gestures we climb aboard
The pickup truck
That our manager in a fit
Of lunacy
Has presented us
And take off for the north,
The north that is magnetic north to the
dreams
And the apparently
Meaningless songs
Of us Neochilenos,
A north—how can I put this?—
Foreseen in a white handkerchief
That sometimes would cover
My face
Like a shroud.
A spotless white handkerchief
Or, no,
One where I saw projected
My nomadic nightmares
And my sedentary nightmares.
And Pancho Ferri
Grasping with both hands
The steering wheel
And making the pickup truck vibrate
While we searched for the exit
Out of Santiago
Asked
If we knew the story
Of these guys Caraculo
And Jetachanco,
Making the pickup truck vibrate as if it
were
The breast
Of Caraculo
Who carried a burden terrible
For anyone to bear.
And I remembered then that the day
Before our departure
We had gone
To the Parque Forestal
To visit the monument
To Rubén Darío.
Goodbye, Rubén, we said drunkenly
And on drugs.
Now banal deeds
Are confounded
With the annunciatory cries
Of true dreams.

But that's how we Neochilenos were,
Pure inspiration
And no method.
And the next day we rolled out
Toward Pilpilco and Lay Lay
And passed La Ligua and Los Vilos
Without stopping
And we crossed the Petorca river
And the Quilimari
River
And the Choapa until we came
To La Serena
And the Elqui river
And finally Copiapó
And the river Copiapó
Where we stopped
To eat fried
Empanadas.
And Pancho Ferri
Returned to the intercontinental
Adventures
Of Caraculo and Jetachancho,
Two musicians from Valparaíso
Lost
In Barcelona's Chinatown.
And poor Caraculo, said
The singer,
He was married and such was his need
To make some money
For his wife and the heirs
To the Caraculo lineage
That he started dealing
Heroin
And a little cocaine
And on Fridays some Ecstasy
For the subjects of Venus.
And little by little, obstinately,
He began to succeed.
And while Jetachancho
Hung out with Aldo di Pietro
Remember him?
At the Café Puerto Rico,
Caraculo observed the growth
Of his bank account
And his self-esteem.
And what lesson can
We Neochilenos take
From the criminal life
Of these two South American
  pilgrims?
None, except that limits
Are tenuous, lines
Are fine lines: faces
Of a reality minted
In the void.
The same void
As horrified Pascal.
This dark
And cold
Geometrical horror
Said Pancho Ferri
To the steering wheel of our racecar,
Forever pointing
North, until
At Toco
We unloaded
The PA
And two hours later
Were ready to go on:
Pancho Relámpago
Y Los Neochilenos.
A minor fiasco
In a nutshell,
Even if some adolescents
Helped us
Put our instruments
Back in the pickup truck: children
Of Toco
Transparent like
The geometrical figures
Of Blaise Pascal.
And after Toco, Quillagua,
Hillarico, Soleded, Ramaditas,
Pintados and Humberstone,
Appearing in empty halls
And brothels made over
Into Lilliputian hospitals,
Something very weird, very few had

Electricity, very
Weird that the walls
Were semisolid, in short,
Places that gave us
A slight sensation of fear
And where the clients
Were devotees of
Fist-fucking (as they say in English)
And feet-fucking
And the cries that flew
From the windows and
Circulated among the cement patio
And the open air latrines,
And corner shops full
Of rusty tools
And sheds that appeared
To soak up all the moonlight
Made our hair
Stand on end.
How can such evil
Exist
In such a new country,
Such a minor entity?
Could this be
The Inferno of Whores?
Pancho Ferri
Wondered aloud.
And we Neochilenos
Didn't know
How to reply.
I was more interested in the question
Of how such New York sexual fetishes
Could have reached
Those provincial
Backwaters.
And with empty pockets
We continued on up:
Mapocho, Negreiros, Santa
Catalina, Tana,
Cuya and
Arica,
Where we found
A little rest—and insults.
And three nights of work
In the Camafeo run by
Don Luis Sánchez Morales, retired
Officer.
A place full of little round tables
And portly little lamps
Painted by the hand
Of Don Luis's mother,
I suppose.
And the only thing
Truly pleasant
That we saw in Arica
Was the sun of Arica:
A sun like a cloud of
Dust.
A sun like sand
Subtly displacing
The motionless air.
The rest: routine.
Killers and converts
Mixed in the same discussion
Of deaf-mutes,
Of idiots undone
By purgatory.
And the lawyer Vivanco,
A friend of Don Luis Sánchez,
Asked what kind of crap we were trying to
pull
With this Neochilenos bullshit.
Neo-patriots, said Pancho
Getting up
From the table
And shutting himself in the bathroom.
And the lawyer Vivanco
Returned his pistol
To his underarm holster
Made of Italian leather,
Exquisite gift from the boys
Of the Ordine Nuovo,
Embossed with skill and care.
That moon-white
Night the group of us
Had to put
Pancho Ferri in bed.
Running a fever of 104

He became delirious:
Now he would prefer our group
To be called not Pancho Relámpago
Y Los Neochilenos,
But rather Pancho Misterio
Y Los Neochilenos:
The terror of Pascal.
The terror of singers.
The terror of travelers,
But never the terror
Of children.
And at dawn,
Like a band of thieves,
We left from Arica
And crossed the frontier
Of the Republic.
To see our faces
You would have said we were crossing
The frontier of Reason.
And legendary Peru
Opened up before our pickup truck
Covered with dust
And filthiness,
Like a fruit with no skin,
Like a chimerical fruit
Exposed to inclement weather
And affronts.
A peeled fruit
Like a teenager skinned alive.
And Pancho Ferri, from
Then on called Pancho
Misterio, didn't escape
From his fever,
Musing like a priest
In the back
Of the pickup truck
On the avatars—Sanskrit word—
Of Caraculo and Jetachancho.
A life slender and hard
Like the noose and porridge of a hanged
man,
That life of Jetachancho and his
Unfortunate Siamese twin:
A life or mere investigation
Of the capricious wind.
And the Neochilenos
Appeared in Tacna,
In Mollendo and Arequipa,
Under the sponsorship of the Society
For the Promotion of Art
And Youth.
Without a singer, humming
The songs ourselves
Or just going mmm, mmm, mmmmmh,
While Pancho sank further
Into the back of the truck,
Devoured by chimeras
And by teenagers skinned alive.
Nadir and zenith of a longing
That Caraculo knew
By way of the moons
Above the drug dealers
Of Barcelona: a deceitful
Flash of light,
A small and vacant space
Signifying nothing,
Worth nothing, and
Nevertheless offered to you
For free.
And if we weren't
In Peru? we
Neochilenos
Wondered one night.
And if this immense
Space
That is our instructor
And our boundary
Were an intergalactic spaceship,
An unidentified
Flying object?
And if the fever
Of Pancho Misterio
Were our fuel
Or our navigation system?
And after work
We went out walking
Along the Peruvian streets,
Among military patrols, and unemployed

Door-to-door salesmen ,
Searching the hills
For the bonfires of the Shining Path,
But we saw nothing.
The darkness that surrounded the
The city centers
Was complete.
This is like a dust cloud
Escaped from the Second
World War
Said Pancho laid out
In the back of the truck.
He said: fibers
Of Nazi generals like
Richenau or Model
Escaped in involuntary
Spiritual form
Toward the Virgin Lands
Of Latin America:
A hinterland of ghosts
And phantoms.
Our own home
Established in the geometry
Of impossible enormities.
And at night we usually
Picked up some girls from the bars:
The 15 year old whores
Descended from the heroes
Of the War of the Pacific
Liked to hear us rattle on
Like machine guns.
But above all
They liked seeing Pancho
Buried in many-colored blankets
And wearing a wool hat
From the highlands
Pulled down so low his eyebrows
Appeared and disappeared,
Helmeted like the knight
He always was,
A guy blessed with good luck,
A great sick lover from the south of Chile,
Father of the Neochilenos
And mother to Caraculo and Jetachanco,
Two poor musicians from Valparaíso,
As everybody knows.
And dawn always found us
Gathered around a backroom table
Talking about the kilogram and a half of gray
    matter
That forms the brain of an adult
Human.
Chemical messages, Pancho Misterio
Would say, burning with fever,
Excitatory neurons
And inhibitory neurons
Inside the vastnesses of a longing.
And the little whores would say
That a kilo and a half of gray
Matter
Was enough, was plenty, because who
Could ask for more.
And tears would fall from Pancho's
Eyes when he listened to them.
And then the rainstorm came
And the rain drew silence
Across the streets of Mollendo,
And across the hills,
And across the streets of the barrio
Of whores,
And the rain was the only
Interlocutor.
Strange phenomenon: the Neochilenos
Continued talking to themselves
And each on his own
We explored the trash heaps of
Philosophy, the arks, the
American colors, the unmistakable style
Of birth and rebirth.
And one night our pickup truck
Headed straight toward Lima, with Pancho
Ferri at the wheel, just like
Old times,
Except that now a whore
Was by his side.
A thin young whore
Named Margarita,
Adolescent nonpareil,

Habituated to permanent
Suffering.
She could equally well have been
called Nimble
Shadow,
That dark shelter
Where Pancho could
Let his wounds heal.
And in Lima we read about the Peruvian
Poets:
Vallejo, Martín Adán and Jorge Pimentel,
And Pancho Misterio went out
On stage and was convincing
And versatile.
And then, however shaky
And sweaty we may have been
He recounted to us the story
Of a novel
By a great Chilean writer.
One swallowed by oblivion.
A nec spes nec metus
We Neochilenos said
and Margarita said:
A novelist.
And the ghost,
The grieving pit
That all his efforts
Turned into,
Wrote—so it seemed—
A novel called *Kundalini*,
And Pancho hardly remembered it,
He made an effort, his words
Rummaged around his atrocious childhood
Filled with amnesia, with gymnastic
Competitions and lies,
And thus the tale was told to us,
In fragments,
The cry *Kundalini*,
The name of a racehorse, a mare,
And mass murder in the hippodrome.
A hippodrome that no longer existed.
An empty space left behind
In a Chile nonexistent
And happy.
And this story had
The virtue of illuminating
Like an English landscape painter
Our fear and our dreams
That marched from east to west
And from west to east,
While we real-life
Neochilenos
Traveled from the south
To the north.
And so slowly
That it seemed we didn't move.
And Lima was an instant
Of happiness,
Brief but effective.
And what relationship obtains, said Pancho,
Between Morpheus, god
Of dreams
And "munch," vulgar term
For eating?
Yes, that's what he said,
Clasping by the waist
His beautiful Margarita,
Skinny and almost naked
In a bar in Lince, on a night
Deciphered and divided and
Possessed
By lightning flashes
From the chimera.
Our need.
Our mouth that opens
So that potatoes
Can come in
And dreams
Can come out: fossilized
Dust clouds
Employing the color palette
Of the apocalypse.
We're survivors, said Pancho
Ferri.
Latin Americans blessed with good luck.
That's all.
And one night before leaving
We saw Pancho

And Margarita
Standing in the middle of an infinite
Quagmire.
And then we knew
That the Neochilenos
Would always be
Ruled
By chance.
The coin
Jumped like a metallic
Insect
From between his fingers:
Heads, to the south,
Tails, to the north,
And then we all climbed aboard
The pickup truck
And the city
Of legends
And fear
Fell behind.
One happy January day
We crossed
Like children of Cold,
Of Changeable Cold,
Or of *Ecce Homo*,
The Ecuadorian frontier.
By then Pancho was
28 or 29 years old
And would shortly die.
And Margarita was 17.
And none of the Neochilenos
Made it past 22. +

DANE PATTERSON, *WEARING CURRENCY*, 2008,
GRAPHITE ON PAPER, 22 X 30". COURTESY OF THE ARTIST.

POLITICS

The Financial Crisis

ANONYMOUS HEDGE FUND MANAGER (I)

Anonymous Hedge Fund Manager (HFM) is a managing partner at a large hedge fund in New York. In the wake of the subprime mortgage meltdown in the summer of 2007, he agreed to talk to us at length about the mechanics of the mortgage system, his own fund's involvement in it, and his thoughts about the future. As the mortgage crisis spread into the heart of the financial system with the collapse of Bear Stearns in March 2008, we visited HFM in Midtown to talk further. We visited again in late summer 2008, just days before the Republican administration took the unprecedented step of nationalizing the mortgage giants Fannie Mae and Freddie Mac, Lehman Brothers failed, and the crisis spread.

OCTOBER 7, 2007
BROOKLYN, NEW YORK

n+1: All right, let's get to it. Is America now a Third World country?

HFM: No, we're a First World country with a weak currency. From time to time, the dollar's very weak; from time to time, it's very strong; and unfortunately what tends to happen is people tend to extrapolate. But in reality, over the very very long term, currency processes tend to be fairly stable and mean-reverting. So the dollar's very weak today, but that's no reason to believe the dollar's going to be weak forever or that, because it's weak today, it's going to get dramatically weaker tomorrow.

n+1: But you, in your work, are not dealing with the long term . . .

HFM: No, we're dealing with the short term. But I'll tell you, in our work we don't trade the G-7 crosses because we don't feel we have an edge on that. Dollar-sterling, dollar-euro, or dollar-yen: it's amazing how many brilliant investors have gotten egg on their face trying to trade the G-7 crosses. I can think of so many examples—where people make these really strong calls, that seem very sensible, and then get killed. A very good example is Julian Robertson in the late '90s being short the yen against the dollar. Japan had just gone through this horrible deflation, the economy was in the shitter, the banking system was rotten. All these things should lead a currency to trade weaker, and he got very very long the dollar, short the yen, and a lot of people did alongside him, and basically there was a two- or three-week period in '98 when they had the financial crisis and the yen actually strengthened 10 or 15 percent. I can't remember the exact numbers, but all these guys just got carried out.

n+1: "Carried out," is that a term of art?

HFM: Carried out . . . like basically they're carried out on a board, they're dead. Another example of that, a personal example:

Generally every year, at the beginning of the year, banks that we deal with will have events, dinners or lunches, where they gather some of their big clients and discuss themes for the coming year. They encourage everybody to, you know, go around the table: "What's your best trade idea for the coming year?" And at the beginning of 2005 I was at a dinner with some fairly prominent macro investors, and it was almost like a bidding war. The first guy would say, "I think the best trade is short dollar, long euro, it's going up to $1.45." At the time, I forget, maybe it was $1.30. And the next guy would go, "No, no, you're so naïve. $1.45? It's going to $1.60!" And it was a competition for who could be more bearish on the dollar and win the prize and be the least naïve person at the table. "It's going to $1.65 and probably higher! Maybe $1.75!" At the eighteen-month horizon.

Now considering that everyone at the table being super-bearish on the dollar probably meant that they were already short the dollar and long the euro, I went back and looked at my portfolio and said: "Any position I have that's euro-bullish and dollar-bearish, I'm going to reverse it, because if everybody already said 'I hate the dollar,' they've already positioned for it, who's left?" Who's left to actually make this move happen? And who's on the other side of that trade? On the other side of the trade is the official sector that has all sorts of other incentives, nonfinancial incentives, political incentives. They want to keep their currency weak to promote growth or exports or jobs; or they have pegs, peg-regimes that they need to defend, and they don't really care about maximizing profit on their reserves, they're not a bank trying to maximize profits, they have broad policy objectives—and infinite firepower.

n+1: So you did well.

HFM: Well, we didn't lose. I mean, I don't bet on this process, but sometimes there are positions you have that have a certain derivative exposure to the dollar-euro, and we tried to be careful not to take too much of that. Because we thought that this consensus, this super-strong consensus that the dollar's got to go weaker, actually represented a risk that the dollar would go in the other direction.

n+1: How do you know all this stuff?

HFM: All what stuff?

n+1: All the stuff you know? Did you go to—

HFM: I didn't go to business school. I did not major in economics. I learned the old-fashioned way by apprenticing to a very talented investor. I didn't even know what a hedge fund was when I started. I'm sure today I would never get hired.

n+1: Really?

HFM: Yeah, it would be impossible because I had no background, or I had a very exiguous background in finance. The guy who hired me always talked about hiring good intellectual athletes, people who were mentally agile in an all-around way, and that the specifics of finance you could learn, which I think is true. But at the time, I mean, no hedge fund was really flooded with applicants, and that allowed him to let his mind range a little bit and consider different kinds of candidates. Today we have a recruiting group, and what do they do?—they throw resumes at you, and it's, like, one business school guy, one finance major after another, kids who from the time they were 12 years old were watching Jim Cramer and dreaming of working in a hedge fund. And I think in reality that, if anything, they're less likely to make good investors than people with more interesting backgrounds.

n+1: Why?

HFM: Because in the end the way you make a ton of money is calling paradigm shifts, and people who are real finance types, maybe they can work really well within the paradigm of a particular market or a particular set of rules—and you can make money doing that—but the people who make huge money, the George Soroses and Julian Robertsons, they're the people who can step back and see when the paradigm is going to shift, and I think that comes from having a broader experience, a little bit of a different approach to how you think about things.

n+1: What's a paradigm shift in finance?

HFM: Well, a paradigm shift in finance is maybe what we've gone through in the subprime market and the spillover that's had in other markets, where there were really basic assumptions that, you know, were wrong.

The thing is that nobody has enough brainpower to question every assumption, to think about every single facet of an investment. There are certain things you need to take for granted. And people took for granted the idea that, "OK, something that Moody's rates triple-A must be money-good, so I'm going to worry about the other things I'm investing in, but when it comes time to say, 'Where am I going to put my cash?,' I'll just leave it in triple-A commercial paper." It could be the case that, yeah, the power's going to fail in my office, and maybe the water supply is going to fail, and I should plan for that, but you only have so much brainpower, so you think about what you think are the relevant factors, the factors that are likely to change. But often some of your assumptions are wrong.

n+1: So the Moody's ratings were like the water running . . .

HFM: Exactly. Triple-A is triple-A. But there were people who made a ton of money in the subprime crisis because they looked at the collateral that underlay a lot of these CDOs [collateralized debt obligations] and commercial paper programs that were highly rated and they said, "Wait a second. Underlying this are loans that have been made to people who really shouldn't own houses—they're not financially prepared to own houses. The underwriting standards are materially worse than they've been in previous years; the amount of construction in particular markets is just totally out of proportion with the sort of household formation that's going on; the rating agencies are kind of asleep at the switch, they're not changing their assumptions and therefore, OK, notwithstanding something may be rated triple-A, I can come up with a realistic scenario where those securities are impaired." And pricing on triple-A CDO paper was very, very rich. Spreads were very, very tight, and these guys said, "You know what? These assumptions that triple-A is money-good, or the assumptions that underlie Moody's ratings . . ."

n+1: "Money-good"?

HFM: In other words, if you buy a bond, you're going to get back your principal. It's money-good. You're going to get a hundred cents on the dollar back.

But in reality this was wrong, and people were able to short triple-A securities very cheaply. They weren't paying a lot to be short and they made huge money on triple-A securities and triple-A CDO paper that now trades at fifty cents on the dollar. I mean that's like the water's not running today, right? *The sun didn't rise.* But if you were trained in finance, you probably are more likely to take for granted that, "The rating agencies have a very sound process, credit analysis, the same process that I've been trained in, all the assumptions that I use are kind of the same as the assumptions they use." In the same fashion, if you assess the attractiveness of a trade based on historical data from a time when people weren't really actively doing that trade, and then suddenly everybody's doing that trade, the behavior of the trade will be different. And if you're trained the same way as everybody else, in general you're all going to behave the same. And when everyone behaves the same, that makes trades a lot riskier: everybody's buying at the same time, you get bubbles, everybody's selling at the same time, you get crashes.

A good example of that is . . . I don't know if you've heard about the problems that cropped up over the summer in a type of business called statistical arbitrage? Stat arb?

n+1: . . .

HFM: Quantitative trading?

n+1: . . .

HFM: Goldman Sachs had a fund that lost 30 percent, and Highbridge had a fund that lost a lot of money. Stat arb is, basically, computerized trading of a huge universe of stocks based on a set of models. And those models can be technical models like momentum or mean reversion, or fundamental models like just, "Buy stocks that have high cash-flow yields and sell stocks that have low cash-flow yields." That's a gross simplification, but the core of it is that there are predictable relationships between stock price history and future performance, or between fundamental variables of a company and stock price performance, and these are broadly reliable. No given stock is going to perform in line with the models. But if you're trading a universe of five thousand stocks, in general you'll have enough of an edge that you'll make money.

n+1: And so the computers themselves are making these trades?

HFM: You build the models and the computer does the trading. You actually do all the analysis. But it's too many stocks for a human brain to handle, so guys with a lot of physics and hardcore statistics backgrounds come up with ideas about models that might lead to excess return, and then they test them and all these models get incorporated into a bigger system that trades stocks in an automated way.

n+1: So the computers are running the . . .

HFM: Yeah, the computer is sending out the orders and doing the trading.

n+1: It's just a couple steps from that to the computers enslaving—

HFM: Yes, but I for one welcome our computer trading masters.

People call it "black box trading," because sometimes you don't even know why the black box is doing what it's doing, because the whole idea is that if you could, you should be doing it yourself. But it's something that's done on such a big scale that a human brain can't do it in real time. The problem is that the DNA of a lot of these models are very, very similar—it's like an ecosystem with no biodiversity, because most of the people who do stat arb can trace their lineage, their intellectual lineage, back to four or five guys who really started the whole discipline in the '70s and '80s.

And what happened is, in August a few of these funds that have big black box trading books suffered losses in other businesses and decided to reduce risk, so they dialed down their black boxes. The black box system started unwinding its positions, and every black box is so similar that everybody was long the same stocks and short the same stocks. When one fund starts selling off its longs and buying back its shorts, that causes losses for the next black box, and the people who run that black box say, "Oh gosh! I'm losing a lot more money than I thought I could. My risk model is no longer relevant; let me turn down my black box." And basically you had an avalanche where everybody's black box was being shut off, causing incredibly bizarre behavior in the market.

n+1: By the black boxes?

HFM: Well, in the part of the profit-and-loss that they were generating to the point where, to give you an example from our black box system, because we have one . . .

n+1: A big black box?

HFM: Actually I think it's gray, and it's not in our main office, it's off site. And we made sure it has no arms or legs or anything it could use to enslave us. But we had a loss over the course of like three days that was a ten-sigma event, meaning it should never happen based on the statistical models that underlie it. Why? Because the model doesn't assume that everybody else is trading the same model as you are. So that's sort of a meta-model factor. The model doesn't know that there are other black boxes out there.

n+1: What's a "ten-sigma event"?

HFM: Meaning that it's ten standard deviations from the mean . . . meaning it's basically impossible, you know? But returns are very fat-tailed, so the joke that we always say is, "Oh my God, today I had a loss that's a six-sigma event! I mean, that's the first time that's happened in three months!" It's like a once-in-ten-thousand-years event, and I haven't had one in the last three months.

n+1: It happens all the time?

HFM: Those kind of things do happen, yeah. And usually it happens because there's a flaw in the model and in the assumptions that people made. Black box trading is small relative to all trading, but there was a ton of it going on and it was all very similar.

+ + +

n+1: So why did all of the hedge funds have this subprime mortgage paper?

HFM: Well, some hedge funds did and some didn't. Some hedge funds made a lot of money being short it. Some hedge funds lost money being long it. Where the losses are concentrated, though, are not so much in the hedge fund world. The losses are concentrated at banks—a lot of European banks, Asian banks. Even the Chinese central bank has exposure.

People talked about this being a hedge fund problem, but it wasn't really a hedge fund problem. There were some hedge funds that were taking pure subprime exposure, but most hedge funds were basically in the CDO business, so they would buy all sorts of mortgage pools. They buy mortgages, and then they package them and tranche the pools of mortgages into various tranches from senior to equity. So basically you have a number of tranches of paper that are backed by the mortgage pools and there's a cash-flow waterfall—the cash comes in from those mortgages, and a certain tranche has the first priority. Then you have descending order of priority, and the hedge fund would usually keep the last piece, which is known as the equity, or the residual, as opposed to the stuff that was triple-A—that's the most senior paper.

So if you had a pool of half a billion dollars of mortgages, maybe there would be $300 million of triple-A paper you would sell to fund that, and then there would be smaller tranches of more junior paper. And the buyers of that paper, particularly the very senior paper, the triple-A paper, were not mortgage experts—they say, "It's triple-A? I'll buy it." These are money market funds; the spread that they're getting paid is very small, so they can't hire a lot of analysts to go and dig in the mortgage pools and really understand them, they just rely on the rating agencies, and that's their downfall.

It's kind of an interesting interaction, in the sense that a lot of this mortgage project was almost created by the bid for the CDO paper rather than the reverse. I mean, the traditional way to think about financing is, "OK, I find an investment opportunity that on its face I think is a good opportunity. I want to deploy capital on that opportunity. Now I go look for funding. I think that making mortgage loans is a good investment, so I will make mortgage loans. Then I will seek to fund that activity, perhaps by issuing CDO paper, issuing the triple-A, double-A, A, and down the chain." But what happened is, you had the creation of so many vehicles designed to buy that paper that the dynamic flipped around. It was almost as if the demand for that paper created the mortgages.

n+1: Created the loans?

HFM: Called forth the loans, because it became a really profitable business. You saw where you could issue these liabilities. Say I could issue these liabilities at a weighted average cost of LIBOR [London Interbank Offered Rate] plus one-fifty, and I know all I have to do is just push that money out the door, LIBOR plus three hundred, and I'll make a huge amount of money from that origination activity or just on the equity piece that I keep, which is highly, highly leveraged. The person who really knows the mortgages is not the person who is really taking most of the risk. The people who were taking most of the risk were the undifferentiated mass of buyers out there.

n+1: Right, and when you say the person who knows the mortgage, meaning the person who knows that the person they find on the street . . .

HFM: May not be a good credit, right? In financial markets, bad things tend to happen when you divorce the people who take the risk from the people who understand the risk. In the subprime market, that distance just increased and increased and increased. It started out that you had mortgage companies that would keep some of the stuff on their own books. Subprime lenders, it wasn't a big business—it was specialty lenders, and they made risky loans, and they would keep a lot of it on their books.

But then these guys were like, "Well, you know, there are hedge fund buyers for pools that we put together," and then the hedge fund buyers say, "You know what? We need to fund, we need to leverage this, so how can we leverage this? Oh, I have an idea, let's create a CDO and issue paper against it to fund ourselves," and then you get buyers of that paper. The buyers of that paper, they're more ratings-sensitive than fundamentals-sensitive, so they're quite divorced from the details. Then vehicles were set up that had a mandate to kind of robotically buy that paper and fund themselves through issuing paper in the market.

n+1: Black boxes?

HFM: No, not the black boxes. But there wasn't a lot of human judgment going on. In reality those guys were so far from the true collateral that underlay the paper—they have no idea. It's like they're buying collateralized paper of a conduit, the conduit's buying triple-A paper of a CDO, the CDO is set up by a hedge fund that's bought mortgage pools from a mortgage originator, and the mortgage originator is the one who realizes that they lent half a million dollars on a house in Stockton, California to . . . someone who makes fifty thousand a year. That's where the specific knowledge about the risk resides, but the ultimate risk-taker is very very far away from that.

So what happened is this machine—the big machine that wanted to gobble up rated paper—needed to be fed. There were people who could make a lot of money feeding the machine, and they were like, "We need to keep originating mortgages, and feeding them to the machine." Someone is hungry for paper, paper will be created. And that's almost never a good thing, when lending decisions are being driven by the fact that many, many steps down the chain there's just someone who wants to buy paper.

\+ + +

n+1: Why was all the press about the mortgage crisis about the hedge funds?

HFM: People like talking about hedge funds. They like to blame us for everything. And there were hedge funds that lost a lot of money.

We've had our share of lumps from the black boxes and subprime at our fund, but we're still standing.

n+1: You lost on the subprime?

HFM: We did. We were involved in creating CDOs.

n+1: You were?

HFM: Yeah, yeah. Not me, personally. But we have people who did it. They would buy mortgage pools, package them into CDOs, and sell off senior liabilities. We kept the equity pieces ourselves, and, you know, those equity pieces are worth—they're worth pretty much zero. But the amount of money we lost was kind of small relative to the amount that was lost on the whole. Because—OK, we had the equity on a CDO with half a billion dollars in mortgage collateral, and we issued paper for, you know, $450 million, and kept $50 million of the most junior piece for ourselves. OK, so we lost $50 million. If that mortgage pool is now only worth $300 million, that's $200 million of losses, $150 million in losses are borne by the people who bought the CDO paper.

n+1: From you?

HFM: From—yeah, from the CDO we set up.

n+1: Are they mad at you?

HFM: Well, our CDO paper performed better than average. So I think they're happy we did a better job than our competitors—but they're not happy they lost money.

n+1: Is the person who ran that—is he going to get fired?

HFM: He was already fired.

n+1: Really? He's gone?

HFM: He's gone. He was a guy who knew the market really, really well, who was a real expert in the nuts and bolts of mortgage lending, and really knew the collateral—but he was a true believer. And there were other people at the firm, say, at the middle of last year, who were not mortgage experts, who were saying, "I see the run-up in housing prices in some of these geographies, and I just don't really get it. I go down to Florida and see the forest of cranes, and I wonder, who's going to be in all those apartments? And I hear about all sorts of friends who are getting loans to buy apartments or houses speculatively and are lying about the fact that it's not a primary residence, and I see these commercials on TV about low-doc, no-doc mortgages—and there is no way, there is no way that this is not going to end badly. And I see that these mortgages are being created by this massive demand for CDO paper, by this robotic bid, and this is the perfect example of a bubble—and we should be short, we should be short subprime paper."

n+1: This is what guys do? They travel around Florida, they watch TV?

HFM: Just in your normal life. I mean, I trade a different market, I don't trade subprime, but I travel for other reasons, and some of my partners do the same thing. And a number of us thought, "This is just crazy. We should be short. This is a bubble waiting to be popped." But the person who was the expert, who traded subprime paper and issued the CDOs, was a true believer in the paradigm: "In 2003, people said that the credit quality of the average subprime mortgage was deteriorating, and now look, those mortgages have performed fine. The subprime market works."

And, hey, he was the expert—you defer to the expert.

n+1: He didn't listen.

HFM: But he's the expert, right? It's a tough thing. If you have somebody who's really trained in the mortgage business, he's been in the mortgage business for fifteen years, in equilibrium he'll do a great job. He'll be able to pick, of the mortgage pools out there, which is the good one, which is the bad one. He did a very good job of that, because the ones that he picked were better than the market. But the guy who's just buried in the forest . . . he's not going to see the big picture, he's not going to catch the paradigm shift.

n+1: And now he's gone.

HFM: And now he—will have plenty of time to think about the big picture.

n+1: [laughs evil laugh].

HFM: [also laughs evil laugh].

ANONYMOUS HEDGE FUND MANAGER (II)

MARCH 25, 2008
NEW YORK CITY

n+1: So this is a hedge fund.

HFM: This is a hedge fund. Now you've seen what a hedge fund looks like: a lot of flat screens, a lot of people staring intently into them, and not a lot of noise. We're quite quiet for a hedge fund. We don't have TVs. That's probably one of the big differences between this trading floor and a typical trading floor—I got rid of TVs some time ago. I don't have a TV at home, and I thought it was ironic that I had gone through all this effort to resist having a TV at home and then I would spend all day watching *Squawk Box* on CNBC, so then we decided, we'll just get rid of the volume, we'll kill the volume, but then I spent my whole day inventing dialogue for Maria Bartiromo, and new texts for the—well, there was this foot fungus commercial that would play on CNBC all the time which was really disgusting, and we were coming up with new variations of foot fungus. So we decided finally we really had to get rid of TVs. Other than that it's pretty standard.

n+1: So how are things going?

HFM: It's been a really turbulent couple of weeks. Obviously the market has been in some, uh, degree of crisis since the last time we spoke, but what's new is that it's really been spreading. I've been doing this for over a decade and I've seen asset prices generally more distressed than they are today, the equity market has been much more distressed than it is today. The particular market that I trade, I've seen prices much more distressed than they are today. But I've never seen the financial system as a whole more distressed. Banks, the sense of panic and despair at the major banks, I've just never seen it before.

n+1: When we talked a few months ago, you seemed OK with things, you thought everything was going fine, America was going to win this.

HFM: Well, I didn't want you to start a bank run with your vast readership at *n+1*. I felt it was my responsibility as a member of the financial community to keep all of literary New York from lining up at the bank or at the ATM the next day.

I still think things will be fine, but I overestimated the degree to which the subprime risk had been off-laid by the banks. I think a lot of it was off-laid—we talked about European buyers and Asian buyers who were the ultimate underwriters of the risk, but as it turns out much more of the risk than I expected was still on the books of the big investment banks. So when you hear about write-downs related to subprime mortgages taking place at Merrill Lynch, Citibank, Bear Stearns, that's a consequence of their having retained risk related to these assets on their books. We thought it had been sold on to Europeans. And it was: the Germans lost a lot of money, and some of the Chinese banks are announcing earnings in the next weeks and the speculation is that a lot of them will have to announce write-downs related to subprime. But Citibank had a ton of this stuff on their books and had to write down a tremendous amount. Almost all of the major banks have.

At the end of the subprime orgy, it became difficult to place a lot of this debt. So the banks would end up warehousing it.

They had a profitable business in purchasing and securitizing these assets, but it was ten minutes to midnight and they didn't know it. They thought they would be able to place it and securitize it when things calmed down. But it turned out the clock struck midnight and these assets turned into—pumpkins. And they couldn't move them, and while all these assets were sitting on their books the real estate market started to deteriorate, and the value of these subprime mortgages started to deteriorate with it.

n+1: How long have they known?

HFM: The biggest write-downs mostly were taking place in the fourth quarter of '07 and they've continued. We've seen some more for the first quarter of 2008. There may be more to come, but for subprime the write-downs may be close to finished. What people are worried about now and what's created a lot of tension in the financial markets is that the rot is spreading to other asset classes. So it's not just subprime mortgages: Now people say, "Gosh, subprime mortgages have performed so poorly that it's weighing on real estate markets and that means that our Alt-A mortgages will perform poorly, that means people should be worried about prime mortgages, too. People should be worried about companies that are exposed to the consumer who is taking out a subprime mortgage, or companies that relied on spending from consumers that was based on home equity, people withdrawing equity from their homes to buy things."

When you're talking about risk management, there's an assumption that not every asset class will be correlated. So, sure, subprime blows up but the bank's OK because prime will hold up, or there won't be a perfect correlation with leveraged loans. But what's going on is that all these credit products are performing badly at once.

n+1: Because?

HFM: Because there are some real linkages. If consumer spending has been supported by people extracting equity from their homes, the mortgage market shutting down will hit consumer spending. And that will hurt companies that rely on consumer spending.

And then there are the financial linkages—hedge funds blowing up so that they can't buy leveraged loans anymore, or banks that got hurt in subprime that have to sell down leveraged loans to generate liquidity, and the buyers are gone.

So that's one financial linkage, but also there's capital—the banks' capital base. Every time a bank takes a write-down, that erodes its capital base, and the bigger the base the more risk it can take. There are rules for that—Basel 2 capital adequacy—and if a bank is writing down 10 billion dollars, suddenly the risk-taking capability is reduced. Assume the capital adequacy ratio for all these banks is 10 percent. So if a bank falls 10 billion below its capital adequacy target, that's 100 billion dollars in risk-taking capacity that disappears.

n+1: And this is regulated by the Fed?

HFM: Yes. The rules can be relaxed—there can be regulatory forbearance—but so far there hasn't been any and there probably shouldn't be, because these rules are there for good reason. A good illustration of what can happen is Bear Stearns. Bear is not a commercial bank, it's an investment bank: it doesn't have these capital adequacy rules, it's not regulated by the Fed, and Bear, if your average bank had a capital adequacy rate supporting 10:1 leverage, Bear is more like 30:1. And that is one of the reasons confidence evaporated so quickly: people looked at the balance sheet and realized that if assets have to be written down even a small amount, Bear can be insolvent. And that creates a panic.

In reality I don't think they had a solvency issue, but when the capital cushion is so small it creates instability.

n+1: So what happened with Bear Stearns? What were the steps?

HFM: Bear was a bank that was very involved in the asset-backed and subprime market. Both as a principal and as an agent.

What happened this summer was funds managed by Bear Stearns—not things on their own books, other people's funds that they manage—were heavily leveraged and invested in asset-backed securities. Those funds blew up—they went into uncontrolled combustion. They failed very quickly. One day they were there, the next all the assets were marked down, then they were insolvent and folded up. Now that's not Bear Stearns's capital, but these were guys sitting in the Bear Stearns office.

n+1: Which is where?

HFM: On, uh, 47th and Madison. Just down the street.

n+1: And they were sitting there; they had a little hedge fund—

HFM: Which means they raised money from outside investors—they get paid based on how the fund does, they get a percentage of the profits. And they traded in subprime assets where the capital was given to them by outside investors.

n+1: These were ten guys?

HFM: I don't know the size of the team, but they were sitting there, buying asset-backed securities backed by subprime mortgages, they were borrowing a lot of money, they used the capital they had, they borrowed outside money, they bought subprime mortgages. They were highly, highly leveraged. 50:1 leverage.

n+1: Why was Bear Stearns in particular doing this?

HFM: Bear Stearns supposedly had an expertise in subprime and asset-backed securities; it is an expertise of theirs. They're still alive.

n+1: Really?

HFM: You know when somebody falls off a motorcycle, and the doctors want to harvest their organs, they're still alive until they harvest the organs? Right now Bear Stearns, there's an EKG, it is pinging, they're technically still alive and JPMorgan is waiting for the healthcare proxy to sign and say they can start harvesting the organs. This is where Bear is right now. They had an expertise.

n+1: So it was $100 billion? How much money?

HFM: I don't know. It was not huge. One to two billion dollars each. In that range. Which doesn't make them huge funds. Modest funds.

But from that moment forth, people on the market speculated as to how many similar kinds of assets Bear Stearns must own on its own books. There was a cloud of suspicion over Bear Stearns. As it turns out, I don't know that they were in that much trouble. They were probably much more careful with their own money than outside money, but once there's a cloud of suspicion the information asymmetry between people outside the firm who don't know what's going on, and people inside the firm, can create a crisis of confidence.

n+1: Can't the firm say, "Look, we have this, we have that . . ."?

HFM: What are they going to do, show you every instrument they have on their books? People don't know what these instruments are worth. Like an asset-backed bond—what's it worth? Nobody knows what it's worth, there isn't a market for this anymore. It's not like there are three bond issues and that's it—there are thousands, and each one is backed by thousands of mortgages. It just becomes an information-processing problem. You simply can't prove to me in a reasonable amount of time that everything's fine.

n+1: They don't have other instruments besides mortgages?

HFM: They do, they have their building, that's one of the things that is probably worth the most. But Bear was involved in a lot of the asset classes that had problems. First it's subprime mortgages, then it's leveraged loans—they're exposed to all these things, thirty times levered, so a very small diminution of the value of these assets could mean that their equity is worth nothing. And it's just going to be impossible for these guys to prove in a short period of time with a high degree of precision that their assets are worth what they say they're worth. There's been a cloud over Bear Stearns for eight months, and in retrospect people were critical of their management for being insufficiently aggressive in trying to persuade people that everything was fine. They simply asserted that everything was fine.

n+1: Did they come here, have lunch?

HFM: No, we're not a big customer, but they did speak to other customers and they did speak in the press, and they came off as—a bit cavalier, I think, and as the credit environment deteriorated the nervousness about them and the rumors about them intensified and it culminated in a process where a lot of customers who had money at Bear Stearns, customers of their prime brokerage business, and regular retail investors, said, "I don't want my money there. Why not move it to Citi or Goldman to be safe?" And once that process starts, as each account withdraws, it becomes even more enticing for the other guy to withdraw because it looks like things are unwinding. And then institutional counterparties start to refuse to take Bear's credit . . .

n+1: Are they an investment broker? If you wanted to take your money out you had to call up your buddy?

HFM: Yeah, and the broker could try to persuade you. And look, "I could be wrong about Bear being in trouble and I could lose a little money moving it around and impose upon myself the inconvenience of moving my money—a little money and a little brain damage. But if I'm wrong and leave it, I could lose a lot of money." That's the balance of risk.

n+1: It'll cause you brain damage?

HFM: Yeah, brain damage. Not literal brain damage but, you know, inconvenience—

brain damage. So on one hand you're going to impose an inconvenience on yourself, but on the other—it unwound very quickly. On Thursday they said everything was fine, on Friday they had withdrawals of sufficient magnitude that they had to go to the Fed. They're not regulated by the Fed, so it's unusual for the Fed to be lending money to Bear Stearns, but an agreement was put in place to try to provide the liquidity to Bear Stearns, and over the weekend a deal was struck for JPMorgan to help.

n+1: The government struck that deal?

HFM: Well, the government had their role. The difference between what happened and a normal takeover is the Fed, because the Fed is providing JPMorgan some nonrecourse financing for Bear Stearns assets. The strange thing about the deal is that Morgan is paying so little for Bear Stearns. Bear Stearns was trading at $170 a share not that long ago, now the deal was two dollars a share. A lot of wealth was wiped out. The question is, why would anyone accept it? Just before you came in today, JPMorgan increased their offer to $10. But a $2 share offer, for the most part it's like, "This is like pennies to me. I'll say no to this deal and maybe I'll do better in bankruptcy." The reason the Fed didn't want Bear to go through bankruptcy is that there are all kinds of interconnections between Bear and other banks. There's counterparty risk, it could lead to panic, it could lead to a whole mess in the financial market, so the Fed just wants the problem to go away, the Treasury just wants the problem to go away. But if I am a shareholder it's not my problem. "Let's go bankrupt, let's see, maybe we can do better than $2!" So everyone here was puzzled that Bear would agree to that kind of a deal.

Now Bear Stearns is unusual in that a lot of the shares are owned by insiders in the company, and the theory we had at the desk here is that the Treasury Department—not the Fed, the Fed's not so tough, but the Treasury Department went to the top guys at Bear and said: "Either a deal gets done that saves Bear and calms the financial system by the end of this weekend, or we will find some reason to put you in jail." And I think one of the things that every officer of a public company is very sensitive to, post-Enron, is jail. There has been a criminalization of failure. And after Sarbanes-Oxley, and in the wake of prosecutions related to business failures, it was like Beria said: You show me the man, I'll find the crime.

So I think for these guys it wasn't just, "I'm risking $2 if I say no," it was, "I'm risking $2 plus anal rape in jail."

n+1: I don't think they put them in that kind of jail.

HFM: OK, then tennis. "I'm risking exposing the weaknesses of my tennis game." So anyway that was the reason that deal was struck.

n+1: And the Treasury, those guys are tough?

HFM: Well Hank Paulson is tough, yeah.

It was very strange because the Fed providing liquidity to Bear Stearns is kind of unprecedented. It's not regulated by the Fed and if it turns out that the Fed finds that an institution like Bear Stearns is so integral to the smooth functioning of the financial system that it needs to bail it out, it makes you wonder whether the regulatory regime needs to be pretty radically overhauled.

n+1: And the Fed has more money than anyone?

HFM: The Fed can print money. They can create money. They can't create value but they can create money. To the extent that there are dollar claims that people have on banks, and the banks can't satisfy those claims—the banks can take assets they have to the Fed and borrow dollars against those assets.

n+1: The Fed can print money over the weekend.

HFM: No, it's not quantitative easing, but in this case they lent treasuries—assets that people will treat just like money—against risky assets that Bear had on its books. That's why they're the lender of last resort, because they have as many dollars as they need to lend. In this case they used Treasury bonds from their portfolio. But if they go and print money promiscuously the dollar won't be worth very much.

n+1 [glumly]: It's already not.

HFM: And one of the reasons the dollar is doing so poorly is that there are worries about our financial system and people anticipate that the Fed will have to run an easier monetary policy in order to deal with it.

n+1: What's going to happen to the guys who worked at Bear Stearns?

HFM: Some of them will wind up working for Morgan and a lot will be laid off, and people talk about it as a bailout but I don't think it's a bailout of Bear's management or shareholders. The shareholders get maybe $10 a share, but they used to trade at $170 per share, so they're pretty much wiped out. The senior management is all gone. And some people say a quarter, some people say half will be laid off.

If you really look at what the Treasury and/or the Fed was doing, they know that they have to protect the financial system from grinding to a halt, but they don't want to create a moral hazard as a result of people thinking they're going to get bailed out no matter what. So yes, there was a bailout of the counterparties, but they needed to take Bear out and shoot it in front of everybody. So they took it out, at a $2 offer, all the senior management is gone, and that's the financial equivalent of taking the shareholders out and shooting them.

From time to time you have to kill a management team to encourage the others. So now Citibank and Merrill Lynch realize that it's unlikely they'll be allowed to default. But at the same time the people who are actually taking risk, the senior managers at Merrill Lynch, know that if a blowup happens, the institutions may be saved, but their shareholdings will be worth zero, and their job tenure will be—done.

n+1: Wouldn't it have been better to let them go bankrupt?

HFM: And let their counterparties face the music? Maybe, but the parlous condition of the financial system as a whole I think persuaded the Fed that this is not the time to experiment and see how interconnected the system has become.

If we were in a calm economic environment and Bear, for nonsystematic reasons, failed—say they put all their money into cheesesandwich.com or something, and they failed for that reason, then it might be appropriate to let them go bankrupt because the rest of the financial system would be stable. Even if it inflicts losses on the rest of the financial system and causes a lot of brain damage for me, it won't be a risk to the system as a whole.

But every bank out there to some degree or another is suffering the same problems that led to the cloud of suspicion over Bear. So this is not a great time to test a proposition that the financial system can cope with disorderly unwinding of all these contracts.

n+1: Why is it that after eight months of suspicion this happened in forty-eight hours?

HFM: That's one of the crazy things about bank runs—it's not clear what triggers them. I was actually in Argentina the day of the bank run in 2000, and I couldn't tell you why it happened that day. It was beautiful weather, and I was having meetings in the office building of a bank called Banco General de Negocios. And everything was great and then when I came down the elevator at the end of the day, late afternoon, there was a line of people out the door of the bank. I can't tell you why it was that day. Argentina had been in economic difficulty for the prior year but that day the bank run started. And then they had to impose basically a deposit freeze.

n+1: Were people mad?

HFM: That's what started the unraveling of the Argentine government; people were standing outside banks banging on pots and pans.

n+1: Did you run from the run?

HFM: There was a big line and I went to the airport.

n+1: And you were here the Thursday that the Bear Stearns run happened.

HFM: We were just sitting here watching. It was amazing how the stock just dove. It had been trading poorly for months but it lost 60 percent of its value in a couple of hours. We were mesmerized just watching on our Reuters screens. And everyone in the market was doing the same thing, the phone stopped ringing, I stopped getting Bloomberg messages, everyone was just watching: "It can't be! What's going on! Stuff doesn't lose that much value on no news in a couple of hours."

And really what was going on was that there was a run on against Bear and people were getting wind of it.

n+1: Can you talk about what the hedge fund might have done to make money?

HFM: We could have been trading the debt of Bear Stearns, which gyrated wildly. Credit default swaps, for instance, are an instrument that lets you trade the credit risk of a borrower. One-year credit default swaps on Bear Stearns at their height were trading at 2,000 basis points, or 20 percent—you would have to pay 20 percent a year to ensure yourselves against the default of Bear Stearns. Today it's about 200. They went from 200 to 2,000 to 200 in the space of a week or so. We could have traded that but we were staring in awe instead of making money! We didn't lose any money, either, so I guess we got some entertainment out of it, which has some value. Now, we could have made money to buy entertainment; instead we just watched screens and got entertainment directly and that's not taxed.

+ + +

n+1: So there's a financial meltdown. Are you worried?

HFM: Worried about what? Specifically? I am always worried. I'm not worried about a catastrophic unwind at this point. Our fund is extremely conservative, we have a ton of liquidity and we've always run our business to be robust to financial crises. We're not directional and we're not highly leveraged. The downside is that in good times we've generated solid returns but we're never, you know, up 80 or 100 percent. It's a low-risk fund by design.

n+1: What about when you lost $150 million in subprime?

HFM: We're not going to talk about that. But that is about as much money as we're ever going to lose. We had planned that that was the amount of risk we would take to that asset class and our worst possible outcome for that asset class happened. I don't want to get into too much detail, but we weren't in the situation where our lenders were pulling lines to us or we couldn't cope with investor withdrawals. We were at a low degree of leverage, so I'm not worried about that.

I do worry about the hedge fund business—I think that it may wind up being a much more difficult business going forward for various reasons. You've had a number of blowups of high-profile funds in the past couple of months. I think that damages the credibility of the asset class. People who invest in hedge funds have thought of it as an asset class that would be robust in any environment, that you're getting the best investment talent, and you're least likely to have these kinds of disasters. But the outcomes of some of these funds give the lie to that belief. So what may happen is that even if you outperform all the other hedge funds—if everyone else is down 10 percent and you're up 1 percent—the structural damage to the asset class is so large that it doesn't matter that you outperformed, money is going to be pulled out of hedge funds.

n+1: A hedge fund is an asset class?

HFM: I think we can talk about alternative investments—hedge funds and private equity—as an asset class.

n+1: Are hedge funds considered more aggressive?

HFM: The reason it's called a hedge fund is that originally the investment would be hedged to broad market factors. Now it's a very plastic definition—just a leveraged investment vehicle—but I think people like to think they're getting the best investment talent, the best risk management, because they're paying a lot more than they would pay for a mutual fund. And if hedge funds have a high probability of spectacular blowup, that makes it a less attractive asset class.

Problem number two is that people invest in fund-of-funds—that is, vehicles that farm out money to several hedge funds on the theory that hedge funds are very uncorrelated with each other, each one has its own investment strategy and their returns won't be correlated—but what we're seeing this year is a high degree of correlation of hedge fund assets. So if I was thinking I'd benefit my diversification by investing in hedge funds but I'm not, if in fact there's a hedge fund factor that underlies the performance of all these funds—then money might leave the asset class and this hurts everybody.

n+1: What about the whole thing?

HFM: The financial system as a whole will be all right—the Fed and the Treasury drew a line at Bear Stearns and the line held. We haven't seen any evidence of the average Joe going to a bank and pulling money out of his checking account. Terrible scenario number one, where the average person loses confidence and the banking system goes bankrupt like in Argentina—the probability of that in the US is close to zero.

n+1: Doesn't everyone also owe credit card debt? They would show up at their bank and ask for their money, and the bank would say, we want *our* money!

HFM: I think people may owe their money to bank x and deposit it in bank y, so it's not actually something they can set off against you. I think another bad path is the Japan scenario—where losses don't get recognized and all these banks are in worse shape than they let on, they don't take risks because they don't really have the capital, but they can't raise capital because they don't recognize the losses, so no one is going to invest in the bank if it hasn't given a true picture of its balance sheet. Then you have zombie banks like in Japan, and that retards recovery, and you have an economy that can never build momentum to grow again.

n+1: They have zombie banks?

HFM: People talk about the banks in Japan post the crash of the early '90s as zombie companies and zombie banks—the bank has a loan to a company that is clearly insolvent, the bank should be doing a restructuring, but the bank doesn't want to admit the company is insolvent so it doesn't restructure the loan to the company, it's in limbo—they're like, undead.

In the situation we have today, where people have made bad investment decisions, where people built houses they never should have built, there's a misallocation of resources. The loss has already happened. The loss isn't what happens on a balance sheet: the loss is what happened when someone cut down a tree, made cement, built a 6,000-square-foot house in a place it should never have been built. So the loss has already happened. The question is: How do you allocate that loss? And if you don't allocate the loss, if you pretend it isn't there, then this has really baleful consequences for the economy. So now we're going through this process of loss allocation. It can be done swiftly, fairly, and intelligently, or it can be done slowly, messily, and inefficiently, or it can not be done at all. The best is to deal with it swiftly and fairly. And when the shareholders get hurt really badly and the banks have to recapitalize at punitive levels, or get taken over at two dollars a share, I think it's fair—the banks made bad decisions, the equity holders are the prime beneficiaries of the activities the bank is undertaking. When things go poorly they should be the primary bearers of the loss, I think that's good.

n+1: They're not going to want to do that.

HFM: They're being forced to do that. The regulations are forcing them to do that and it's happening. I mean, Citigroup, Merrill Lynch raised capital, they did it at prices that I don't think they're happy about.

n+1: Their share prices went down.

HFM: They went down and they raised capital at that lower price. I think it's fair that those guys should bear the loss. Now who else can take loss? Foolish borrowers—they lose their homes or wind up having to sell assets to pay back their debts. Or taxpayers can take the loss, through paying for some kind of bailout or through inflation, which isn't fair, but which is likely to happen to a certain degree. What's important is that this is done quickly and that when it's done there's certainty that loss has been recognized and that losses have been distributed, and then we can start moving again.

n+1: Otherwise we have zombies?

HFM: Otherwise we have these zombie banks that can't lend, zombie companies that shouldn't exist, and resources that should be released aren't being released. When Russia defaulted on its ruble debt in '98, we knew of a Japanese company that had bought a lot of it. And we noticed that they never publicly disclosed the loss. Not just us, other people knew, too. And somebody asked the management, Didn't you own hundreds of millions of dollars of GKO? "Yes." So aren't you going to take a loss? "No . . . we plan on holding the debt to maturity." It was defaulted! That's failure to confront the problem. So we're going through this loss recognition and liquidation—it's a painful process and you want to do it in a way that doesn't inflict further damage but you also do have to do it.

I was just in Florida and it was amazing to see all the new housing that's just empty. I was visiting relatives in a relatively upscale property development in south Florida that is 2,500 homes. The initial phase sold out quickly, and many people who lived there decided to invest in the last phase of development and buy some units in order to resell them—and it's like it's a movie set or something. It's like a neutron bomb went off, there's no one there.

n+1: Could we squat in them with our magazine?

HFM: I wouldn't encourage you to break the law but I do think that squatters in the East Village or wherever, we should tell them they're better off there—they don't need to live in a building with no power or water and rats and garbage. You can live in a nice building with a pool and sunshine.

DAVID HARVEY

Trained as a geographer, David Harvey (born 1935, Gillingham, England) is a leading Marxist thinker and an exponent of what he calls "historical-geographical materialism." His most important theoretical work, The Limits to Capital *(1982), reconciles the account of industrial capitalism offered in Volume One of Marx's* Capital *with the somewhat confused and contradictory reflections on financial capitalism in the later, posthumous volumes of Marx. This contribution has gained in importance over recent decades, as financial services have displaced manufacturing as the largest sector of the American economy; as levels of consumer indebtedness have neared or surpassed annual GDP in several wealthy countries, including the US; and as wracking financial crises have migrated from Latin America to Southeast Asia to the heartland of global capitalism.*

If Marx in the Communist Manifesto *ironically produced an unsurpassed hymn to the bourgeoisie, Harvey's* Limits *gives stirring testimony to the wonders of finance: "Credit can be used to accelerate production and consumption simultaneously. Flows of fixed and circulating capital can also be coordinated over time via seemingly simple adjustments within the credit system. All links in the realization process of capital bar one can be brought under the control of the credit system. The single exception is of the greatest importance. . . . There is no substitute for the actual transformation of nature through the concrete production of use values." Credit—including housing finance—is created in vain unless wage laborers continue to convert the natural world into commodities at increasing speed. Otherwise, an economy is literally banking on fantasies.*

JULY 14, 2008
NEW YORK CITY

n+1: We'd like to start by asking you to take us through the subprime crisis. Build it from your analytic perspective.

David Harvey: How far back do you want me to go? To its theoretical roots? It might be useful to do that, because part of the problem is that the explanations that are given are very much about, "Oh, it was predatory lending," or, "Oh, it was excessive optimism on the part of consumers." Instead of saying there's a systemic problem here, which periodically erupts in the history of capitalism, we tend to look at this as a peculiar incident of the present. But property market crises have played a very crucial role historically in triggering major downturns in particular economies, and sometimes the global economy.

For instance, the global downturn of 1973—everybody says, well, it was oil. But actually the recession started about six months before the oil embargo, and it started with a global crash in property markets. If you look at what brought the Japanese economy down at the end of the 1980s, it was speculation in land and property markets. If you look at the recession in this country during the savings and loan crisis—which was huge, something like a thousand banks were on the watch-list—it was a property market thing.

Very frequently when there's excess capital around, and nobody knows what to do with it, it goes into some sort of asset building. And asset building in property markets is a good place to go. One of the reasons is that when you build something, the rate of return stretches way into the future, so it displaces a current surplus of capital with long-term capital investment. So you only find out what you've done—bought too much of it—sometimes four, five, six years later.

Now if you look at property markets in this country, you see that they were taking off in the middle of the 1990s. And by the time you get to the high-tech crash—1999, 2000—you see even more money flowing into property markets. Property markets are debt-financed—you have to borrow in order to build condominiums and to buy. So the debt structure becomes terribly important; there's a correlation between the buildup of excessive liquidity within the financial system and the tendency of that liquidity to flow into property markets. That's not the only place liquidity can go. It can go into military expenditures. It can go into raw-material commodity bubbles, too, and we're seeing a bit of that right now, sort of displacing the property-market bubble. Food prices are shooting up, energy prices are shooting up, so we've got a lot of excess liquidity flowing into those sorts of things as well.

This is not unique in the history of capitalism. What is different this time around is the extent of it, and the degree to which the financing changed its manner. For instance, when the property market crashed in 1973, it was mainly local banks that got caught out, because if you had a mortgage, you had it with a local bank, and the developer would also borrow from a local bank, so the mortgage market was localized. During the 1980s the mortgage market became securitized, and they started to put together all these mortgages and push them into organizations like Fannie Mae and Freddie Mac, or they would get packaged into collateralized debt obligations and then sliced up and sold to some innocent party in Norway, or a pension fund in Florida, or a bank that had excess liquidity in Germany. So the mortgage market became really global.

That was supposed to spread risk, which to some degree it did. But as it spread risk, it also built more risk. People at the financial institutions, I think, really did start to think that because you'd spread risk, you'd eliminated risk, which of course you hadn't done. And then you have all of these practices of gulling people into home ownership—those have been around for a long time, but, predictably, they began to crop up more and more frequently, and then people couldn't pay because of the employment situation and all the rest of it, so suddenly you get the unraveling. Everybody says, "It's safe as houses," but it turns out that housing finance is not that safe—it was destined to run into trouble. I was sure it was going to burst about two or three years before it did, and I was going around saying, "This can't possibly go on."

n+1: So you stopped flipping houses?

DH: Actually I was in a difficult situation. I needed, for all sorts of reasons, to buy into the New York market. And I said, "Delay it, because there's going to be a crash." And I kept on delaying and delaying until last summer, which was the peak of the damn thing! So don't trust me on predictions. Timing is everything. Of course a lot of people who did flip things made a lot of money, and a lot got caught.

n+1: It might be useful to talk about where this overaccumulated capital that sought an outlet in real estate came from in the first place.

DH: In a competitive economy, capitalists find themselves forced by competition to devote their gains to further expansion of the system. So the history of capitalism is a history of continuous expansion—unless there's a crisis, in which case the expansion comes to a stop. So we tend to think that growth is a normal condition of capitalism. You look at the financial press, and if the growth rate is low, everybody starts saying, "This is terrible. The world is awful."

Capitalist economies are committed to growth, which means there are always surpluses which have to be absorbed. And there the question arises, well, where do you put these surpluses? Can you still make the same commodities you made yesterday, or do you have to make something different? An argument I make is that one of the things you do with yesterday's surpluses is build cities. The whole history of city building is connected, if you like, to absorbing these surpluses in profitable ways. Rebuilding the property market is one place where you put your surplus capital.

n+1: There's a distinction to be made between surplus capital and fictitious capital,* yes? Because it seems that there's a certain amount of surplus capital that's prompted

* "Fictitious capital," in Marx's usage, is capital created in anticipation of future revenues, but treated as an already-existing commodity. CDOs, which treat debt claims as assets, neatly illustrate the concept.

all this speculation, but also an unprecedented amount of fictitious capital.

DH: One of the ways I think you should look at that is to say, you know, all capital is speculative. You make a commodity, and you don't know if you're going to sell it. You speculate that there's going to be a market for clothes or shoes or whatever, and if the bottom drops out of the market, your speculation goes to nothing. So speculation is a normal practice in capitalism, and I think that's something we have to get into our heads. If we say, "Well, there's capitalism, and then there's excessive capitalism, called speculation," then we could say, "OK, we'll get rid of the problem by getting rid of the excess." And I'm saying you can't do that, because all capital is speculative in some way.

House building, for example, is inevitably a speculative enterprise. A developer will take a huge tract and build a thousand houses and then hope to sell them. And if you can sell them, then the speculative capital, which is fictitious, becomes real, because you've managed to complete the cycle; you've sold the product successfully at the end of the day, so your speculation turned out to be successful, and so nobody calls it speculation anymore, they call it normal entrepreneurial practice. The interesting question is, what happens when the property developers who built those thousand houses suddenly find that they can't sell them? Or can't sell them at a price which covers their costs? Then suddenly everyone's saying, "Well, that was because they were being speculators." But actually this is just normal practice. It becomes unhinged when developers can't find a marketplace for their houses—when there's nobody to buy them.

n+1: So with what's happening now—the housing market collapses, and foreclosures start to happen—who gets screwed by this? Who bears the brunt of this devaluation?

DH: Technically, everybody should. But we have a structure of state power which is dedicated to protecting the integrity of the financial system. So in effect what happens is that the state uses its power to bail out the financial institutions. And of course it can't do it totally, since there are serious losses in the financial institutions, but they can't possibly let the financial sector crash. The credit system is awash with lubricant, and if you took away the lubricant, the friction in the system would become so tough that capital accumulation would grind to a halt. So you need the credit system, but right now it's not as fluid as it was. It's constricted, and a little bit of constriction has catastrophic consequences. As soon as things stop moving, capital stops flowing in this easy way, and you're in real, real trouble.

There's an analogy to what happened in the wake of 9/11. On 9/11, this city stopped. There were no flows of money, no flows of goods. Everything stopped for about three days. Then all of a sudden Giuliani and Bush and everyone come and say, "For God's sake, get out your credit cards and start shopping and get the whole thing moving again!" In a way, what happened in the wake of an event like 9/11 is a very good example of what happens in general when the credit system starts to gum up.

n+1: And wasn't it a basic policy response of the federal government after 9/11 to keep interest rates extremely low?

DH: Oh, absolutely. Pump liquidity into the market. The Federal Reserve immediately said, "We've got to pump money in here to keep the credit flowing." So that's what's happening right now. Meanwhile, nothing so far—although legislation's now finally being passed in Congress, I think, or is about to be passed—nothing is really being done to help those people foreclosed upon. I don't have sufficient information to say what proportion of the people who got foreclosed upon were themselves flipping or speculating. Some of them were, in some parts of the country—in California, for example, there was quite a bit of that going on.

But in a city like Baltimore, that was not going on. It was largely a low-income, African-American population that had been pulled into the dream of home ownership, and they've been wiped out. And in effect if you look at cities like Cleveland or Baltimore the foreclosure wave has been like a series of financial Katrinas. You've wiped out low-income neighborhoods, in many instances populated by African-Americans and Hispanics. I'm very familiar with Baltimore, and I have a map of the foreclosures in Baltimore, and it's clear who's being affected. A lot of it affects women, particularly single, head-of-household women—they're just being completely destroyed.

There's been no attempt until now to prop up the populations being most affected. Notice we're getting the legislation now—when this problem is beginning to percolate into the middle class. The first tsunami wave, if you like, has hit the very lower classes, and they've been wiped out. The million and a half foreclosures so far have really seriously affected them. Now we're beginning to get legislation because the next two million foreclosures are likely to affect people who are slightly better off.

n+1: You talked earlier about Fannie Mae and Freddie Mac, which seem to have garnered a lot of their political support over the years from the fact that both parties very strongly support homeownership, almost as a sort of right. How do you feel about that?

DH: You might well think a little bit about the whole history of the mythology of homeownership—I'll call it that, the myth of homeownership—and where it came from, and how it spread, and the role of housing in a capitalist system. There's always been, obviously, a very important association, which goes back to the seventeenth century if not before, between private property and individual liberty and so on, and the United States has always had that as part of its founding mythology.

But what I think is interesting is that up until the 1930s or so, if you went to large urban areas, most people were renters. And actually, in terms of mobility of workforce and all the rest of it, renting is much more sensible than ownership, so there wasn't much incentive to move from renter status to homeownership. But a program which launched in the 1930s, which became very strong in the 1940s, was about homeownership for the working class, and all these institutions got set up—financial institutions, the Federal Housing Administration, and all the rest of it, to support homeownership. And one of the arguments made very explicitly back then, and this was also true in Britain in the 1920s, is that debt-encumbered homeowners don't go on strike—that encouraging homeownership, particularly at a time of great political stress in the 1930s, had a political and ideological objective. And then there was the whole issue of what was going to happen to all of the soldiers coming back from the World War—were they going to face unemployment, what were they going to get into? And so you got a G.I. bill of rights that supported homeownership.

One benefit was that, for state reasons, this creates a little political stability. And secondly, it allowed that segment of the population that became homeowners to build equity, so the house no longer was simply a home, it also became a form of savings. You could save, and eventually when you became a full property owner and you paid off your debt, you had an asset. And so it was a way of saying to the working class, "You can have an asset," which is a capital asset, sort of, for your old age, and you can pass it on to your kids, and so on. So this builds up in the 1950s and 1960s, until by the time you get to the 1960s, the majority of people are homeowners, with all kinds of political consequences.

Now, what are most homeowners interested in? They're interested in the protection of the value of their property. So what kind of politics come out of that? You keep immigrants out; you keep African-Americans out. Not-in-my-backyard politics, and the homeowners associations become very politically conservative.

Then by the 1980s, the house is no longer seen merely as a long-term asset that you build, but for some people, it starts to be a short-term speculative game. How do you build political solidarity in one of those neighborhoods in Stockton, California, where everybody is only there for a few years to flip houses? There's no local cohesion; the only local cohesion's going to be around the defense of private property rights, and maintaining housing value by not allowing someone to put, I don't know, a drug-treatment facility in your neighborhood. So you move from the idea of a house as a home, which all renters had, to the idea of a house as a vehicle for long-term savings, to the house as a short-term speculative gain.

Now you think of the political consequences of that—in terms of political attitudes and subjectivities—and you don't have to be a crass Marxist to see very quickly that, actually, the politics of this is terribly important, and I think that gulling people into homeownership has been part of the political objective from the 1930s onward. It's important to see this in the long term, about what this does to political attitudes in the country, political allegiances and so on. Now we've reached a point where people are indeed desperately concerned to defend the value of their property.

n+1: So maybe we should own the means of production but rent our houses?

DH: Well, you know, that's the interesting thing about property. Marx is not against property in the sense of the right to appropriate things—he very much encourages that. What he's against is private property. And in a sense, renting is a form of property you appropriate. And particularly if you have a large segment of social housing, as was the case in Britain, for example, up until Margaret Thatcher, you have proprietary rights; you can't be kicked out, except for malfeasance or something of that kind. You have right of residency, but you don't have right of trading. I was thinking about this—some of these people who were flipping properties had kids. I wonder what their kids' idea of home is.

n+1: You may see a new world of squatting. In Colorado, for instance, there's been a lot of pre-fab homes built in the suburbs, the economic viability of which seems pretty unclear right now, and you wonder whether, if some of this stuff is sufficiently devalued, you might have some of these suburbs just turn into unclaimed housing.

DH: You may get that. Actually, there's a very interesting phenomenon right now in some areas of Europe, which is the phenomenon of shrinking cities. In places like Leipzig, what you've got is a serious loss of population, and just empty tracts. So the city government takes tracts, buys them out, demolishes them, and builds a park. We may find the phenomenon of shrinking cities—probably not so much in the United States because of immigration. But if they shut off the immigration stream, as some people seem to want to do, you'll find quite a few places with shrinking cities.

But this is a global process now. As you'll see from the pictures of the Olympic games in Beijing, property development has not come to a halt globally. Dubai, the Gulf states are building like crazy. There are still booms on in India as well as China. If you're in Moscow, you'll see that there's a building boom there. So the interesting question is, is this just us? There was a huge crash in East and Southeast Asia in '97–98, which didn't affect us, and we all kind of looked at it and said, "Well, they've got Asian flu, you know; they've got crony capitalism; it's confined to that area of the world." Actually the United States made a lot of money out of that crisis, buying up properties very cheap. Now the crisis propensities of capitalism have come home to roost here, and there's a big, interesting question as to whether this is going to be so big as to pull down, say, the growth rates in China and India. And there are some signs of that. But, at the moment, the building booms are still going on in those places, big time. So global capitalism is kind of saying, "Forget the United States. We could all rush off to Dubai, or the Emirates, or we can rush off to Shanghai and Beijing."

It's a very interesting moment. We are very cognizant of the fact that we are in a crisis. But it's not yet the case that it has become a total, global crisis. Capitalism has some outlets, and the uneven geographical development of the capitalist system is such that it's pummeling this part of the world right now, and some parts of Europe—Britain is in trouble, Ireland and Spain are in trouble. And all of them, by the way, are in trouble because of their property markets. My guess is the decline in consumer demand in the United States is likely to have serious implications for the BRIC countries [Brazil, Russia, India, and China]. But it hasn't gotten there yet, and I think the hope is that somehow or other that is going to help stabilize the situation because, again, look at all that surplus money that is piling up in the Gulf states. What is it being used for? You've seen the images of Qatar and Dubai and so on—a huge building boom is going on.

n+1: Islands. They build islands.

DH: Yes! They build whole islands! I mean, it's an astonishing kind of construction boom! With a lot of American companies heavily involved, a lot of American financial institutions relocating into the Gulf states. And the Gulf states are saying, "This is our moment, this is going to become a financial center, because this is where all the oil money is piling up, and why funnel it through New York when we can funnel it through financial institutions located in Qatar and Dubai?"

n+1: We wanted to ask you about oil. It seems a lot of people from a left perspective are reluctant—though this is changing, obviously—to think too much about resource constraints, or think it smacks of Malthusianism, and I was struck reading *The New Imperialism* with your description of the Middle East as the spigot of the global economy. And I thought, that's a descriptive and not an analytic term, and as such slightly unusual in your work, and I wondered if you lend credence to the idea of a peak in global oil production, and if so, what you think this might do to the global economy.

DH: One of the interesting parts of Marx's *Grundrisse* is a very serious discussion of the relationship between barriers and limits. Barriers can always be transcended, overcome, got around. Limits are absolute. One of the things he does in the *Grundrisse* is to point out that capital is always facing what look like limits, and it's been very adept at turning them into barriers. You can think of a limit on, say, labor supply. Through technological changes and so on, it's turned what might have been a limit into a barrier and it's circumvented it. The same thing applies to the whole relationship to the environment. What looks like a limit, capital has a habit of being able to turn into a barrier. And my disagreement with Malthusians, or the Malthusian strain, is the tendency to think in terms of absolute limits, instead of thinking of barriers that need to be circumvented or overcome.

When you think about the ways in which capital can deal with, say, an environmental limit of some kind and turn it into a barrier, then we see some of that going on right now. When T. Boone Pickens says, "We're going to cover Texas in windfarms," I mean, how quickly people started to move on this sort of stuff! A lot of these new technologies we're suddenly hearing about have been in the pipeline for some time. So now all of a sudden people say, "There's a limit," and then they say, "No, it's no limit, it's a barrier, and here are the ways we can get around it." There's a technological fix, there's a social fix, there's a political fix. There are some barriers right now in oil production, but a lot of that has to do with the failure to invest in expansion of the oil-producing capacity during the 1990s, and the fact that oil was relatively cheap during those years, it was very cheap. You've now got a situation where it's suddenly becoming very expensive, but oil is not the kind of thing you can go and just open the spigot—it takes a few years. Many people would say, "Well, in five years' time, it will be less of a problem, because investment will have been pushing in with high prices."

n+1: Toward the end of *A Brief History of Neoliberalism*, you talk about "the unthinkable but not impossible" chance that the United States could suffer a crisis the way Argentina did a few years ago, and then you give a couple scenarios of how that might play out, in terms of a bout of hyperinflation, or a more prolonged devaluation. To what extent do you think this would be a localized problem, or to what extent would it wipe out a lot of value that belongs to people outside America and Britain, too?

DH: Clearly, the United States has been borrowing at the rate of two billion plus dollars a day for about the last ten years, and its indebtedness to the rest of the world is huge. A lot of that is held by the central banks of Asian countries and Gulf countries, some from Europe. That debt is being wiped out by the devaluation of the dollar. And at some point or another, you have to ask yourself: why would these countries continue to fuel the US debt economy? I think the Chinese central bank, for example, owns a good chunk of Fannie Mae. And the share value of Fannie Mae has collapsed, and a handful in the Chinese government lost a lot of money.

n+1: We have to bail out the Chinese government—the US government has to.

DH: No—in effect, what's happening is that the US government's being bailed out on the backs of the Chinese working class, because they're the ones who are producing the value. And that value is then returning to China in terms of excess funds, the surpluses that the Chinese have, and then the Chinese invest it in consumerism in the United States. Or have been. And of course they've been funding the Iraq war, funding the US government debt. About 50 percent of US treasuries are now owned by foreigners. The United States is essentially owned by foreign central banks, and this creates, I think, a real serious problem for the United States in terms of its room for maneuver politically. Obviously, those central banks have no interest in crashing the US economy—they have a lot of interest in keeping the US economy afloat, but at what price?

There's a lot of chatter about to what degree we're going to face an inflation crisis in the next few years. My guess is yes, we are. I don't see any way out of that. People argue no, because wages have not been pushing up very high, there are other forces which are keeping prices down, but I just don't see it. This kind of very low interest rate regime is, I think, really fueling inflation. And by the way, I think the official inflation figures are phony. When your bagel costs 50 percent more than it did two years ago, this not a 3 or 4 percent rate of inflation! This is big stuff. The real rate of inflation is significantly higher already, and to the degree that people feel that inflation, I think we're going to see some serious adjustments in the way people spend their money. They have to adjust, because wages are not going up, but costs are going up. It's not only gas; some other things are going up remarkably.

n+1: If big capital in the United States could get its money out of the country before a major devaluation took place, and then bring it back in, and scoop up things at fire-sale prices—in some ways this would seem the ideal outcome from that point of view. Do you think there's a chance of something like that happening?

DH: I'm sure there are elements of big capital that are already doing that. I'm sure there are a lot of elements of big capital that put their money in euros over the last seven or eight years, and that means it's now gone up twice the value and they can come back in and buy assets relatively cheaply. Strange as it may sound, from the European standpoint, property in Manhattan is relatively cheap. One of the things keeping the property market going here is European money coming in and buying condominiums!

n+1: A Norwegian friend of mine wrote me the other day that everyone in Oslo is saying New York is the new Berlin.

DH: Yes.

n+1: Which do you think is more likely—a monetarist* response, or a deliberate bout of inflation?

DH: I suspect that the inflation path will be more politically feasible, because you can always say, "It's the greedy oil states," or "It's the speculators," or "It's the Chinese" who are pushing raw material prices up. You can always blame somebody else for that, whereas if the government undertook really strong fiscal austerity, then people would blame the government, and no government wants to be blamed. So the easiest path out is through inflating away the debt—easier politically, I suspect, than the straight auster-

* Monetarism as an economic philosophy emphasizes the preservation of the value of money, primarily through tight control of the money supply.

ity path. And, remember, those places that adopted austerity in the past could always blame outsiders. Mexico could blame the IMF—there's always someone else to blame. Or they could blame the United States, or they could blame the financial institutions elsewhere. The problem in this country is, who would you blame for fiscal austerity?

n+1: And when this devaluation-by-inflation happens, people's savings and pensions won't be worth much.

DH: They'll be devalued. Actually, already the return on money market funds is barely 2 percent, while the official inflation rate's now close to 4 percent, so you're losing 2 percent of the value on any money you have in a money market account. You've got to have your money in an account that's earning more than 4 percent in order to be making anything, and it's hard to find a rate of return that's higher than 4 percent, if you're investing savings right now. So there's already a devaluation of savings going on, and it's been going on for a couple of years, and it's going to accelerate. So one of the best things right now is to be in debt, because then your debts get inflated away.

n+1: So austerity and slow default are the two worst-case scenarios. What's a best-case scenario?

DH: I don't think there is a best-case scenario for the state of capitalism right now. I think it is between a rock and a hard place. You can have deflation or you can have inflation. From the standpoint of capital, I guess the best-case scenario would be that the growth processes which have taken off in China and India and all the rest of it will be sufficiently strong, sufficiently powerful, to make the United States and Britain and Spain and the rest a localized problem rather than a global problem—that's the best-case scenario, I suspect, from the standpoint of capital. From the standpoint of workers, however, and the population in general, I think the best-case scenario is actually starting to think about what kind of alternatives there can be to the capitalist organization of production.

The history of capitalism has always been about growth, and if you look at it since about 1850, you see compound rates of growth around 2 or 3 percent per annum for the whole capitalist system. Now "the whole of the capitalist system" in 1850, that's about twenty square miles around Manchester. You have a different story when it's the whole globe. Just imagine what the world's going to be like, fifty years down the way, at 2 or 3 percent rate of growth—and what the ecological, political, social consequences are likely to be. I think this is the kind of moment when you need to look at the system and say, "Look, this system is unsustainable into the future." We have to think about a zero-growth economy, and a zero-growth economy is incompatible with capital accumulation in perpetuity.

All societies need a surplus. I mean, very primitive societies that don't have a bit of surplus—they're very vulnerable to climatic fluctuations and all the rest of it. The problem right now is that the surplus, insofar as it's in private hands, has to get reinvested in making more surplus. It's not a constant thing; it's continually expanding. Now, the Swedes had a wonderful plan, which was to tax part of the surplus and put it into a worker-controlled fund, which would then invest back in the corporations. After twenty years, the capitalist class would have disappeared, and you would have had a worker-controlled production system. That was what scared the bourgeoisie in Sweden, and that's when they started giving Nobel prizes to Hayek and Friedman and all these other people, and trying to set up big institutes to back them!

It was a very interesting plan. But if the state controls the surplus, then you've got to have democratic control over the state. Otherwise you get the Halliburton phenomenon—you don't know where the state begins and the corporation ends. So if the state is going to control more of the surplus—and I think that's inevitably going to be the case, given what's going on right now—then democratizing the state becomes a terribly important initiative. If you want a peaceful transition as opposed to a total, revolutionary kind—which by the way there are signs of in many parts of India, and we've seen it in Nepal—then democratic control over the state apparatus starts to become a crucial objective for any kind of political movement.

We have to think about a revolutionary solution—which is going to deal with questions of social inequality, with questions of environmental degradation, and it's going to deal with this whole issue of growth in perpetuity, which cannot continue. Otherwise we're going to get more and more of these fictional, speculative growth spurts, followed by more and more serious collapses. If you go back to 1970,* we didn't have these kind of collapses like Mexico in 1982 and 1995; we didn't have Indonesia in 1997 and '98; we didn't have Argentina in 2001 and the United States in 2007 and 2008; we didn't have that kind of thing going on. What you see is the system is beginning to get rockier and rockier, and it's time that people started to say, "Look, this system cannot continue in this kind of way." So the best-case scenario is the growth of a political movement.

* In the early 1970s, both the gold standard (which pegged the value of the dollar to gold) and the Bretton Woods system of international exchange rates (which pegged foreign currencies to the dollar) were abandoned. The instability of exchange rates in the years since has factored importantly in increased speculative activity across national boundaries.

ANONYMOUS HEDGE FUND MANAGER (III)

SEPTEMBER 4, 2008
NEW YORK CITY

n+1: We're back in your office above midtown. Last time we looked out people were being fired, people were jumping out of windows . . .

HFM: And it's continued largely in that vein. The credit crisis that was underway is still underway, and the recognition of losses is continuing—but it's still continuing at a pace that means that the situation is not resolved. We haven't reached a point where people feel like all the bad news is out of the way. It's like a rainstorm of shoes: the shoes keep dropping, and there are still clouds in the sky, and there's still going to be more shoes dropping, and until the footwear stops falling, you know, the crisis will continue.

n+1: You were optimistic that companies were announcing their losses, were dealing with the bad news. Was that not correct?

HFM: No, they are, they are, but people's estimates of the size of those losses have increased. If you talk about subprime, most of those losses have been recognized. But the losses extend beyond subprime, they extend beyond leveraged loans. So now people are worried about prime mortgages, they're worried about development loans, mortgages of commercial property, so the losses have not really been recognized, or the loss recognition process there is only just beginning. Then you have the whole issue of Fannie Mae and Freddie Mac: their equity is definitely wiped out, these things are insolvent, the equity has been burned through—you have negative equity. You have to recognize that. If you marked all their assets to market and said, "What are the assets worth?," you'd find that the assets are worth less than their liabilities, which means that the equity is worth nothing. If that were a regular company—and not a company that plays this really important infrastructural role in the mortgage market—they'd go bankrupt. This company goes bankrupt. The equity should be wiped out and maybe some of the debt should be wiped out, and it needs to be restructured. But instead it's like the zombies, they're zombie companies. These companies are very politically powerful and also they're important, and there's fear that if they failed or if the equity holders were wiped out, it would lead to a horrible shock in confidence. But in the end, if you have a dead body in the room, and I keep saying, "That person's not dead, that person's just resting," and pretty soon it starts to smell and decompose—there's only so long we can pretend before the odor becomes overpowering and we have to run from the room.

n+1: And when we talked about whether this was going to spread beyond the credit market—that seems to be happening?

HFM: Well there are two kinds of linkages we can talk about in the ways the rot has spread. One is the financial linkages. So does it spread to other asset classes? And it has—there was a problem in subprime, and then it moved to Alt-A, and now people are worried about prime and commercial mortgages. So there definitely has been a financial spreading. The other linkage you worry about is, "Do the problems in the financial system spread to the real economy?" To a certain extent, obviously, right? The financial system is a way of accounting for what's going on in the real economy. And so we see foreclosures, and unemployment ticking up and job loss, but I think people have actually been surprised at the extent to which the real economy has been stable in the face of all this. I mean, technically we don't even have a recession yet! We haven't had negative GDP growth! And that's kind of a mystery. People in the financial community have been saying, "Gosh, things are so bad, pretty soon it's got to spread to the real economy." At a certain point if that recession never comes, then people will convince themselves that it's not going to come. But right now, the fact that it hasn't happened yet has not really changed anybody's assessment in the financial world that that damage is still coming.

n+1: And is it just that people are still maxing out their credit cards?

HFM: No, but one of the things that has been very beneficial for statistics in the US has been exports. Exports have been a real bright spot because the dollar has been weak and the rest of the world has been strong. The rest of the world is continuing to grow. People have talked about China being a very large source of growth, and some of the countries that have done well with high commodity prices—Brazil, Russia, India. Growth has held up pretty well in these countries, and so that's been supportive to the real economy in the US. That may be changing—the emerging markets are starting to slow down and running into some more problems. And Europe, too. If you look at what's happening to the euro versus the dollar, it tells you that people are concerned about growth in Europe.

n+1: The euro is weakening?

HFM: The euro is weakening. The first time we talked it was interesting because everyone was saying, "The dollar is going to get killed, it's going to be the end of the dollar." And I think I said, you know, it's very hard to project the future of the currency based on its recent past. The currency market tends to be ahead of events; it's a very forward-looking market. And so, the dollar—in spite of all the prophecies—the dollar's been on a tear in the last couple of weeks, even the last two or three months. That is because currency traders look at the rest of the world and say, "What the US is going through, the rest of the world is going to start to be affected by that." So suddenly it's not so attractive to short the dollar along with everything else.

I think we had this year of people robotically selling dollars and buying every other currency in the world. First out of a sense of optimism about the emerging markets: "There's so much growth potential there; I want to be exposed to the currency." Then out of pessimism about the US: "The financial situation in the US is so terrible, the banks are in such rotten shape, I want to be out of dollars." So there's been a huge flow out of dollars. The world is, you know, short the dollar. Now suddenly people look at the world and they're panicked, and they want to reduce risk. They just want to get back to flat, right? "I don't want to have any positions at all. I'm too scared," you know, "I just want to curl up into a ball." And when that happens, if everybody was short dollars, then people have to buy dollars back to flat down, and that's one of the things that have pushed the dollar stronger.

n+1: And so if these other markets are slowing down, is their slowdown going to slow us down here?

HFM: It will probably have an impact on exports in the US. And this is of course the nightmare scenario, that the whole world slows down simultaneously and you get into a vicious circle.

n+1: And then what?

HFM: And then you have the Great Depression! I don't think that's going to happen. But the nightmare scenario is basically that there's no source of growth anywhere in the world, you have a shrinking of demand, a spreading wave of risk aversion all over the world, and you get into a liquidity trap. That's still a very extreme scenario.

n+1: When does this begin to feel like less of a cyclical thing, like the weather, and more of a permanent end of the world kind of thing?

HFM: When you see me selling apples out on the street, that's when you should go stock up on guns and ammunition.

n+1: You make it sound like people just have to come out to the public and say, "We lost all this money." But the consequences actually would be, ah . . .

HFM: There would be some bankruptcies, yeah, there would be bankruptcies. And shareholders would be wiped out and management teams would be out on their ear. But that probably should happen.

It's interesting, because how should policy react? And you could break people into two camps. There are people who say, "There needs to be robust government intervention. The government needs to prop up asset prices in order to keep banks solvent. There needs to be a buyer of last resort, and that buyer of last resort is going to be the only player with the balance sheet to do it: it's going to be the government, it's going to be the US government, the Treasury." And then there are people who say, "No. What needs to happen is that we finish this process of loss recognition, the faster the better, so that there's full transparency as to the true financial condition of banks and companies and everybody, and then prices (financial assets) get marked to levels that reflect their true condition and that don't have embedded in them this entrenched expectation of continued decline." There's some price at which the consumer knows it's a bargain: everything's just been marked down.

And which camp you fall into isn't a matter of ideology; it's a matter of how bad you think the problem really is. Because, you know, if you had a factory, and you're like, "The factory is having problems," one of the ways of recognizing loss is to say to the equity holders, "Sorry, the equity holders' claim is worth nothing, it really now belongs to the debt holder." What you're doing there is shuffling claims—you're not doing anything to the factory, you're shuffling claims. And once you're done shuffling, and everybody knows the financial condition, the factory can continue producing.

What if, though, instead you just go in and you just, like, smash all the equipment in the factory? Then you've done real damage, right? The factory doesn't work anymore.

And when you talk about financial institutions, if you say we can mark everything down to its true condition, you're saying the markdowns themselves don't cause damage to the institution. The institution is still there, the bank is still there. There's still people that show up to work, you haven't lost all the intellectual capital. These banks continue to exist.

But there's some people who think the problem is so bad, that if you actually recognize the losses, that it's akin to smashing the equipment in the factory. Because these institutions can't exist anymore, right? That for a bank, if you say, "Look, you can't exist anymore. You're so deeply insolvent that everybody's fired and everybody's got to leave"—at that point, financial intermediation won't work anymore. It doesn't matter that you've marked everything down to the level that makes sense—you don't have a financial system anymore. And a lot of people think that's one of the reasons the Great Depression was so difficult to get out of, was that the financial machinery was smashed. So I think which camp you fall into depends a little on how bad you think the damage is.

n+1: Of all the companies in the world a bank is the least likely to want to go bankrupt.

HFM: Yeah, because the whole business model is based on trust, it's based on the appearance of solvency. The structural damage you can do to a bank, through bankruptcy, is much larger than the damage you can do to a factory through bankruptcy. So there are reasons that have to do with the fundamentals of business, not just the interests of management. Banks are going to struggle much harder to avoid admitting that they're bust, and that's why the regulators have to step in and say, "You're bust." Which has happened for IndyMac Bank and a couple of other community banks—FDIC has been taking them over, so you are starting to get that process of recognition. But we're not at the end of it.

One way that people try to get a handle on how big the losses could be is to look at the profits to the financial industry in the US relative to GDP over a long historical period. And you see that as a percentage of GDP it has tended to be pretty stable over time, but in the last five years it became a much larger proportion of GDP. So you can say, "Well look, if the true profits really should have been at the historical trend, how much excess profit was made which was really phony-baloney and probably needs to be reversed, you know, CDOs, subprime, this kind of stuff?" If you do that analysis, you get to a number between $1.25 trillion and $1.5 trillion. The write-downs so far are on the order of 500 billion, OK? Risk capital has been raised, there's been something like $350-400 billion raised; so new equity has been raised to cover those losses. But I think people do that analysis and say, "There must be more, there must be more to go."

n+1: You're feeling pretty low?

HFM: I'm feeling pretty low, yeah. "Low" is probably the wrong word. I'm feeling pretty nervous and I'm feeling a certain degree of frustration that this situation is stretching on as long as it has, because the losses, the true losses, were inflicted a long time ago, when people built houses they shouldn't have built or built the park buildings they shouldn't have built or bought cars they couldn't afford or whatever. Those losses were created a long time ago.

n+1: When you're talking about recognizing these losses, how much of that is connected to the real economy and people actually losing their houses?

HFM: Some of these houses aren't even occupied. It's about misallocation of resources, right? I mean, yeah, some of that was people being put in houses they couldn't afford. Now what is that house worth? It was sold to some poor schlub for $400,000 because he was able to get a $400,000 mortgage. His ability to get the mortgage is what created the price. In reality, this guy can afford to carry a mortgage on a $150,000 house, and there's nobody else to buy this house, based on where it's sited and what its features are. And yet if you had to write down the mortgage, you'd have to sell the house to someone else who can afford that $150,000, or you'd need to come to an agreement with that guy and say, "Look, your payments are now commensurate with a $150,000 mortgage." The loss needs to be recognized. The house shouldn't have been built. Now that it's built, what's the maximum value you can get out of it? That's what it's worth.

n+1: But, you know, some of this is gonna mean . . .

HFM: That people are kicked out of their homes? Some of it will. But to the extent that there's nobody else to occupy those houses, then the process involves turning those people back into renters or writing down their mortgage, giving them a forgiveness on that. It doesn't help anybody—let me put it this way—it doesn't help get a better recovery on the value of those assets, like those houses, to keep them empty. So somebody is going to maximize the value of that house, somebody is going to occupy it. Maybe it's the same family who lives there now, maybe it's a different family, but it's certainly not going to be anybody who buys the house for

$400,000. It's going to be somebody who pays a lot less for that house.

n+1: OK, a last question, a more general question. You know, you have a beautiful mind. I listen to you talk, and then I read over the transcript, and I'm just amazed at the way your mind works. And now we're living through a crisis in capitalism, possibly a historically bad crisis. And do you feel, you know, do you feel that your mind is being used right now in history in the best way it possibly could?

HFM: Well, where do you think it would be used better? I mean, I think if there's a problem here, this is the place—this is where the problem is. +

JESSICA BIEL AT THE 2008 OSCARS.
COLOR PHOTOGRAPH. ASSOCIATED PRESS.

JESSICA BIEL'S HAND: THE CINEMATIC QUAGMIRE

A. S. Hamrah

FOR TWO MONTHS THIS SUMMER the only movies I watched were movies about the war on terror. While other moviegoers were enjoying cinematic treats like *You Don't Mess with the Zohan* and *The Happening*, or the revival of Kobayashi's *The Human Condition*, or that Norwegian movie about Norwegian yuppie writers that everybody liked so much, I was immersed in the backlog of global-war-on-terror movies released since 2002. The only summer blockbuster I saw was *Iron Man*, a war-on-terror movie and therefore allowable.

I watched three dozen of these movies and maybe 15 percent of them were any good. The rest, like the war itself, represented an enormous waste of manpower and resources that would have been better spent on something good for people, like entertainment. When I say this I do not mean any disrespect to the three thousand men and women who died on September 11, 2001, or the over four thousand American soldiers who have died overseas, or the tens of thousands of Iraqis who have been killed, or the unknown number of detainees who have been tortured in prisons. But watching these movies was like being buried under rubble while working in an office, like being stuck in the desert far from home, invaded by an occupying army, left tied in a stress position for days.

You ask why I put myself through this. Like some kid fresh out of high school sauntering into a recruitment center just to check it out, I wasn't exactly coerced. I wasn't drafted. A suggestion was made, I volunteered, I didn't want to seem like a wuss. Here was the story of our time, they said, told cinematically. Wasn't it my duty to cover it? It might be, I answered. So they signed me up, they put my name on a contract.

Fortunately for me, I cannot be stop-lossed. American soldiers continue to die in Iraq with no power to make it end, but I can simply file this report, turn my back on the cinematic quagmire and walk away. I know it's unfair. It's criminal. But if there's one thing we've learned these past seven years, it's that fairness has nothing to do with it.

THE FIRST IRAQ WAR MOVIE was *Fort Apache,* a western John Ford made in 1948. It was also the first Vietnam movie. A thinly veiled retelling of Custer's defeat at Little Bighorn in 1876, *Fort Apache* holds up the ordinary cavalry soldier, represented by John Wayne's Captain York, against an oblivious commander, Henry Fonda's Colonel Thursday, who foolishly leads his men to doom at the hands of Apache warriors. In *Fort Apache,* the soldiers of the Seventh Cavalry do their duty, "riding the outposts of a nation," as it says in another Ford western, while a commander who refuses to listen to his officers charges blindly into death.

Wayne's York gives what amounts to a press conference after the defeat. He doesn't lie to the assembled reporters who consider the dead Thursday a hero—we can't picture John Wayne lying in a movie made in 1948—but he doesn't tell the truth, either. What he does is let the reporters believe what they want to believe. The reporters don't really listen to what York says, anyway. Instead, they tell him what happened in the battle, even though they weren't there and he was. York's response, a soliloquy about dead soldiers and the permanence of the US Army, delivered by John Wayne as he looks out a window, ends the film.

The Apaches carry *Fort Apache*'s moral weight, rejecting peace to fight with honor. The movie preserves the dignity of the US Army, however, which is portrayed as separate and apart from Thursday's stupidity even as it's subject to it. Ford shows Thursday was wrong; he shows how regular soldiers get killed. What makes the film tragic is that it doesn't matter. In their victory the Apaches remain the enemy, in defeat Thursday remains a hero. After a while nobody remembers the dead soldiers' names.

John Ford fought in World War II and filmed the landing at Normandy, but *Fort Apache* was not about the war just ended. It was about a much longer war. What we see in movies about the war in Iraq and Afghanistan, in movies about the so-called global war on terror, is that we are still playing the *Fort Apache* game—cowboys and Indians and reporters.

MAYBE ANOTHER FILM, MADE CLOSER to the events at hand, a film with no moral weight at all, is really the first Iraq war movie. In 2001, less than four months before the destruction of the World Trade Center, *Pearl Harbor* came out, to much fanfare, on 3,200 screens.

Brought to us by the men who made *Armageddon, Pearl Harbor* existed to celebrate, in costly and spectacular fashion, the fliers who avenged the attack that got us into World War II. But it also existed to do away with the very idea of moral weight, to make war look like late-'90s action-adventure, something that happens while Ben Affleck and Josh Hartnett argue over a girl. In *Pearl Harbor* Michael Bay and Jerry Bruckheimer celebrated war from the sky, a kind of war like the first Gulf War, the kind Jean Baudrillard could claim didn't really take place because the soldiers fighting it were never in any danger.

Who wants to remember *Pearl Harbor* now? After seven years of this new war that isn't so new anymore, nobody does. Looking back on that obnoxious and innocent time when *Pearl Harbor* was the first blockbuster of 2001, and being able to see the last blockbuster of that summer looming on the horizon, *Pearl Harbor* becomes an insult to everything—life, death, war, the movies. Why was that entertainment?

The truth is it wasn't entertainment. Is any summer blockbuster? Summer blockbusters are civics lessons, collective work we do for the economy, grim torture-filled slogs like *The Dark Knight* or the war in Iraq. The lesson of *Pearl Harbor* came in the form of dialogue delivered by Colonel Jimmy Doolittle, played by Alec Baldwin in the last role he had where we were supposed to take him seriously as an authority figure. "Victory belongs to those who believe in it the most and believe in it the longest," he says in *Pearl Harbor.* "We're gonna believe. We're gonna make America believe, too."

In the year or so before 9/11 that's what all our blockbusters were telling us, from *X-Men* to *Bring It On.* It was a message we were ready to hear. Boys and girls had to get together as a team, learn from the old dudes, and kick some ass. Why? We didn't know why. But it's good to be prepared.

Soon enough we found out. And pretty soon after that, just like in *Duck Soup*, we had a war we were promised would be both easy to win and endless.

RIGHT AWAY ENTERTAINMENT BEGAN TO TAKE OVER. Already there was no other way to see anything. Everything had to fit into the world of entertainment, even though TV, the source of entertainment, kept saying the world had changed forever.

On September 11, 2001, two French brothers, Gédéon and Jules Naudet, who were working on a documentary about a firehouse in downtown New York, filmed the destruction of the World Trade Center right from Ground Zero. They caught the planes going into each tower, the initial rescue efforts, with the sound of bodies thudding on the pavement outside. Jules Naudet, trapped with firemen inside the North Tower when the South Tower collapsed, continued filming.

It was like filming the exact moment of the Big Bang, but in reverse: the end of the world. The buildings were gone, there was nothing but white smoke and sirens. Spreadsheet confetti fell endlessly, like volcanic ash. "The building collapsed to dust," says one firefighter in *9/11*, the TV movie that emerged from the Naudets' footage. "No desks, no chairs, no telephones, no computers . . . you find a foot."

The footage is frightening and tragic, put together in a thoughtful way that gives every firefighter his due, and yet something's missing. You feel bad for even thinking so, but it's true: something's missing. The Naudets' footage, as essential as anything that's ever been filmed, became the basis for a TV special. Set within the context of TV it strives to be really good TV, and it is really good TV, and now who ever thinks about the Naudets or their footage anymore?

WHILE JULES NAUDET WAS FILMING IN THE NORTH TOWER, a thousand miles away, in Sarasota, Florida, George W. Bush was sitting in front of an elementary school classroom reading along with second graders as they followed a story called "The Pet Goat." After his chief of staff whispered to him that a second plane had struck the Twin Towers, the President just sat there for over seven minutes. He continued to read silently or stared into space.

This footage is as essential as the Naudets' footage of the end of the World Trade Center. It too deserves to be seen in its entirety. Instead, it was taken over by Michael Moore, who was afraid we would be bored by it. So instead of letting us see this thick chunk of dead time in which the President of the United States squirmed, he spoiled it in *Fahrenheit 9/11* by showing only sections of it, adding an on-screen countdown clock to time the President's inaction, and talking over it, telling us what we were already seeing: "Mr. Bush just sat there."

Whatever we would have thought about this footage on our own was not good enough for Michael Moore. He ruined it in the name of entertainment, encouraging us not to think while he showed pictures of a man he claimed wasn't thinking.

THE FIRST TWENTY-FIVE MINUTES OF OLIVER STONE'S *World Trade Center*, which take place on the morning of September 11 before the first tower was hit, are an evocative and even beautiful remembrance of New York City—evocative and beautiful because we know what's going to happen. Haunted shots accumulate and create a strange tension the rest of the film can't sustain. Stone wisely introduces the towers from the deck of the inbound Staten Island Ferry; we see that romantic view that is gone forever. Soon the shadow of a plane passes over the side of a building with a billboard for the movie *Zoolander* on it.

World Trade Center has the unintentional effect of reminding us how much TV we watch. So much of the film consists of families of trapped policemen watching TV that you begin to see this as a fundamental part of Stone's view of humanity. History is a slag pile they stare at without understanding. (The firemen called Ground Zero "the Pile.") Stone forces regular people to watch and rewatch the catastrophe over and over, as if he's saying, "See? See?" He makes his characters submit docilely to TV news, then presents the rest of their lives as a series of Hallmark moments that weren't worth filming.

THESE ARE THE TROPES OF WAR-ON-TERROR MOVIES: fake Middle Eastern music, constant TV news and radio commentary, scenes of combat shot in Morocco instead of Iraq, actors we don't recognize speaking Arabic with subtitles, videos of men in ski masks proclaiming in Arabic while they hold a Westerner hostage, American soldiers accidentally killing an Iraqi woman or child, vets losing their shit in their hometowns, a constant resort to cell phones, a scorpion fight, titles identifying every location change, a cut to black to avoid showing something horrible, a precredits wrap-up crawl that tells us what happened later, blonde wives back home. It's amazing how everyone has a blonde wife back home. You'd think al Qaeda made these movies.

Shaky-cam always reminds me of TV cop shows or coffee commercials, things that are on in the background. There's a lot of shaky-cam in *United 93*, so like TV it has an ambient quality. It's almost calm. A storm is brewing but all people do is look at computer screens and talk on cell phones. Then they turn on CNN. Back on the plane, a hapless passenger is buttering a muffin while one of the hijackers puts together a bomb in the restroom.

The hijacker's bomb is a fake meant to frighten the passengers into submission, a prop in the movie but a prop in real life, too. It makes you think about how all the cell phones in the movie are props. The actors scream and cry into their fake phones, yet they are not famous actors, maybe not actors at all, and you put yourself into their situation so much you can't believe they actually made a movie about this. If Kevin Costner were on the plane, you might have cheered it on its way, wanting it to crash as he calmly dialed his wife. His presence would have contradicted this strange radio commentary from the Naudets' *9/11*: "What you see here is right out of one of those movies you would see in Hollywood: people walking around with cell phones in tears." The cell phones cried that day and it seemed like Hollywood.

United 93 is an exploitation film in the form of a safety-instruction manual. It manipulates us mercilessly but blandly. When Flight 93 crashes the screen cuts to black. The only decent thing to do at that point would have been to end the film right there and flip on the lights in the theater. But miles of credits roll like they always do.

ROBERT REDFORD'S *Lions for Lambs* is as close to the purely didactic as Hollywood gets. Yet since it doesn't quite know what it wants to say, this salutary didacticism is really a lost cause. It's like a play that examines every viewpoint it can think of in the most boring way possible. I admired that about it, but if it were a person doing that instead of a movie, you'd leave the room. Maybe the same thing does happen with the movie. It's hard to imagine someone watching it. It's like an art installation called "Robert Redford Political Movie."

Tom Cruise is exceptional as a US senator who wants to escalate the war. For some reason, he's very good at playing very serious self-convinced loonies. Redford, however, gives the scariest aging-star performance since *What Ever Happened to Baby Jane?* At one point, while calmly discussing something with a student in his office (he plays a college professor), he suddenly jerks his hand upward to reveal a huge scar on his forehead, then barks out lines about getting "fifty-four stitches protesting in Chicago" after he came home from Vietnam. That was as harrowing as the plane crash in *United 93.* It was so unexpected and frightening I jumped out of my seat like it was wired. I know he's an actor playing a part and all, but in the 1960s Robert Redford was a handsome movie star who made a lot of money by not being in Vietnam. I don't know if he was at the 1968 Democratic National Convention, but somehow I doubt it. Wasn't he filming *Butch Cassidy and the Sundance Kid* then? He thinks we all have short memories. That's probably why we allowed another Vietnam to happen.

THE AMERICAN CINEMA has been producing bullshit for so long now it's no longer capable of dealing with a situation like this. That's the message of *Home of the Brave.* The vets in this movie who return home and have trouble adjusting to civilian life are a sad mirror for Hollywood's inability to cope with the war in Iraq. In *Home of the Brave,* one of the vets even gets a job selling tickets at a cineplex. "I sell these stupid tickets to these stupid movies," he says. "But I don't go see any of them."

In 1946, right after the war, William Wyler cast a man named Harold Russell in *The Best Years of Our Lives,* a movie about the problems vets faced returning to their hometowns. Russell, an army vet, was a nonactor who lost both hands in an explosion during the war and was fitted with prosthetic hooks. When you watch the movie you can tell Russell is not a professional actor yet his performance as sailor Homer Parrish is unsentimental, affecting, and unforgettable.

In *Home of the Brave,* pretty Jessica Biel plays a vet who has lost one hand. The actual Jessica Biel, it goes without saying, has both her hands. Her stump, which we see, is a prop stump she covers with another prop, a fake hand. When a coworker at the school where she teaches gym tries to help her with something by saying, in all seriousness, "Hey, let me give you a hand," the audience laughs. If somebody had laughed at Harold Russell in 1946, he would've gotten his head bashed in. That is the difference between then and now—not just in terms of how we think about veterans or about the current war, but about the movies, too, about whether acting is taken seriously and about the way actors move through the frame or are moved through the frame by directors. The story in 1946 was that Harold Russell's Homer was a good guy who faced his problems the only way he knew how, by trying to get through life like everybody else. In the film from 2006, there is no story; there is a message. The message is that if you lost a hand in Iraq, Jessica Biel might play you in a movie. Any veteran who laughed at her deserves a medal.

THERE IS A DIFFERENCE BETWEEN ACKNOWLEDGING that many veterans come home with post-traumatic stress disorder and wanting them to come home with it. Fortunately for Hollywood, many vets do come home with psychological problems, emotional adjustment issues that lend themselves to drama. *In the Valley of Elah*, which is based on a true story, is noteworthy for how sordid and amoral it is, how sordid and dull.

Paul Haggis, who wrote and directed it, seems to have consciously drained the film of all the effects that ruin contemporary filmmaking. *In the Valley of Elah* is quiet, low-key, precisely framed and carefully lit, shot in long takes. It has things besides Tommy Lee Jones in common with *No Country for Old Men*: its brutality and its southwestern setting. Jones is better in this than in the Coens' film. He gets to be typically authentic but also an uptight asshole. He's got a face like a dog, with black beady eyes, jowls and lines, and he looks shrunken, pale, and mottled. An excellent actor named Victor Wolf, who plays a Latino soldier from Jones's son's unit, gets to spit a question in Jones's face: "Wouldn't it be funny if the devil looked just like you?"

When the film sticks to amorality it's pretty good. When it gets to lecturing Salvadoran janitors about raising American flags upside down to signal distress, it gets pretty bad. The film refuses to condemn the war outright. It does so instead by equation. The war must be wrong if it turns a soldier's best buddies into psychos who will kill him for no reason, then chop him up and set him on fire to get rid of the evidence. This is a case where "based on a true story" really works for Hollywood. It gets you to shut up and keep your complaints to yourself.

EMPIRES IN DECLINE NEED IMAGINARY CADS who are also superheroes. They send them out into the world preening and being casually brutal so we can all pretend the empire's doing fine. The English have James

Bond, a 1960s import to the movies from postwar British fiction, and now America has Robert Downey Jr.'s Tony Stark, a.k.a. *Iron Man,* an import from our literature created in the Vietnam era and updated for the war in Afghanistan.

Because of Robert Downey's charm we care only about Tony. When he puts on the *Iron Man* suit we lose interest; he becomes a steroidal C-3PO and he's gone. But Tony Stark fascinates. He needs a fake heart to keep him alive, the fake heart powers a superhero carapace that makes him all-powerful—he's a metaphor for how Hollywood movies work at the box office. The metal suit is as much an excuse to give Robert Downey a good part as it is a touching industrial fantasy. Tony Stark and *Iron Man* are two separate things. When he's out of the suit, he's free, he can act, do interesting things other actors don't do when they play superheroes because they are always too much the costume. What's also touching is Tony Stark's very American desire to make everything right in the world, a desire he doesn't share with James Bond.

To the extent that *Iron Man* is a war movie about how Yankee ingenuity and super-technology will make things right in Afghanistan, it's interesting. When it becomes a clash between competing business executives in giant metal suits, it's boring. And when Tony Stark returns home and asks for a hamburger after being tortured and held captive in the caves of Tora Bora, and somebody gives him one from Burger King, and Robert Downey has to act like he likes it, you have to wonder what's the point of being a billionaire playboy at all.

GRACE IS GONE IS A CURIOUS FILM. It had the potential to be the best of the homefront Iraq war movies—certainly it's the best acted. It's under eighty minutes long, but that's not its problem. The problem is that it gives every indication of having been tampered with or left slightly incomplete. Scenes seem truncated, and actors in the cast list aren't really in the movie. It emerges as a film that was worth making, wasn't fully made, and is only half worth watching.

Another problem has to do with one of the film's locations, a small amusement park that to me was clearly a substitute for Disney World. It's too bad Disney World would never let a film like this be made there. That would be something, a poignant indictment more to the point than a lot of documentaries. It's too bad in general that although going to Disney World is a big part of a lot of people's lives, it's an experience that can't be represented cinematically outside of home movies. God forbid we should see somebody unhappy on the spinning teacups.

John Cusack plays a schlumpy, tentative Home Depot manager in the Midwest who doesn't know how to tell his two young daughters that their mother, a soldier, has died in Iraq. He decides to put it off as long as possible by taking them to Enchanted Gardens, the Disney World substitute. As the three drive through a landscape of big-box stores, motels, and chain restaurants, we see the beige landscape our soldiers are fighting for in Iraq. The only other recent film I can recall showing this landscape is *The Brown Bunny*, the film in which Chloë Sevigny gives Vincent Gallo a blow job. I don't necessarily recommend pairing them as a double feature.

In Cusack's other wartime effort, the near-future satire *War, Inc.*, he plays a weary corporate hitman going through the motions in a war-torn country named Turaqistan. It's to his credit that Cusack wants to make movies that investigate or indict contemporary reality, but *War, Inc.*'s satire is hesitant and chaste. It gets lost in set pieces that only try to replicate the things they're supposed to be mocking.

A meal Cusack shares with Marisa Tomei (canny left-wing reporter) and Hilary Duff (whorish Turaqistani pop star) at an abandoned château should have been a Renoiresque highlight, the heart and soul of the film. Here we get the first inkling the trio constitutes some kind of sexually tense family. Instead, it turns into a tribute to the torture scene in Reservoir Dogs, which is emerging as the primal scene of all Iraq war–era movies and maybe the entire era in general.

I SAW THE DOCUMENTARY *The War Tapes* on DVD and made the mistake of watching the bonus features first. One of the bonus features turned out to be résumés for director Deborah Scranton and producer Chuck Lacy. Scranton is a former director of network-TV sports who graduated from Brown with a degree in semiotics. She's also a former member of the US Ski Team who lives on a farm in the mountains of New Hampshire. Lacy, the former president of Ben & Jerry's, runs a venture capital fund and in his spare time breeds grass-fed cattle and imports yerba maté from Paraguay. After I read that I had to take a day off before I watched the film so I could evaluate it without prejudice. Also to reassess my life.

Scranton and Lacy made *The War Tapes* by giving small video cameras to soldiers in a New Hampshire National Guard unit stationed in Iraq in 2004. The film uses footage shot by three of the soldiers: Mike Moriarty, an unemployed forklift operator who would like his kids to see him "as a good man who was brave"; Steve Pink, an acerbic carpenter whose graphic letters home reveal a good writer; and Zack Bazzi, a serious-minded liberal who moved to the US from Lebanon when he was a child and wants to be career soldier.

All the footage these men shot is riveting, even when it's boring. Sometimes little is going on and the men just horse around or complain about KBR and Halliburton. Then comes the poetry of burning trucks, then sickening incidents. Riding in their Humvee one night, the men strike and kill an Iraqi woman as she's crossing the street carrying a box of cookies. Scranton and Lacy are not content to let the soldiers' footage speak for itself. They add ominous music and turn it into an Iraq-based episode of *Ice Road Truckers*, abusing the pact they seem to have made with these soldiers by giving them cameras.

The three men are inherently interesting, even after they return from the war. Bazzi remains unflappable, opposed to the war but not the military and concerned about the way the media portrays vets as PTSD-addled head cases. Moriarty takes a lot of pain medication for injuries he sustained in Iraq and goes through a couple of jobs before settling down into a good one with the town where he lives. Pink seems bitter about his experiences; he rants about how the war is about money and oil, "and somebody better get some pretty soon besides Dick Cheney or none of those lives were worth it"—1,800 soldiers had died when Pink said that and gas cost $2.23 a gallon.

THE GROUND TRUTH TAKES US THROUGH the process of joining the army, going to war, and coming home with your face burned off or without your legs. Although this documentary is unapologetic about emphasizing the last part of the process, it doesn't neglect the first part. *The Ground Truth* exposes US Army recruiting as a form of unregulated advertising and Marine Corps recruiting as out-and-out fraud. The film portrays basic training as psychological torture designed to obliterate personality. It shows how new recruits, naturally opposed to taking lives for no reason, learn to enjoy singing songs about killing, with ethnic slurs that make them easier to memorize.

Once they were in Iraq, one soldier notes that "the killing of civilians started to pile up." Another points out that "peer-pressure group killing is not necessarily courage." They are different people when they get home. A 23-year-old veteran hangs himself because he can't stop thinking of himself as a murderer. Another laments, "Even if I become a Muslim, if I read the Koran every day," it wouldn't bring back the woman he accidentally killed.

This grim film ends on a heroic note when a soldier named Camilo Mejía decides his conscience won't allow him to return to Iraq for another tour of duty. Mejía defies the rule that once in the armed forces you must continue to fight in an illegal war. Patricia Foulkrod, the film's director, does not defy the rule that documentaries must include sentimental music, photo montages, and stock footage.

THE SITUATION CLAIMS IT WAS THE FIRST fiction feature to deal with the war in Iraq. The film is set in Morocco, the pretend Iraq, and features fake Middle Eastern music. The strapping, apple-cheeked Danish actress Connie Nielsen plays a courageous war correspondent caught between two men. In crucial scenes, I was distracted by a large silver ring she wears. *The Situation* has an air of Hollywood glamour and self-congratulation that it tries to efface at every turn. And it's not even a Hollywood film. A couple of lines in the end credits sum up these problems. Special thanks go to *Sa Majesté le Roi Mohammed VI, Roi du Maroc* and Cynthia Rowley Sunglasses.

THE KINGDOM IS UNABASHED overkill entertainment. Made during wartime and dealing specifically with the global war on terror, it seems more like a prewar film, straight-up Hollywood action-adventure fantasy from another time. It's far too gruesome for what it wants to be, and too late.

A crack FBI team goes into Saudi Arabia to investigate the bombing of an American workers' city. Two of the team are mock-squabbling Jennifer Garner and Jason Bateman. Chris Cooper, the senior guy, rubs team leader Jamie Foxx's chest: "Feels like you got a beast in there." Later Jeremy Piven feels Foxx's chest, too. This was written by the screenwriter who wrote *Lions for Lambs*, a unique talent. Some of his dialogue, post-bombing: "My five-year-old boy, when I got home, had a box of Band-Aids and was trying to put his mama's mouth back on."

RENDITION ASKS US TO OPPOSE something everybody is already opposed to, the torture of innocent people. If the Egyptian-American who's whisked away to an unnamed Middle Eastern country (Morocco) to be tortured had in fact been a terrorist, this film might have worked. We would have had to ask ourselves if we were opposed to the torture of viable suspects in the war on terror. But in *Rendition* we get the torture-porn thrill of watching an innocent man be interrogated—blonde Reese Witherspoon's husband, no less—at the same time as we get to deplore that this happens.

Jake Gyllenhaal, an unlikely CIA bureau chief, watches with increasing desperation as interrogation techniques become enhanced. His subplot mirrors *The Devil Wears Prada*. When he finally quits his demeaning job, he throws his cell phone in the water, just like Anne Hathaway did in that movie. Maybe next he goes and gets a job at the *New York Sun* or the *Village Voice* or wherever it was supposed to be.

EVEN THOUGH *GHOSTS OF ABU GHRAIB* came out more than a year before Errol Morris's *Standard Operating Procedure*, which covers the same subject, I saw the Errol Morris film first. It's striking how similar the two films are, not just because they both deal with the torture of prisoners at Abu Ghraib and the scandal that broke when photographs of the abuse appeared in 2004. The main difference between the two films, and this is not to Morris's credit, since *Ghosts of Abu Ghraib* is straightforward, TV-style documentary and not great art like Morris makes, is that *Standard Operating Procedure* is obsessed with infographically investigating the photographs and has Lynndie England in it.

Rory Kennedy's film, more of an exposé than an investigation, is the better of the two. That Morris's film got a theatrical release and Kennedy's premiered on HBO says something about what is deemed worthy of theatrical release in this country, and why. Kennedy's film uses the same techniques as TV news shows, which makes her film more overtly cheesy than Morris's, which, with its barking-dog and creaking-chain reenactments, was also cheesy. But in Kennedy's film we get the sense that she feels these techniques are being put in the service of finding out the truth, whereas in Morris's film we get the sense that he's looking at people like they are bugs, *then* finding out the truth. They are stand-ins for Bush, Cheney, and Rumsfeld, whose victims they are. It's these higher-ups who are guilty—and here the sound editor cuts in the loud thwack of a rubber stamp—GUILTY! Morris's attitude raises the question of why he doesn't make a film about Bush, Cheney, and Rumsfeld, and of course the answer is that he can't because they would never talk to him. So *Standard Operating Procedure* tortures Lynndie England with Morris's Interrotron camera, using her (and her fellow soldiers) as replacements for the people he'd really like to pin down.

Ghosts of Abu Ghraib takes the visual simile of "ghost" detainees—detainees brought in off the books so they can be tortured in secret—too far. But so did Morris's film. Why do all American films, even American films made by intelligent documentarians, have to literalize everything? Maybe that has something to do with why Morris used Danny Elfman for his score. We automatically associate Elfman's music with Tim Burton, the great literalizer of childhood imagination. The problem is that scary music—and the music in *Ghosts of Abu Ghraib* is pretty scary—makes too much obvious sense. Abu Ghraib may remind us of certain scenes in *Carrie*, but it is not *Carrie*, it is real, and that's the point. What happened at Abu Ghraib may be the product of a culture formed by Stephen King, but in making films about it, serious filmmakers would do better not to indulge their inner *Cujo*.

Certain people appear as interview subjects in a number of different war-on-terror documentaries—the prison guards from Abu Ghraib, anti-abuse navy men Alberto Mora and John Hutson, legal scholars and authors like Scott Horton and Alfred McCoy, the infamous John Yoo, who is always bland and calm. Their various appearances in these films were shot probably only months apart, but seeing each of them one after another in different films, in different jackets under different lighting, we watch them age before the camera with the strain of telling their stories again. Meanwhile, we see the same clips of George W. Bush saying he's going to "smoke 'em out and get 'em runnin'," or Donald Rumsfeld saying he was only kidding about standing up eight to ten hours a day. They are frozen in those moments when they appear stupid and evil, yet these clips take them out of life and into some timeless realm of official TV where no one is ever punished. Maybe punishment is what happens on home video, then on YouTube, like it did to Saddam Hussein.

IF, BY JULY 2007, YOU HAD NOT HEARD there was a war going on in Iraq, then *No End in Sight* was the documentary for you. The film had a real audience of maybe two people—two people, by the way, I would be happy to meet. The film is meticulous in establishing that the war was a botched job from the beginning, and it gets a lot of well-known people to appear on camera to support that extremely noncontroversial viewpoint. Then it concludes that, since American soldiers have died in this war or were horribly maimed or crippled for life, we have got to find something good about it. It is easy to get confused and emotional when you are dealing with veterans whose lives have been permanently altered for the worse, but you've got to figure things out a little more than that before you make a movie.

A DOCUMENTARY FROM THE EARLY 1980S called *The Atomic Cafe* changed everything. It introduced the idea that history could be told via stock-footage orgy, a fun combination of clips strung together for maximum hilarity at the expense of the people who shot them. Industrial films, TV commercials, military films, TV news footage, scenes from B movies, home movies—detritus from the lower rungs of film history could be marshaled into formation to make glib points about things we are against.

Most documentaries do this now, even if that's not all they do. So for instance in *Why We Fight*, a documentary on the militarization of our culture and how that led to the war on terror, if the narrator mentions "cities" and "work" we are treated to sixty-year-old stock footage of people flooding into the lobbies of office buildings.

What we are seeing when this happens is America's Greatest Hits, an exercise in nostalgia that shows up our era in favor of a time when the average person dressed a little better and his most cherished goal was not to grow up to be Jimmy Fallon. This is lazy filmmaking, but it can be pretty entertaining. In *Why We Fight*, we get to see a Halliburton promotional film from 1951 in which the original narrator chirps, "There she is—oil! That's what all the fuss is about."

One of America's Greatest Hits was President Dwight Eisenhower's farewell address, which he delivered live from the Oval Office on January 17, 1961. The former general warned the country about the creeping influence of what he called the military-industrial complex. The country, the film notes, didn't listen. Of course we don't see the whole speech—that would be boring. Instead, we get to see bits of it photoshopped into TV screens in stock footage of 1950s living rooms. As Oliver North once said: *Neat!*

It's not that *Why We Fight* is wrong. It's a collage, but it's not wrong. No, it invites us to contemplate its rightness even as it contemplates its rightness itself. Given the subject matter, it does that in a pretty serene way. It demonstrates that there is no point of radicalism from which it could do anything else. So "*why we fight*" also means "why we don't fight," why we are passive, why we don't rebel.

Today people are very concerned about where their food comes from. They want to know that the ingredients in it are fresh, organic, locally grown, all that stuff. That's how I feel about documentaries. Where did all this footage come from? Wouldn't it be better if the director made it all himself? Or maybe making films like this is like making your house out of straw, sticks, and brick, and then putting aluminum siding on it and columns out front. Funny, yes. A little scary. I wouldn't want to live there.

TAXI TO THE DARK SIDE OVERWHELMS YOU with detail so repellent and frightening that by the end of it you are fully convinced that no punishment could be painful enough for the Bush administration. The film calls them murderers and makes the charge stick. It too often relies on ominosity (the American cinema has become an ominosity machine) but the depth of the information presented here excuses the film's excess. Who knew Guantánamo Bay had a gift shop where you could buy T-shirts that say GUANTANAMO BAY BEHAVIOR MODIFICATION INSTRUCTOR CUBA? Who knew the enhanced interrogation techniques used there included forcing detainees to wear pointed birthday hats? Alex Gibney, the film's director, covers his subject more thoroughly than any book or article I've read. It is without question the grimmest film on the war, and that's saying something.

It's best, however, when it sticks to its main story, essentially an onscreen autopsy. Dilawar was a taxi driver who was stopped by Afghan warlords in December 2002 and turned over to US forces for money. Chained in the prison at Bagram, he was beaten for days until he died. His legs were so "pulpified" by the beatings that had he lived it would've been necessary to amputate them. His guards beat him so he'd shut up because he was screaming in pain and continued beating him after he'd died because they thought he was faking immobility. They jumped on his back until they were tired, took breaks, then beat him some more. He was shackled the whole time. Dilawar didn't have a last name but back in his village he got one on his gravestone: THE MARTYR.

Gibney traces these techniques up through the chain of command, where Donald Rumsfeld stands all day and tells reporters "life goes on." A lieutenant general explains enhanced interrogation techniques, inadvertently describing the war on terror at the same time: "It was California avocado freestyle. I mean, it was just a free-for-all."

IRAQ IN FRAGMENTS IS SO GOOD I'm surprised people even recognize it as a movie. It's devoid of the clutter other documentaries rely on for visual interest. (Most documentaries are radio with pictures.) The person who made it, James Longley, also shot it, recorded the sound, and edited it. His cinematography is so superior to the cinematography in any of these other documentaries that he must be a Martian. Longley made his film in Iraq, not in a TV studio or in Morocco. He does not have to thank *Sa Majesté* or Cynthia Rowley for anything. The film's stars are the Mahdi Army and the people of Baghdad and Kurdistan.

If only for the way the movie reveals Iraq as a country of colors instead of just the tan dust we see in other Iraq war movies, this film would be exceptional. These vibrant images switch between the tranquil—fruit and vegetables for sale in a market, fish in an aquarium—and the violent—the scarves covering the faces of the Mahdi Army vigilantes kicking the alcohol sellers, the strings of colored lights lining the streets at night as flagellants parade by, beating themselves with metal chains.

Longley lets things play out, even speeches and the harangues of clerics. The sound in the film is unlike that in other films, too. Longley makes sure the sound always works in tandem with the images to evoke the places where they were shot, not to explain them. In the film's final third, shot in Kurdistan, where the sky is full of smoke from brick kilns and the fields are covered with sunflowers, Longley's filmmaking pares things down to an elemental level reminiscent of Dovzhenko: images of fire, the moon, snow, bones, and blood. The film ends in twilight with a Kurd reminding us that "nobody can escape America's reach" and that when it's all over, the winners always let you know God was on their side.

BRIAN DE PALMA'S *REDACTED* aroused controversy when it came out in late 2007, the kind of ridiculous controversy that is the hallmark of our time. The film found no audience and played on few screens, but the right-wing media howled.

Bill O'Reilly and others called for De Palma and the film's producer, TV and sports magnate Mark Cuban, to be arrested for treason and sued for defamation. In an attempt to hit them where they live, right-wingers demanded fans boycott the Dallas Mavericks, one of Cuban's properties. Later it emerged that Cuban had in fact cut the film's final scenes, fearing they would cause "emotional distress" and result in lawsuits from the families of real soldiers. TV personalities getting together to decry a basketball team because of a movie that's already been expurgated by its producer—we don't have censorship in this country, we have synergy.

Redacted fictionalizes the Mahmudiyah rampage, in which five American infantrymen gang-raped and murdered a 14-year-old Iraqi girl after killing her parents and her sister, a toddler. De Palma goes for a new kind of annoying realism by showing this played out in various media, including the ones that went on to attack him, yet at the same time *Redacted* feels stagy. The film is a clunky combination of De Palma's Vietnam movie *Casualties of War* and the amazing "Be Black, Baby" section of his underrated *Hi, Mom!* For a film of such urgency, *Redacted* is inferior to the De Palma movie that preceded it, the trashy *Black Dahlia*, also a fictionalized account of an infamous real-life rape and murder.

SHOT IN JORDAN, NOT MOROCCO, *Redacted* moved in the direction of Iraq, not Hollywood. *Battle for Haditha*, also the reenactment of a war atrocity, also shot in Jordan, moves even closer. Improvised around the story of how marines murdered twenty-four innocent Iraqi men, women, and children in al-Anbar province in November 2005, *Battle for Haditha* is the best Iraq combat film yet made, which is to say the only good one.

The British director Nick Broomfield, known in this country for documentaries like *Kurt & Courtney* and *Biggie and Tupac*, interlaces three stories in a way that owes more to neorealism than "hyperlink" cinema, that already forgotten term for movies like *Syriana* and *Babel*. Broomfield presents a middle-aged ex-Baathist, the insurgent who plants an IED that leads to the bloodbath, as an irked, confused speechifier without reducing him to pure villain status. I didn't get the name of the actor who plays this difficult, thankless role. The names of Arab actors are too easily buried and forgotten, like the names of the Arab dead. Elliot Ruiz's portrait of a competent, intelligent 20-year-old soldier who is nonetheless guilty of murder is flawless. To successfully improvise a part this grueling without going over the top is a sign of real distinction.

A throwaway scene in *Battle for Haditha* sticks in my mind: a marine forced to drop and do push-ups while chanting "I will not be funny anymore." For me, this quick scene encapsulates something real that it's glib to acknowledge: the war on terror is one group of Americans punishing another for the 1990s—in another country, with lots of collateral damage.

YOU CAN SHOOT A REENACTMENT FEATURE where it took place, even if it took place in Pakistan and Afghanistan. But what if part of it took place in the prison cells and interrogation rooms of the Guantánamo Bay detention facility? Michael Winterbottom and Mat Whitecross, British directors like Nick Broomfield, knew they would not be allowed to film in Camp X-Ray and Camp Delta, so they re-created the Guantánamo center in a hospitable country near where they were already shooting: Iran.

The Road to Guantánamo, one of the essential war-on-terror films, begins unpromisingly as extreme-travel TV or the first episode of *Real World: Guantánamo Bay*. We meet the Tipton Three (although they are not called that in the film), young British men of Pakistani decent who were kidnapped by the United Front in Afghanistan. Quickly the film shifts tone, the story becomes more and more harrowing as the photography of landscapes and faces becomes more beautiful. Thoughts of *Harold & Kumar Escape from Guantánamo Bay* dissipate well before the three (now played by actors) are trapped inside a truck that's filling up with blood as dozens of prisoners scramble over each other to avoid the bullets Afghani soldiers shoot through its walls.

Once in Cuba, the three are subjected to abuse that includes the nonstop yelling of their fascistic American guards, whose evident fear of being looked at tends to impart demonic power to the boys' collective gaze. "Don't let 'em look!" and "Face away from us!" are the commands of powerless people who are afraid to be seen because they know what they're doing is wrong. Two years later, the guards still harangue them as they are driven by bus past the HONOR BOUND TO DEFEND FREEDOM sign and taken out of the prison camp to be set free: "Don't look out the window!" The film makes those five words as sickening as anything that's happened in the war on terror.

In 1981, the English band Au Pairs had a song called "Armagh," about an Irish woman tortured in a British prison. The first lines went:

> We don't torture, we're a civilized nation.
> We're avoiding any confrontation.

Is their country's experience in Northern Ireland the reason British filmmakers are making better films about the war on terror than Americans?

MAYBE. BUT RIGHT AFTER *The Road to Guantánamo,* Michael Winterbottom, without Mat Whitecross, made *A Mighty Heart,* from Mariane Pearl's book about the kidnapping and murder of her husband, the journalist Daniel Pearl, by terrorist jihadis in Pakistan in early 2002. Shot in Pakistan and India, the film strives for the kind of grainy shaky-cam realism on which *The Road to Guantánamo* did not rely.

A Mighty Heart stars Angelina Jolie as Mariane Pearl. The first half of the movie is like a documentary about Jolie playing Mariane, the reenactment of a reenactment like *The Road to Guantánamo.* We watch her acting, she walks around with a prosthetic pregnant belly, underplays her phone reaction to Daniel's boneheaded parents, who think everything is going to work out fine. The third quarter of *A Mighty Heart* is a very good episode of *Karachi Vice*—"I love this town," an American intelligence agent exclaims. The last quarter is back to Jolie. Her lower lip is dry, later almost split, illustrating the film's arc of emotional destitution.

Mostly she's on the phone. Not just her; everyone in *A Mighty Heart* is on the phone. The film is an investigation into cell phone use among Westerners who live in big houses in Karachi; it's a film about manners. The cell phone is the instrument the Westerners use to control the world around them, a world where they make everyone their servant. Even when Daniel is out working, his nice-guy unctuousness gives him away as a privileged Westerner. He might as well be ordering organic pizza in a restaurant in Brooklyn. He's always all "Yeah, no, I'm good" and "I'm gonna let you go, OK?" Still, he depends on his cell phone less than the others, and the film implies he's punished for it. When he's kidnapped, Mariane loses phone contact with him, a sign of grave danger.

In bed at night, with little hope, she continues to send texts he'll never read: "I love you."

What Winterbottom intended is unclear. He does the best he can under the circumstances, working with the biggest star in the world to help her tell the most important story on earth, ambiguously undercutting it with repetitive actions showing Americans as both all-powerful and ineffectual. Were the Pearls really like this? By the film's end, after Mariane gives birth, we see her and her child as a unit complete without Daniel. Wistful music from the band Nouvelle Vague plays. Is this supposed to be melancholy, or is it a testament to the superfluousness of the Western male, or both?

A MIGHTY HEART ENDS WITH A BIRTH, *The Hills Have Eyes II* starts with one. A cinematic coincidence, but maybe it's in trash like this that we'll find the truth of the situation. After all, it's the torture porn of the *Hostel* and *Saw* franchises, made concurrently with the prisoner abuse at Abu Ghraib, that exposed certain truths about American culture before the Abu Ghraib photos did.

Even better, *The Hills Have Eyes II* is explicitly a war film. National Guard troops on a training exercise in the New Mexico desert, which we're initially led to think is Afghanistan or Iraq, run around yelling "America number one, bitch!" Soon they begin to get picked off Indian-style by relatives of the mutant family from the first remake of *The Hills Have Eyes*. This is a promising start, but the movie ends up being less effective than it should be. Too bad producer Wes Craven assigned it to a director of videos for Nickelback and Sisqo when it needed a John Carpenter. One gory image lingers, a dead guy with his wallet shoved into his head.

WOULDN'T IT BE FUNNY if it turned out that World Wrestling Entertainment had made one of the best films about the war in Iraq? That's the kind of dumb hope I had going into *The Marine*. John Cena, the professional wrestler, a bulky Matt Damon delivered by forceps, plays the title role, a veteran of the war in Iraq. Returning to his blonde wife in South Carolina, he finds the only job he can get is security guard. After he's fired for throwing somebody through a plate-glass window, he goes home and confesses his biggest fear: sitting around at home doing nothing.

Triton (that's the marine's last name) is like the United States. He's never learned that all men's miseries come from not being able to sit quietly in a room alone. The couple decides to take a road trip in their Lincoln Navigator, a preposterous vehicle for them to own, but I guess not more than it is for anybody else. A gas station blows up, Triton's wife is kidnapped—significantly, he is robbed at a gas pump. Now Triton is back in his element, once again doing what he was trained to do in Iraq. For the rest of the movie he is shot at thousands and thousands of times and not hit once.

WITH THE EXCEPTION OF TRASH MOVIES, war-on-terror films are so grim, dismal, and tragic that when you have contempt for one, you feel bad about it. *Gunner Palace*, a documentary in the form of a music video, promotes the war in Iraq as crazy fucked-up shit that nobody but the grunts and a few haji good guys understand—and the film's director, who narrates in a cool-guy whisper that sounds like he's auditioning to dub *Two or Three Things I Know About Her* into English.

Right off, this sub-Godardian voice-over is childish and filled with hokey attitude. "Most of us don't see this on the news anymore. We have reality TV instead—*Joe Millionaire, Survivor.* Well, survive this: a year in Baghdad without changing the channel." When the filmmaker tells us, "Unlike a movie, war has no end," we don't bother to sort that out because we are glad that at least movies have an end. In a piece from 1955 on Soviet films, Robert Warshow wrote that "the commentator is one of the diseases of our time and must be endured; he will be there at the end of the world to say into a microphone: 'This is the end of the world.'" But Warshow didn't know the commentator would be hip.

Making a film this bad helps no one. It's also inappropriately lame. When a soldier shows an Iraqi orphan a SpongeBob SquarePants doll, a title appears over the image: SPONGEBOB. The film becomes human when the soldiers *Gunner Palace* follows around are allowed to speak for themselves. The hilarious slacker SPC Stuart Wilf tells us that it's better to be in Iraq than to be a loser in his hometown, where he'd be doing nothing because there's nothing to do. This 19-year-old combat veteran speaks for everyone who's from a place like that, and the sanity of his position is only bolstered by the way he dances around in a Saudi robe he bought on leave in Qatar. Wilf comes across as all-American and a total fuckup, a much more appealing figure than John Cena's ludicrous marine, and more heroic.

KIMBERLEY PEIRCE'S 1999 FEATURE DEBUT, *Boys Don't Cry*, was as assured and fully achieved as Nicholas Ray's debut was fifty years earlier. Like *They Live by Night*, *Boys Don't Cry* showed a flair for drama that was intimate but explosive, and had a true understanding for the pain outsiders feel in love. Why, then, nine years later, is Peirce imitating *Gunner Palace*? *Stop-Loss* had the potential to be the best movie about the war in Iraq. The combat scenes early in the film are the best-directed combat scenes in any war-on-terror movie. When they end, *Stop-Loss* resorts to an MTV-inspired version of media realism—soldiers' video diary footage and interludes of rap—that has nothing to do with the story Peirce wants to tell, and has everything to do with keeping the attention of her perceived audience so she can tell them an important story. The film has to jerk itself out of this mode whenever it wants to be a film at all.

WHEN ACTOR-DIRECTOR LIEV SCHREIBER and his producer on *Everything Is Illuminated*, an adaptation of the Jonathan Safran Foer novel, go to the airport to pick up an intern coming to work on their film, we are witnessing not just a historic first in the history of interning but also the beginning of one of the best movies about the war on terror. Nina Davenport's documentary *Operation Filmmaker* is only tangentially related to the actual war in Iraq, but it has more to say about the issues animating it than most films dealing with it directly.

Having seen a young Iraqi film student named Muthana Mohmed interviewed in Baghdad by MTV, Schreiber gets the genius idea to hire Muthana and fly him to Prague, where Schreiber's film is shooting. Soon Muthana, the Stuart Wilf of international film production, is charged with tasks like mixing vegan snacks in little plastic cups for producers who must constantly be treated like babies. Producer Peter Saraf, unhappy with the slacker Muthana's attitude, schools him: Muthana has to learn to make himself invaluable to his bosses. He must fawn over his producer and director. For instance, to ingratiate himself, he should bring them coffee in the middle of meetings—but discreetly and quietly. That's how we do it in America, Saraf explains. Nothing demeaning about it. Totally normal. We all came up that way.

A better portrait of how people who think of themselves as Good turn the disadvantaged into their slaves has never been put on film. *Operation Filmmaker,* the entire thing a subtle metaphor for the way America helps Iraq by occupying it, damns everyone it touches, including Muthana and the filmmaker herself. After Muthana expresses his admiration for George W. Bush, the producers of *Everything Is Illuminated* pretty much abandon him to fend for himself. He stays in Prague, gets a job on a movie based on the video game *Doom,* and convinces its affable star, Dwayne "The Rock" Johnson, to pay for him to go to film school in London. The Rock may have been conned by Muthana, but why should he care? The Rock's a movie star, he's got money, and he can give it out any way he chooses. In *Operation Filmmaker* a professional wrestler really does come to the rescue, and Davenport has the grace not to make the ironic but obvious point that the Rock is a Republican and Saraf and Schreiber are Democrats.

MAYBE IN MOVIES RIGHT NOW the war is best approached obliquely. *Full Battle Rattle,* by Tony Gerber and Jesse Moss, documents what happens at the National Training Center at Fort Irwin, a thousand-mile tract of the Mojave Desert comprising thirteen replica Iraqi villages. The army sees this as a stage set where soldiers learn how to handle themselves in the real theater of war. A Lieutenant Colonel McLoughlin, training there, explains: "Our number one priority is to provide hope to the people. All our bright thinking here is all for naught if we don't control the crowd."

These soldiers learn to control the crowd by playing cowboys and Indians in a landscape where Indians used to be. The center employs 250 Arabic-speaking Iraqi-Americans, who are given character biographies and scripts so they can portray townspeople, insurgents, and Iraqi policemen. In one scenario, the son of the deputy mayor is accidentally killed by American firepower. Negotiations begin that are more like *The Price Is Right* than a war movie. American soldiers carry around $2,500 in play money to pay off relatives of the dead. Then the brass steps in for further smoothing, awkwardly rehearsing for the real thing. "I have a contract for a sewage system," says Lt. Col. McLoughlin. "It's worth over $280,000—*approved!*" He seals the deal: "Have some fruit. This is our best fruit."

It's not just the soldiers who believe in this fiction the army's created. The middle-aged Iraqi man who plays the deputy mayor longs to be promoted to the status of full mayor. At work in the Mojave his dignity is restored. Later we see him at his other job, manning the cash register at a liquor store in a desolate San Diego neighborhood.

This beautifully composed documentary provides the most human and balanced view in any of these films. It's a hopeful, even utopian film that takes place far away from the Green Zone and Abu Ghraib, strangely touching and sad. A doctor shows us mannequin limbs with carved plastic wounds. "These injuries are exact replicas," he says. The limbs snap back into place. By the time the film was done, five of the soldiers in it were already dead.

DICK CHENEY HAS TOLD US THIS WAR will not end in our lifetime. An era of endless war chokes off the kind of evaluation that in the past has produced the best war movies. If the war on terror never ends, those films cannot be made. Evaluation will be left to movies like *The Dark Knight*, which indulge our longing for relief from war at the same time as they replicate its stasis and reconfigure its atrocities as blockbuster entertainment.

You always hear conservatives say Hollywood hates America. To me, what proves Hollywood hates America is the way they keep making Batman movies. Meanwhile, no Hollywood filmmakers have gone to Iraq. All the 1990s World War II films Hollywood made, the *Saving Private Ryan*s, with their Pentagon advisers and Department of Defense equipment they got at the cost of script approval, were made by people pretending they wanted to go to war. *If only we had a war*, they seemed to moan. *Ach, we were born too late!*

Here was your chance, Hollywood, to emulate the Greatest Generation filmmakers you professed to admire so much. What you made instead were things like *War of the Worlds*, a film that reveled in the destruction of New York, then hightailed it through the woods to grandmother's house. Sleep tight. +

JOHN DIVOLA, FROM THE *VANDALISM* SERIES, 1970,
COLOR PHOTOGRAPH. COURTESY OF THE ARTIST.

THREE POEMS

Frederick Seidel

HOME

The homeless are blooming like roses
On every corner on Broadway.
I am unclean.
I bathe in their tears.

The homeless are popping like pimples.
They're a little dog's little unsheathed erection sticking out red.
It makes us passers-by sing.
Ho ho. It's spring.

West Siders add fresh water
But feed the flowers with urine.
Sir, can you spare some change?
Can you look at me for a change?

Uncooked hamburger
Erupts when he lowers his trousers.
It's his song.
It's raw oozing out of a grinder.

He looks like a horrible burn from Iraq.
His wound ripples
In a hot skillet.
America doesn't look like that.

He bends down to eat garbage.
I bend down with a bag to clean up after the dog.
I take the shit out of the bag
And stuff it back up inside the dog

And sew the anus closed,
And put the dog in a two-fifty oven to scream for three hours.
The homeless are blooming like roses.
I'm hopeless.

I bathe in their screams.
I dress for the evening.
My name is Fred Seidel,
And I paid for this ad.

PAIN MANAGEMENT

I'm a liar with a lyre. Kiss me, life!
Even if I vomit
When you try to bring me back with mouth-to-mouth.
Even if the mouth-to-mouth
Vomits in my mouth, it's life!
A fellow in the elevator
Jokes about global warming and it being 84°
Outside. *But what did you expect? It's late October!*
The corpses put out leaves.
Leaves don't leave the trees. New Guinea in New York.

The Caribbean nannies in the park are savage sausages
On cell phones.
Boudins noirs. Blood inside a casing. Caretakers.
The children stand around in little cages, waiting whitely.
The Caribbean nurses at the hospital are expressionless bone
Nose rings behind the white Formica counter
When bed 229B calls the Nurses Station a second time, a third time.
It is too early to give the poor woman more morphine.
The masks hide the heart
Inside each human being's head. A liar with a lyre.

The nurses in the park ignore the ruin they've got slumped
Next to them on the bench—and talk on their nonstop tom-toms,
On their cell phones that are jungle drums.
The old on their walkers inch forward inside their cages
With their nurses. The nurses at the hospital are expressionless
Behind the Formica in 5 Central when 229B
Howls this time, but really howls.
She will get something
When the pain management guy
Rounds with his team.

And the dog walker doesn't walk the dogs.
He sits on the curb not doing the job.
His innocence flotilla on leashes surrounds him
Like a parachute on the ground

After a landing, panting.
The pure of heart stare at Adolf Hitler with their honest eyes.
Poor United States of America.
The nurses stand outside the hospital on their break
Where they can smoke.
These ones are mostly white, wearing green.

There's something about the sight of nurses lighting up.
Do nurses think nurses are protected?
They inhale the horn of the charging rhino.
I also do impersonations
Of righteous persons.
My righteous fall like rain,
And grow like grass.
I impersonate myself. I'm a liar with a lyre.
Sto mentendo.
(I'm lying.)

A man still wearing his solar topee
Is being boiled alive in a jungle pot.
Needless to say, the man is white.
With one chop, the Aztec priest splits open the Spanish captive's chest
And, reaching inside, yanks out the still-beating heart,
Which he sets on an alabaster plate, and which God starts to eat,
Who, needless to say, is wearing a solar topee.
Needless to say, needless to say,
Never mind what I'm saying,
I'm lying.

It's my physical therapist friend at the other end of the telephone trying.
To tell me something crying.
Her husband is back in the hospital, not dying.
But with his whole left side suddenly paralyzed.
The doctors at New York-Presbyterian don't know why.
It is exactly as if he'd had a stroke—though he is young.
But his speech and cognition are unimpaired.
But he can't even use a bedpan or sit up in bed.
Art throws the dog a bone.
I am ashamed of my poem.

"SII ROMANTICO, SEIDEL, TANTO PER CAMBIARE"

Women have a playground slide
That wraps you in monsoon and takes you for a ride.
The English girl Louise, his latest squeeze, was being snide.
Easy to deride
The way he stayed alive to stay inside
His women with his puffed-up pride.
The pharmacy supplied
The rising fire truck ladder that the fire did not provide.
The toothless carnivore devoured Viagra and Finasteride
(Which is the one that shrinks the American prostate nationwide
And at a higher dosage grows hair on the bald) to stem the tide.
Not to die had been his way to hide
The fact that he was terrified.
He could not tell them that, it would be suicide.
It would make them even *more* humidified.
The women wrapped monsoon around him, thunder-thighed.
They guide his acetone to their formaldehyde.
Now Alpha will commit Omegacide.
He made them, like a doctor looking down a throat, open wide,
Say Ah; and *Ah,* they sighed;
And out came sighing amplified
To fill a stadium with cyanide.
He filled the women with rodenticide.
He tied
Their wrists behind them, tried
Ball gags in their mouths, and was not satisfied.
The whole room when the dancing started clapped and cried.
The bomber was the bomb, and many died.
The unshod got their feet back on and ran outside.
The wedding party bled around the dying groom and bride.

POSTER, C.1943

WORK PROJECTS ADMINISTRATION POSTER COLLECTION (LIBRARY OF CONGRESS).

ON FOOD

Mark Greif

FOOD RIOTS HAVE BROKEN OUT in Haiti, Egypt, Mozambique, and Bangladesh. In New York, eight million people look into the refrigerator wondering what to eat.

Rice prices soar on the international market as shortages trigger unrest among people for whom rice is a dietary staple. The packaging of the rice on my pantry shelf tells a story about pristine fields and rare cultivation. "To keep our rice select, we inspect each grain. . . . This may seem like a lot of extra work to you, but we care."

"Care" is one of the fluctuating words of our time. As CARE, it is an international rescue organization; as demotic speech, a matter of whim and interest; in official talk (as of health care), it essentially means nursing or medicine. In one sense, I could care less if I have rice. In another, I care (and care for myself) a great deal: I put all kinds of worry and concentration into whether I will have white rice, brown rice, basmati, arborio . . . Does brown rice leave more of the fibrous husk (for health)? Is polished rice more suitable to the Cambodian cuisine I'll cook tonight (for experience)? And should I have salmon, which, with its omega-3s, is said to be good for my brain, heart, and mood? Or tofu, with its cholesterol-lowering soy protein, its isoflavones and selenium? Thus from taste or "choice" we stray outward to a vantage from which the wrong choice at dinner looks like death, where care becomes ambassador for compulsion.

Two generations ago, progress in the realm of food split along dual tracks. For those who don't yet have enough, the goal remains to gain plenty by any technical means available. For those whose food is assured, the task becomes to re-restrict it. This second movement has been underacknowledged.

Having had our food supply made simple, we devote ourselves to looking for ways to make it difficult. The more we are estranged from the tasks of growing and getting food, the more food-thought pervades our lives. It is a form of attention that restores labor, rarity, experience, and danger to food's appearance (its manifestations in the market and at the table) and its refusal (our rejection of unfit foods, our dieting). This parallels the new complication of other phenomena of bodily attention, specifically modern exercise and sex. It will be objected that the care for food is a fascination only of the rich; this is false. Stretching from high to low, the commands to lose weight, to undertake every sort of diet for purposes of health, to enjoy food as entertainment, to privatize food-care as a category of inner, personal life (beyond the shared decisions of cooking and the family dinner), have communicated new thought and work concerning food to the vast middle and working classes of the rich Western countries.

I think there is something wrong with all this. Underlying my opposition is a presumption that our destiny could be something other than grooming—something other than monitoring our biological lives. Many readers will disagree. Their disagreement is only legitimate if they are prepared to stand up for a fundamental principle: that what our freedom and leisure were made for, in our highest state, really is bodily perfection and the extension of life. One of the main features of our moment in history, in anything that affects the state of the body (though, importantly, *not* the life of the mind), is that we prefer optimization to simplicity. We are afraid of dying, and reluctant to miss any physical improvement. I don't want to die. But I am caught between that negative desire and the wish for freedom from control. I think we barely notice how much these tricks of care take up of our thinking, and what domination they exert.

THE REASON TO EAT FOOD is no longer hunger. There is now no point in your day when if you were to go without a meal you would fall into physical jeopardy. You "get hungry," to be sure, but probably from birth to death never *go* hungry, though enough people in the world still do.* This is a change in life.

---

* To put this in concrete terms: In 2005 USDA statistics, about 4 percent of American households, at some point during the year, found their normal eating habits disrupted because of lack of money to buy food. About one-third of those households faced disruption in one or two brief episodes; another third experienced disruption frequently. In the developing world, the problem is different—there, portions of the population may face starvation or disease from the inability to buy food. The World Food Programme

Confusion arises around any need that never gets fully activated. We know we have to eat because otherwise we will die. We direct our thoughts to the activation-point, the terminal condition, even though we'll never approach it. We act as if we are under compulsion for decisions none of which are determined by this need—as if our provisional necessity were a fatal necessity. We have to eat; but we don't have to eat anything in particular, so extensive are our food choices, any of which is sufficient for life. (Traditional societies always existed subject to conditions of scarcity; choice was circumscribed when one's food was given by whatever would grow.) We have to eat; but we don't have to eat at any given moment, so regularly do we eat, so lavish are our meals. (Though of course you get hungry just hours after eating—from sitting, or waiting, or being. Hunger is recalibrated in half-inches where once it was measured in yards.)

It's now considered possible for some of us to get ourselves to states in which eating once again feels medically necessary, even with respect to the timing of daily meals. "My blood sugar must be down." "Remember to stay hydrated." You become "hypoglycemic," that is, lacking in sugars. You become "dehydrated," that is to say, thirsty. You reach a point where you get lightheaded, sick, unhappy without your food.

Truer states of privation can be achieved through exercise. (A kind of confusion is deliberately maintained between thirst, which activates in shorter timespans, and hunger, which is slow-building and diverse in its fulfillment—so that a glass of orange juice becomes a palliative to thirst that also contains, in the solids and sugars and vitamins and tangible substance, a kind of food.) But you don't even have to wear yourself out to feel changes inside you. Enough of us monitor ourselves this closely in daily life. We become patients in a hypothesized emergency room, in which we move as specters.

These reduced states, and the ability to identify the feelings of them, go with a degree of discernment and class distinction. Lower-class people get hungry, and "we" get hypoglycemic. The redevelopment of biologically necessary hunger is considered morally superior to its widespread alternative, the lazy hunger of an addiction to abundance. The poor say they want lunch. Don't believe them. Put aside the hun-

---

puts the proportion of the developing world that experiences undernourishment at 16 percent of the total population.

ger of these people who endlessly crave "junk foods" and "drug foods," fats and sugars—the obese overeaters, one of the last classes of people it's socially acceptable to despise. The exalted need of the momentarily dizzy armchair athlete is counterpoised to the cravings of the obese underclass.

HISTORICALLY, THE *MODERN* PROJECT OF FOOD has always been associated with an end to scarcity. Before modernity, the multiplication of food meant that the supernatural had entered the mundane: as with the miracle of the loaves and fishes, Jesus' carbs and proteins. Not until the 18th and 19th centuries did plenty come into view as a practical possibility. Its realization crept up on theorists by gradual developments. Malthus declared it impossible that agricultural production's carrying capacity (arithmetically increasing) could ever catch up with the level of population (geometrically increasing) less than two decades before capacity proved him wrong. Malthus wrote in 1798. The last major "subsistence crisis" to strike the Western nations en masse, according to the agricultural historian John D. Post, occurred in 1816–17. (The starvation conditions in 1845–47 in Ireland and parts of Central Europe because of potato blight he disqualifies as an isolated last catastrophe.) Periodic famine would no longer be a recurring feature of Western life, though it had been a basic condition for all human societies since the early Holocene.

The early years of the 20th century ushered in a second transformation. The embrace of agricultural mechanization spurred a transition from the mere end of famine to the permanence of plenty, even over-plenty. The United States led the worldwide change, which took place from about 1915 to 1970. The application of machine power, specifically the arrival of tractors, made labor hours drop despite ever larger harvests. Crop yields increased per amount of acreage cultivated, massively so with the introduction of hybrid strains of corn. Bruce L. Gardner, reanalyzing most recently the agricultural and economic data for the period, notes that US farms produce seven times the amount of food they did in 1900, while having shed two-thirds of their laborers. "As late as 1950, food consumed at home accounted for 22 percent of the average US household's disposable income. By 1998 that percentage had been reduced to 7," while we manage to eat more.

We live far enough after the period of the modernization of food to condescend to its achievements. The technical achievement of superabundance led to a predictable but short-lived celebration of technicized food itself: a commercial fetishism of the techniques of freezing and refrigerated transport, Swanson dinners and Birds Eye vegetables, and a lust for the re-engineering, preservation, and shelf stability that made Cheez Whiz and the Pringle out of smooth Wisconsin milk and bursting Idaho potatoes. Corresponding to modernization was an *early modernism* of food, a recognizable trajectory through attitudes well known to us from painting or design or writing. Postwar modernization theory held that modernizing was exclusively an economic-technical achievement, one which stood apart from the sorts of aesthetic regimes that succeeded one another in progress in the arts, but it was not so. "Food science" represented a moment of human progress, recognized and regnant, transformed into culture. When mid-century food technics are satirized today by right-thinking people as kitsch—Tang, fish sticks, and Wonder Bread—a moment of utopian progress is reduced to folly, as can happen with so much of the naïve ecstasy and radiance of all products of the machine triumphant.

Today we participate in a *late modernism* and even a *postmodernism* of food. We witnessed, after the triumph of a previously unquestioned project, a characteristic latecoming struggle around the nature and direction of progress. First, in the late 1960s, came reactions against the inhuman technical character of food science and "agribusiness." Critics in this phase pitted themselves against consumer capitalism. This initial reaction was romantic and primitivist, associated with the counterculture and the movement "back to the land," just a few decades after productivity gains had led an agrarian population to leave it. It brought a call to the East for mystic authenticity in the culture of "health foods"—tofu, brown rice, yogurt, seaweed, wheat germ, made from the live spirits and microbes excluded in industrial processing. (These were the parts that were said to live and germinate, against an antiseptic modernist technics of death: the Bomb and pasteurization were made by the same culture. The historian Warren Belasco has extensively documented both the actions and the imagination of the early food counterculture.) This counterculture, too, introduced its own counter-technics of food-medicine, in remedies either Western but crankish and eccentric (like the chemist Linus Pauling's early championing of Vitamin C, a scandal in its time), or Eastern against the West (macrobiotics, acupuncture).

Soon a more flexible capitalism proffered a new set of options which allowed the dissolution, or simply the side-by-side juxtaposition, of opposites, and a new field of cooperation. The standard of "health" perhaps foreordained that the dropouts would deliver themselves back into the hands of experts. Proselytizing pioneers of the counterculture became the arbiters, physicians, and best friends of an expanded version of the Western capitalist culture they believed they had critiqued: figures like Andrew Weil, MD, the "healer," and the organic "growers" of Cascadian Farm. The conceit of magic pre-existing "natural" remedies and supplements and minerals (red wine, chocolate, "fiber," "antioxidants," et cetera) was brought under the mantle of medical testing and food enhancement. Food scientists and processors ceased to fight their former opponents, as they were licensed by the counterculture to formulate new concoctions and mine new markets evaluated, not by opposition or refusal, but along the common metric of health. The postmodern moment can be identified whenever the tug of war between "scientific" food progress and "humane" food reaction produces more business for both sides. In our moment, the options exist in plural, and the most self-satisfied individuals graze from two troughs, the scientifically fashioned and the organically-romantically grown, with the same rationale of "health" for both.

(Food science, to make this clear, was not intrinsically evil nor flawed, and the food counterculture was not just about optimizing toothsomeness and health, but about opposing an established order wherever it had become complacent. Whenever utopians present the substance of their wishes, a fair number of their dreams do come true, though sometimes in forms other than the ones they had anticipated. The Victorian prophet Winwood Reade in 1872 predicted that three inventions would transform the world (the wording comes from Lewis Mumford's later summary): "a fuel substitute for coal, aerial locomotion, and the synthetic composition of food." Each came to pass or was obviated within a hundred years. Small-scale petroleum drilling had already begun in the 1850s and 1860s and was sufficient as a coal substitute until recently. The Wright brothers made their successful experiments in aerial locomotion in 1903. The synthetic composition of food didn't become necessary because of the revolution in productivity. Rather, "synthetic" food became possible in another way—not synthesized ex nihilo but through the chemical refashioning of foods that existed in "natural" form. Reade concluded with two "further triumphs . . . left for man": "The extinction of disease and the achievement of immortality." We must recognize that the 21st-century enterprise of health is an open attempt at one (the end of disease) and a covert search for the other (immortality). Health today cannot be understood apart from its refusal of mortality—not through the discovery of a fountain of youth, but through the bargain that, if men and women will obey health guidelines and regulate themselves as they are told and buy the right products for care, they can lengthen their life spans without any absolutely fixed term.)

THE CONTEMPORARY TRANSFORMATIONS OF FOOD are associated with a new impersonality imparted to the field—making of eating a "hobby," one pastime among others.*

New food entertainments have changed the character of the tradition devoted to cooking and dining. Food generates constant discourse. It has given interest in food an increasingly abstract character, as a "spectacular" function of food can be divided off from its practical, gustatory function. We are learning to take our foods at a remove. First, the contemplation and nutritional analysis of our foodstuffs becomes a semi-autonomous "scientific" sphere independent of any particular meal or mouthful. Second, our entertainments create a standpoint of satiety or disinterest from which we can contemplate food without hunger and find pleasure in that contemplation.

We've had an explosion of "food writing," as the bookstore category is renamed from "cooking" to "food." We have memoirs in food, novels

---

* A beauty pageant on television broadcast a short video of the young women contestants talking to the camera about their favorite occupations when not keeping up with their schoolwork or doing pageantry. What were their hobbies? Many listed eating. It was jarring but ultimately unsurprising. By having young women say "eating" and not "cooking" is their hobby—is that an advance for feminism, in a way? It would be, unless for these women eating holds such a special place only against the background of socially compulsory starvation. These women must constantly *not* eat for the sake of their figures and their competitiveness. It has often occurred to me, when I hear other women describe food as a hobby, that the gender character of this devotion may not be because of the social reproduction of an old sexual division of labor—that women used to cook (and still do) and are still taught to care for food in a way that men do not always—but because the burden of taboo, self-restriction, and even outer social policing around *not* eating falls disproportionately on women. I suppose if someone praised me for studying and preparing for, say, my natural proclivity for flower arranging, and it afforded me sensual pleasure, and then the same authorities said, "Now you must be very careful when you actually *do* flower arranging, and choose carefully how many flowers you're allowed to arrange, and take fewer than you would like, and watch out whether you have accidentally arranged flowers *at the wrong time* or taken *too many*"—well, I might turn it into a "hobby" too.

with recipes, high literature which expands to absorb a "canon" of 20th-century food writers from A. J. Liebling to M. F. K. Fisher to Ruth Reichl. Chronicles appear of a single comestible through history, cod or salt. The newsstand purveys magazines that range from the scientific purism of *Cook's Illustrated*, to the aspirational luxury of *Gourmet*, to the academicism of *Gastronomica*. The Food Network delivers twenty-four-hour TV programming devoted to cooking and eating: interminable specials on barbecue, semi-celebrities peddling the delights of chipotle. (In *Harper's* a few years ago, a well-meaning critic devoted himself to exposing that channel's programming as "gastropornography," trapped by the same leveling action between food and sex that makes all of our basic bodily desires into just one thing.) And late at night on TV, between the other paeans to desperation ("Been in an accident?"; "Foreclosure problems?"), are the pitches for miracle metabolism supplements, fat-burning capsules, and colon cleansers.

It may seem odd to think of food warnings and diet plans as entertainment, too. Certainly they've taken on the same spectacular character, though, and offer a linked way to spend your time. Should we eat wild or farmed fish; is chocolate healthy, and is red wine? Last month, the magazine *Health* featured an advertisement for its website: "Trying to figure out what fish or vegetable is safe to eat this week?" It wasn't a joke. Nor was it just about contamination—it concerned a *weekly* shift in knowledge. The whole idea of food "news" announces the end of thousands of years in which there couldn't be such a thing as "news" in food. On one channel, we have competitive eating, broadcast as sport; on another, a weight-loss game show, *The Biggest Loser*. On one, how an automated factory makes Ho Hos; on another, the nutrition report. The point is not that we're "schizophrenic" about food, as some say—celebrating gluttony and advocating dieting. The point is that although we're collectively amused along two separate tracks, both may have a common meaning and, perhaps, purpose.* Their meaning lies in making food "discursive" along every axis. Their purpose? They may constitute a more fully integrated system at the level of social regula-

* This raises the matter of commensurability. Right now, your actions every day become foods, or the wiping away of foods, their eradication. If you do a certain number of minutes on the treadmill, measured in calories, that wipes out a bagel. But so does having sex wipe out calories. We're frequently told this, too, by the health magazines. With the three central bodily activities of our time (exercise, food, and sex), whatever draws the links to make them all expressible in a common measure contributes to the underlying attitude.

tion, underlying what look like contradictory temperaments and local interests.

Kant's aesthetics required aesthetic contemplation to be disinterested. A viewer must not take the aesthetic object to have a use, and must not conceive of the object's physical desirability. Beauty must not be confused with attractiveness. A painted bunch of grapes should not inspire hunger. One should not think how well a painted horse would ride. In principle, real food should never be aestheticizable under this regime, because it will always be seen as an object to be enjoyed. Part of what is astonishing about the present order is that it does make food available, at times, for something more like disinterested aesthetic appreciation. And this allows the step backward from immediacy that perhaps lets us think of our mortality, our bodily incarnation in its journey toward death, as likewise groomable, accessible to recipe—and preparation, and taste—if not yet subject to an absolute choice of when we die.

THE MOST MODERN AND ELITE of our eaters find that careful discriminations, taboos, and rigorous exclusions still lead down both paths without contradiction: toward the totally engineered and compressed vitamin pill; and toward the organic, sourced, inherited, unmodified "whole" food—not "made" but harvested, not altered (in this imagination) except by joyful labor. You can eat your PowerBar, product of an engineering as peculiar as any the world has known, and wash it down with unpasteurized unfiltered cider pressed by Mennonites, and on both fronts, you find it good.

° ° °

Which leads to a troubling question: why *would* it be necessary or useful to express all the forms of bodily life in common metrics? The instinctive suspicion is that when incommensurable goods and activities are modified to be expressible through some common medium, it is because the transformed goods are easier to "monetize," or to render accessible to either commercial or social-functional intervention. Because it is a way of reducing all things to a common coin, outside our control, when all the processes of the body are evaluated in the same metric, which we have no access to on our own, it helps the effort of convincing someone that he needs tangible equipment, or intangible expert knowledge, to accomplish what he did previously without it—for example, eat. Whenever formerly private and habitual practices are penetrated by a need for outside equipment and specialized knowledge, the individual hands himself over to experts, and integrates both his time and his spending power into the wider system.

THE FOOD IMAGINATION of our moment is different than we think, and needs to be excavated, category by category.

Food dreams: A friend of mine sighs and says he wishes he didn't have to eat. He wishes he could take a pill that would cover all of his physical hunger for two weeks, say, or a month. Then he would only have meals when he wanted to, purely for pleasure: he would be completely delivered from the bodily responsibility to consume food. Another friend wishes for a magic food that could be eaten all the time, in satiating quantities, in different flavors, that would require exactly as many calories to chew and digest as it contained. This is the rumor about celery—that it has just as many calories as must be burned to process it. "Celery-food" would be calorically null. Then she would not have to monitor what she ate; then she could eat as large a quantity of food as she wanted, to gratify any hint of hunger, without it being incorporated into her body as weight.

Interior visualization: We've learned to picture our insides; and the pictures get better and better. "Beautify your insides": an advertisement to young women for Metamucil, illustrated by a presumably gut-emptied fashion model complacently reclining against a drape. In forensic television like *House* and *CSI*, we see first the sick patient in the hospital bed, or the expired corpse on the slab, diagnosed by the team; then a computer graphic of the insides of the stomach or heart wall or liver in churning color; then the modifications to show the new pathological state: ugly, green-infested, bacteria pinging like lottery balls. We want, ourselves, never to approach that bad state. Never to be corroded. At such times, we really do want our insides to look beautiful. We have somehow seen our own healthy stomachs, hearts, or livers, and feel a longing for them, as we learn what has gone wrong for some fictional person.

Food fears: When a third friend is about to eat a food that has fat, especially meat fats or hydrogenated oils, he imagines the interior arteries of his heart becoming clogged with a yellow-white substance, like margarine or petroleum jelly. When he eats calories or fats, he imagines individual particles entering shrunken fat cells in his belly and sees them stretch and become oblong. When he eats meat, he imagines it passing through his colon with a rough texture that scrapes the walls, roughening them, to make them susceptible to cancer. He conceives an evil superfat, beyond palm oil, soybean oil, and trans-fatty acidic frying oil, that can spread from food into every cell, hardening the arteries, clotting as plaque, making him obese.

Dogma of total effect: We've moved toward a dogma of total effect when it comes to food. There is nothing that goes into your body, on this view, that doesn't permanently affect its makeup. Nothing fails to be incorporated. "Everything that goes into food goes into you," runs the frightening apothegm of one health-food advertisement. It is as if the somatic record registered all the adulterations and processes of our foods even more than the ingredients. Perhaps, too, the type of labor that went into them—even the intention with which that labor was done. It's like the idea of a perfect fossil record or perfect calculation of what you consumed over your whole life, as if your body grew or aged differently based on every single item to pass your lips. Not for us, the quite reasonable supposition that the majority of what we eat doesn't change us; that human beings have been digesting so much for so long that they eat disparate foods with identical outcomes.

Healthy taste: Taste is conditioned by ideas. The physiological base emerges in infancy and is shaped by one's "native" cuisine. Sweet, salt, sour, and bitter are said to be physiological universals. Subsequently taste is conditioned by will and effort. The savors of coffee, bitter chocolate, wine, beer, anchovies, brine, sharp cheeses, Brussels sprouts, all have to be learned with intellectual and physiological effort—for some people with more difficulty, for others less. The taste of health is one of these. A healthy taste will be the aggregate of all the carrots, apples, breakfast bars, protein shakes, fruit smoothies, chewable vitamin C tablets, tempeh, green tea, and zinc lozenges you've ingested. It is a rubbery ball of taste, added to and modified by each new item that's "healthy" that crosses your lips.

The most confusing foods to taste now are those that are bad for you but delicious and those that are "natural" or rare but flavorless. You learn to taste artificial grape flavor as "cheap" or chemical-like. With "refined sugar" or fried food, you say, "I enjoy having a Coke and onion rings, but I get a headache afterward"—and then you get the headache. Taste also becomes a product of comparison and decision. At a highway rest stop, I wanted a hamburger, but I bought a turkey sandwich. The roll was cardboardy, the turkey metallic, the lettuce white; but underneath it all, because of the self-denial and the act of choice, it had a peculiar flavor—it *tasted healthy*. When you eat the supermarket tomato that tastes terrible, it is "terrible"; when you bite into the heirloom tomato that happens to be tasteless and watery, you adjust it to taste "real."

The Jetsons: When George and Judy Jetson wanted to make a meal, they entered the kitchen, reached under the counter, and pulled out a little pellet, a pill. They put the pellet in the food oven, closed the door, opened it again, and now it was a steak. The pellet always became some very basic food—a plump turkey, a bowl of mashed potatoes, or an ice cream sundae with a maraschino cherry on top, for Elroy. Something unmarked; something common. And something whole.

This vision of an ideal food future managed to get our real food future wrong in exactly the right ways. We have experienced a bifurcation of food along Jetsonian lines. The Jetsons had a pellet. Now we eat the pellet. We call it a PowerBar or a multivitamin pill. Every "nutrition facts" statement on a label reminds us that our foods are assembled of thousands of elemental sub-parts, fat and protein and carbohydrate and vitamin and mineral parts—more pellets that displace the whole. We have *constituent* foods, fundamentally.

On the other hand, we have *provenance* foods: foods with names and locales, that passed through particular hands to take their current forms, and carry something of their geographic and personal attachments with them anywhere they go. We don't get turkey and mashed potatoes. Instead, Vermont organic fingerling potatoes with Sardinian olive oil, and a free-range grain-fed turkey raised cruelty-free. Food with origins, and sourced foods that carry with them a certain way of life and experience. What you're doing when you're eating these foods is also eating Vermont and Sardinia, and the labor performed in those places. Or, more genteelly, you're imagining what sort of lifeways, which you experience vicariously, go on in such places of origin. It's not labor but a kind of bliss, with fish leaping into nets and grains bending to the scythe. Perhaps you even imagine what goes on in the consciousness of the animals in the lands where the turkeys range free.

Gourmet vs. foodie. The gourmet of past decades wed himself to a single place: Western Europe, and more particularly France. He learned to cook a single alien cuisine, French, and his time and attention went toward two basic activities, cooking and importing. He cooked a limited palette of dishes and learned a set sequence of techniques. The gourmet knew foods that lent themselves to travel: wine, cheese, sausages (or charcuterie), pâtés, later coffees and chocolates. He would have a shop in his wealthy town that sold these items ("the gourmet shop"; the "wine and cheese shop"), and as an "expert" he could match wits with the experts who worked and shopped there. Julia Child exemplified the old gourmet.

The foodie differs in having the whole world at his fingertips. There is no one other region. There is the globe. If his cookbooks are European, they gravitate first to Europe's warm and "savage," uncivilized places: Provence, Southern Italy; then quickly slide to brightly illustrated new books carrying him to Turkey, Morocco, Vietnam, India. No single tradition exists for him to learn, no singular importers to patronize, but an ocean of ingredients that wash up on his shores—in the high-end supermarkets, which pretend to adventure among wild foods (the one nearest the *n+1* office is called "Foragers"; Trader Joe's represents the supermarket as a colonial trading station), in the old gourmet shops which survive on sufferance, and in the ethnic groceries, where the "ethnic" food may even include the foodie's native, childhood cuisine. The foodie wades out and swims in possibility. And then, surprisingly, many a foodie will deliberately restrict his range. He begins to set rules or laws for himself that make the quest for food harder and the thinking more complex. Undiscovered foods only; "authentic" restaurants only, or kitsch diners, or barbecue joints; organic food only; local or farmers' market food; historically reconstructed food; raw food or slow food only. A foodieism even exists of carnivorousness, or disgust: eating body parts that have become disreputable or rejected. Anthony Bourdain, traveling five thousand miles in business class to eat a sheep's eyeball, is one type of foodie hero, the authenticity-, nature-, and experience-devouring buccaneer who acknowledges disgust only by offending cautious philistine eaters. The rules or laws of his restrictions may be contradictory, operating in different food spheres, yet the true foodie can keep several going simultaneously, or slip from one regime to another. Not everyone undertakes the path of restriction, or follows it rigorously, but enough do, and the trait is essential.

The gourmet was always close to the snob. He wanted to be an aristocrat and identified with tradition. The foodie comes after the eradication of tradition. He is not like an aristocrat, but like someone who has stumbled into obscene wealth by what seems to him happenstance—as, judging globally, any of us in the rich countries has stumbled into wealth by the luck of where we live, and into food-wealth by our system of cheap overabundance and our access to all the migrant cuisines that shelter in America and Europe. There is no food we can't access. There is no food, moreover, that can't be further enchanted by our concentration, restriction, choice, and discrimination between better and worse specimens. We add the value of our intellectual labor, our "finishing" of the world's raw materials. Foodieism is a natural hobby for first-world professionals, ostensibly taking up the world, but referring back to the perfection of the enriched, corporeal self.

IT WOULD BE DISHONEST to suggest that we have not had critiques of the new food order. They come in two forms, and can represent a kind of fraternal warfare. First, we have exposés of our "fast food nation" and brilliant critiques of the national addiction to corn syrup. These come from the partisans of "nature," who fight industrial or mass food. Second, standing against them, the chef-, kitsch-, or ethnic-food worshipping gourmands occasionally strike back. They accuse the nature-lovers of tampering with pleasure, acting like killjoys, or speaking condescendingly from a position of wealth (from which the gourmands also speak, but never mind). It is a specimen situation of what Bourdieu called the "law of mutual lucidity and reflexive blindness" among practitioners of critique.

The most notable voice from the side of the gourmands may be UCLA sociologist Barry Glassner. His strategy in his book *The Gospel of Food* (2007) is to let nutrition scientists contradict each other in such a way as to create a chaos of knowledge. In this chaos, the best solution for eaters—until better information is available—may be to eat what you most enjoy, which, for Glassner, happens to be expensive Southern California restaurants in the contemporary foodie mode.

The most important voice in the "nature"-oriented critique of food is the journalist Michael Pollan. His *The Omnivore's Dilemma* (2006) seems to be the *Silent Spring* of this decade. It takes its great moral gravity from the orientation with which Pollan starts: that of the public good, the good of the environment, even the interests of animals. He does the investigative work to convincingly establish a critique of corn overproduction caused by the US's celebrated mechanization of agriculture and planting of hybrids. The consequence of reliance on a single crop and the necessary introduction of artificial fertilizers has been land damage. Tractorized corn farming causes overexpenditure of fossil fuels in an artificial economy sponsored by the state (leading to carbon pollution and fuel depletion). It makes for the cheapening of feed for food animals, particularly beef cows and broiler chickens, whose expanded ranks add wastes to the environment, while their removal from dependence on grassland allows humans to abuse them in ever more confining pens. The subsequent lowering of the price of meat leads humans to eat too much flesh, because they can afford it, and thus suffer new health problems. Meanwhile, the processing of large quantities of corn into too cheap a form of "unhealthful" nutrition, in the use of corn syrup to sweeten and calorify just about every processed food—sweetening foods beyond what is needful to the palate—creates obesity and ill health by a second route. And corn is further processed into all sorts of food-products (fillers, binders, emulsifiers) which are not easily found on their own in nature.

The difficulty with Pollan's argument is that he winds up moving from the large-scale phenomena of environmental effects to the small-scale phenomena of human body composition and health. One of the shocking moments in his book describes a chemical test that proves how much of the average American body has been built from molecules originating in corn. It's a scene made for horror, and more than one person I know who has read it developed a visceral disgust for corn products in foods. (As with Upton Sinclair's *The Jungle*, a novel about labor abuses in the meatpacking industry, with which Sinclair famously "aimed for America's heart and hit it in the stomach," Pollan's discoveries may often lend themselves less to solutions for the collective good than to immediate, personal self-protection.) It's worth remembering that this kind of use of corn was one of the great dreams of progress in food: a single source of nutrition that could feed everyone, or be broken down and recreated in any form—a dream of humankind since the time of God's manna. Pollan's critique can become purely privatistic (in the worries about individual weight gain and disease from meat and corn syrup) or turn into a hostility to progress and the widespread, easy provision of food itself. His book goes on to treat the large-scale success of organic farming, which he believes has cost the organic movement its soul; be that as it may, Pollan's only successful alternative, a "grass farm" where all livestock farming depends on the successful management of grass, seems to represent a model that simply can't be scaled up for a multitude of eaters. It depends to a high degree on charismatic genius simply to run from day to day.

After this, *The Omnivore's Dilemma* becomes essentially self-directed. Can Pollan forage food? (He learns to pick extremely expensive mushrooms.) Can he kill his meat? (He hunts a wild boar.) How will he enjoy his book-ending meal, a dinner so maddeningly elite (the fava beans don't help) as to make one momentarily sympathetic to Pollan's most petty critics—those who say that he defends "nature" in the form of food, not for the good of mankind, but to justify the sort of egotistic luxury trade that pays the rent on a thousand Whole Foods Markets.

Whether or not one admires the path Pollan takes, one thing is clear. In his solutions, and in his reasoning about first principles, he is anti-progressive. He no doubt votes for Democrats; supports the right causes; has the right attitudes. He defends "nature" but moves quickly from outer nature (trees, earth) to an inner nature (or "human nature") which he believes is fixed in crucial respects. The invariant parts of human nature, for Pollan, are rooted in our evolutionarily acquired attitudes to just such things as food. As is true for much other conservative thought about human nature (conservative with a little *c*), Pollan has a fundamental belief that past practices are likely to be superior simply because they were the past, "our" past. They must suit us in some deep way. He holds an underlying preference for the "nature" to be found beneath the vanity of reason. The line of thought in his short *In Defense of Food* (2008) intensifies this feeling. Pollan gets away from contemporary ever-changing studies of nutritional science (the material Glassner employed to sow doubt) by appealing to his evolutionary model, in which human beings are adapted to eat many very different traditional diets, so long as their diet is not the new "Western diet" of 20th-century invention. He seems to believe, against present food culture, that adopting any traditional diet of his grandparents' generation or earlier would lead us now, when combined with modern medicine, to live longer than we will on our own current diet (post–World War II Western foods). He has much to say in this book that is more honest than what other mainstream figures will allow themselves to say—for example, that food anxiety is beneficial to "the food industry, nutrition science, and—ahem—journalism" but not to eaters. But Pollan's philosophical commitment to "tradition" as his truest guide, and the imputation that reason is always inadequate to decide anything "complex," like human dietary or social practices, distorts his thought in a particular way.

The most progressive food philosophy of the present day, in the strict sense of progress as opposed to conservation, is vegetarianism. On the basis of reason and morality, it calls for a wholesale change in the way that human beings have always eaten, and a renunciation of a central part of the human dietary past and all its folkways. Vegetarianism has not given up on utopia. The point in *The Omnivore's Dilemma* at which Pollan must lose the goodwill of many of his readers, I think, is in his discussion of vegetarianism. I speak as a non-vegetarian. (Non-vegetarian because I am immoral, not because I think there is any good argument for carnivorousness. It is not true, what some philosophers say, that genuinely to hold a belief is necessarily to act on it. I hope I will learn to be moral, by and by.) Everything in Pollan's book concerning meat animals and their damage to the environment points to the conclusion that we should stop eating meat in any serious way. It is at this point that Pollan's traditionalism splits with his hope for social change, and one sees which comes first. He will not stop eating meat, because humans have always eaten it.

Non-dogmatic vegetarians are often the eaters who seem to have the greatest stake in *progressive* food production and food chemistry while still paying attention to the socially harmful forms of overproduction that critics like Pollan identify. For them, Quorn (protein made of fungus) and Boca Burgers (protein made of soy) and multivitamin pills all have their place in a rational and future-oriented diet, just as heirloom lentils do, or quinoa, or Thoreau's beloved beans.

Pollan really possesses, as his true endpoint, not social change for the sake of the social, but change for health. Health may be expanded to include what our medicalized culture calls "quality of life"—satisfaction of the palate, crumbs of happiness, dinner table sociability, and Pollan's sort of natural piety—but it never ceases to be health. Its fulfillment may require progress in science and progress in medicine. But it is always, fundamentally, progressive in an antisocial way. Though it claims to purify and strengthen the body politic, health has nothing to contribute to (horizontal) solidarity and democracy. It always leads individuals back into themselves, as those selves try to meet the (vertical) demands of experts. Any focus on optimization and purity has a way of contravening the attitude of democracy. Democratic imagination desires that which is unlikely, unfitted to itself, unfit; it incorporates the sick and unknown not just for the sake of justice, but for a reckless joy.

IS THERE ANYTHING I KNOW that Pollan and Glassner don't? I know that each of them can only escape the system of flawed nutritional science by looking for more and different science. And yet if one were really to get out of this system, one would have to embrace a will to discover a different source of value.

The rules of food, of sex, of exercise, of health, give us ways to avoid facing up to a freedom from care which we may already have within reach. This would be an accomplished freedom from biology, lacking nothing, which we simply don't know what to do with. What if life were not really a possessive commodity that came in quantities that you gained or lost by your efforts? What if there were no further overcoming of some obstacle (disease, mortality) still to be attained, and we are now *in* the era of life assured and made free? If so—well, how should we act?

WHAT IS HEALTH? It is stored care.

It is good foods intaken, converted into a kind of currency, with your body as piggy bank. It is vile careless pleasures kept from the mouth, rejected.

It is a set of predictions about the future of your body based on correlations from others' lives. It is a set of attitudes and feelings about your body as it is now, based on introspection, feeling, combined with chancy outside expert information.

It is putting in the hours of exercise to keep your heart pumping far into your old age. It is not bad, nor good. It is not assailable, nor is it the only truth.

I can't help but want to live longer. I also want to live without pain. This means I want "health." But when I place myself at a point within the vast constellation of health knowledge and health behaviors, I can't help but feel that these systems don't match up with my simple projects of longevity and freedom from pain. There is something too much, or too many, or too arbitrary, or too directed—too doom-laden, too managerial, too controlling.

° ° °

THE ULTIMATE QUARRY and ultimate obstacle in any different way of thinking about food is this concept of health. How would one truly get outside of the rules of the game? By rejecting health as a goal, and choosing some other reason for living?

We have no language but health. Those who criticize dieting as unhealthy operate in the same field as those who criticize overweight as unhealthy. Even those who think we overfixate on the health of our food call it an unhealthy fixation.

But choosing another reason for living, as things now stand, seems to be choosing death. Is the trouble that there seems to be no other reason for living that isn't a joke, or that isn't dangerous for everyone—like the zealot's will to die for God or the nation? Or is the problem that any other system than this one involves a death-seeking nihilism about knowledge and modernity, a refusal to admit what scientists, or researchers, or nutritionists, or the newest diet-faddists, have turned up? . . . As their researches narrow the boundaries of life.

Health is our model of all things invisible and unfelt. If, in this day and age, we rejected the need to live longer, what would any one of us rich Westerners live for instead? +

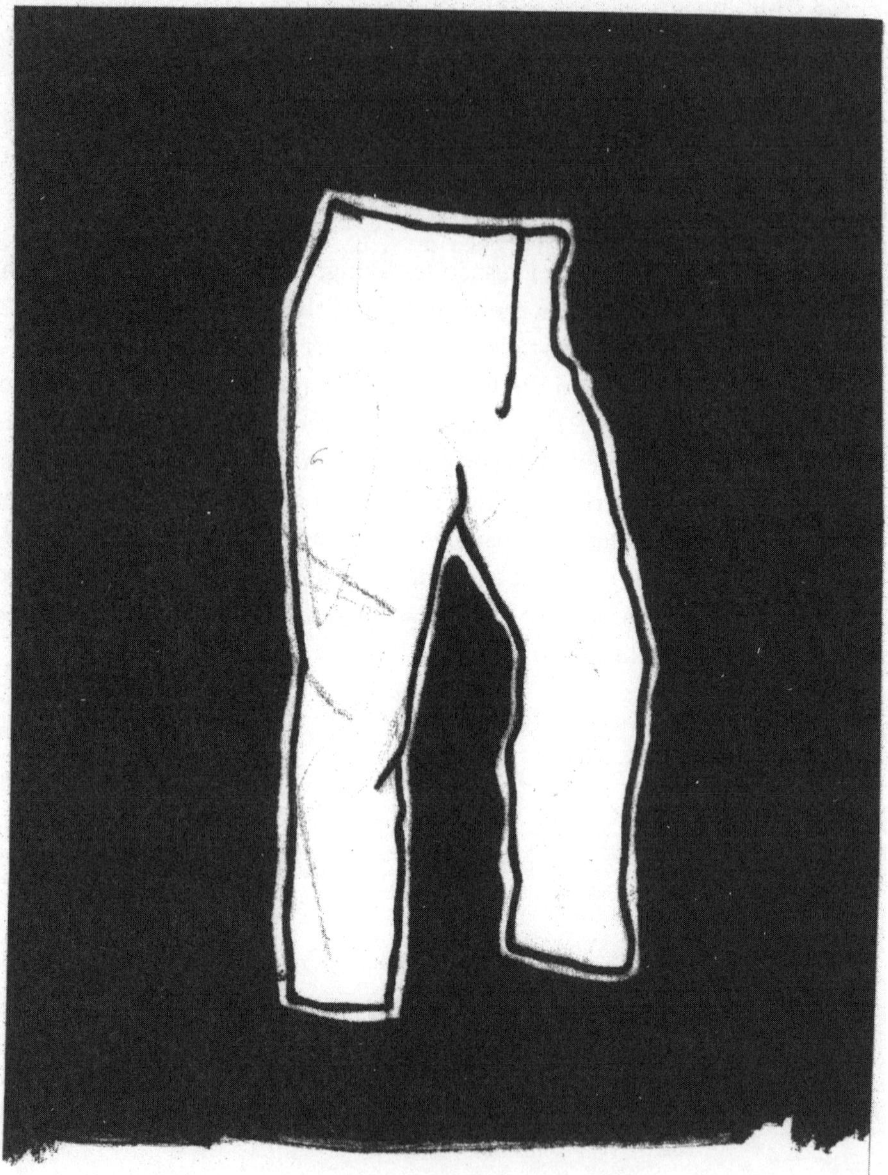

HEXIT/MJK, *GHOSTPANTS*, 2008,
INK ON PAPER. COURTESY OF MR. AND MS. HEXIT.

CLAUS PEYMANN BUYS HIMSELF A PAIR OF PANTS AND JOINS ME FOR LUNCH

Thomas Bernhard

Vienna

PEYMANN *after trying on six pairs of Zegna light summer pants in a boutique on the Graben and eventually buying the second pair and wearing them out of the store, with his old pants under his arm, walking quickly but not frantically toward the Plague Column*

A pair of pants that fits
can make you feel better than anything else
don't you think so Bernhard

ME

That is the truth

PEYMANN

On the one hand a pair of pants that fits
on the other hand *Richard III* in your head
it makes you feel good Bernhard
So all right then let's take a little walk Bernhard

enchanted by his new pants

Trying on trying on trying on Bernhard
that's the thing
it's exhausting of course
with pants it's like with *The Winter's Tale*
it's like with *Leonce and Lena* with pants
putting on a pair of pants is exhausting of course
putting on Shakespeare is exhausting in exactly the same way
when we put on a pair of pants it's exhausting exactly the same way

as when we put on Kleist or Shakespeare
When we have on a pair of pants that fits like this
a pair of pants that really sits well Bernhard
it's the same feeling of happiness
as when we've brought into being
a Shakespeare that fits
a Kleist that fits
a Schiller that sits well Bernhard

stops and looks down at his new pants

They sit well sitting down too these pants

tries them out sitting down so to speak

Nice aren't they
sit excellently
good store don't you think
When you're over forty
you only buy top-notch
well-fitting pants

straightens up again

Buying pants has always been a tragedy
I don't know
is it more appalling to put on Shakespeare
or six pairs of pants Bernhard
I don't know
This city tempts you to buy pants
They really do fit well Bernhard these pants
don't you think

his face twisted with doubt

don't you think

ME

They fit excellently
Zegna makes the best pants
An Italian cut suits you
You have absolutely the wrong body type
for an English cut
Your body type
was made for an Italian cut Peymann

PEYMANN
You think

ME
Definitely
you look best in Zegna pants

PEYMANN
Years back I was running around in rags

ME
Forty years ago you were running around in rags
in the winter twenty-two below zero
you had nothing on but frayed jeans
and a so-called Coca-Cola cut-off
until you put on *Iphigenia* in Stuttgart
after *Iphigenia* you were suddenly very elegantly dressed
You underwent this transformation in Paris

PEYMANN *happy about his new pair of pants*
Seriously Bernhard
do these pants fit

ME
Clothes make the man Peymann
should I carry your old pants for you

PEYMANN
No
nonono

ME
You know what
let's go get lunch at the Zauberflöte

PEYMANN
At the Zauberflöte

ME

The Zauberflöte is an establishment
where you can get top-notch food at a reasonable price

PEYMANN

Well then let's head there Bernhard

ME

I've always
hated buying pants

PEYMANN

Me too

ME

Every time I've tried on a pair of pants
I've had a choking fit
It's not just one pair of pants
we try on you know
there are always several pairs
there are lots of times I've tried on seven or eight pairs of pants
and every time I thought
I'd have a stroke in the changing room

PEYMANN

But you never did have a stroke
You're tough Bernhard
I hardly know anyone tougher
Ten or fifteen years ago
you were already saying
you were going to have a stroke

ME

The pants changing rooms are too narrow
there's no air in them
There have already been so many strokes
in pants changing rooms

just ask the garment guild
they'll confirm it for you
People go into a store
and want to try on just one pair of pants
and they try on seven or eight
and have a stroke that is the truth
clothing establishment changing room strokes are the most
common kind

PEYMANN

It's like if I
rehearsed *The Winter's Tale* for three days and three nights

ME

Just ask the doctors in the cardiology ward
Cardiac fatalities while trying on pants
are no rare thing
If we could read the cause of death
on people's gravestones
then every time we looked at the gravestones
no matter which cemetery
we would read
Cause Of Death Trying On Pants
If you're honest
you have to admit
that this trying on pants is more exhausting
than trying out a play
a rehearsal is nothing compared to pants
People go into a pants store
and all they want is to buy a pair of summer pants
an especially light pair of summer pants
as they say
and they try them on and try them on
and have a stroke
When trying on pants
extreme caution is recommended
We just try on a light pair of summer pants

and Death comes to get us
It's interesting death
in men's changing rooms is much more common
than in women's changing rooms Peymann
women slip into their skirts so easily you know
whereas for men it takes serious effort
On the other hand it's in changing rooms like that
that I've come up with the best ideas
I was trying on pants once
when I had the idea for a novel
a novel I wrote too
in Würzburg believe it or not
but it's true I put it aside immediately
and threw it out
that is the truth
I've thrown out more novels than I've published
not to mention all the other prose
that I've written and thrown out
and not published
We just try on a pair of pants
and we conceive of a novel
or a stage play
Ghastly this term "stage play"
The word "stage" in general
but the word "play" too
and especially "stage play"
I hate the word "theater" too
and "actor" there's no word I hate more than "actor"
everything that has to do with theater
I hate it more than anything

dramatically

I hate the stage
I hate the actors on the stage
I hate the world of the theater

PEYMANN

I can't agree with you there

ME

That's true
After all you're a theater person
as they say
but I'm not a theater person
Body and soul
and with your whole heart
you love the theater
you're crazy about the theater
I hate the theater body and soul
and I loathe it more than anything
nothing is more repellent to me
but that's exactly why I'm in its clutches
I hate the theater
and everything that has to do with theater
and have been handed over to it
You are in its clutches from love
I am in its clutches from hate

PEYMANN

The theater is my world

ME

It's not my world

PEYMANN

The theater is my passion Bernhard
nothing but theater

ME

With me it's just the opposite
I loathe the theater
it draws me in
because I loathe it
You love actors
I hate them
You love the public
I hate it

You love the stage
I hate it
Everything you love
I hate
everything you loathe
I love
I love everything
you loathe

PEYMANN

A good beef soup Bernhard
that's what I'm in the mood for
when it's hot
you want a hot beef soup
Austria is the land of beef soup
nothing's better in Austria
than the beef soup
There's no country in the world
where they have better beef soup Bernhard

ME

Shouldn't I carry your old pants for you

PEYMANN

What are you trying to say Bernhard
you think I'm not even strong enough
to carry an old pair of pants by myself
What do you think I am
At the end of the day I'm the Director of the Burgtheater
so I must be stronger
than I'd need to be just to carry my old pair of pants Bernhard
walks faster down Kärtnerstrasse toward the Opera House
As Director of the Burgtheater
it's a constant test of strength
I'm not afraid of it Bernhard
The Burgtheater is a heavyweight Bernhard
A heavyweight that's what the Burgtheater is
how on earth could you think

that I can't even carry my own old pair of pants
when I'm the Director of the Burgtheater
The Director of the Burgtheater has to carry
the whole Burgtheater day in day out Bernhard
figuratively speaking Bernhard figuratively
just imagine that
day in day out the whole Burgtheater as it lays and stands there
Bernhard
this whole Burgtheater overflowing with actors and dramaturges
to pick it up early in the morning
and lift it high in the air
and keep lifting it higher and higher Bernhard
always higher and higher Bernhard
and always higher than the other directors lift their theaters
the Director of the Burgtheater has to lift the Burgtheater
just imagine that Bernhard
You wake up early in the morning and you know
you have to lift the Burgtheater high into the air
and in fact always higher and higher
and in any case as Director of the Burgtheater to lift the
Burgtheater higher
than all the other directors lift their theaters
these ridiculous stages Bernhard
these ridiculous stages in Germany and Switzerland
all these ridiculous European stages
every day I raise up the Burgtheater so high
no other theater director can raise his stage to that height

ME

Yes you're a real Kraftlackel

PEYMANN

What's a Kraftlackel

ME

A Kraftlackel is someone
who doesn't have anywhere near as much strength
as he needs
but shows more strength than anyone

PEYMANN

That's a Kraftlackel

ME

Yes that's a Kraftlackel

PEYMANN

These Austrian words
are unbelievably funny
lots of things here almost everything
is unbelievably funny
it seems to me that here
nearly everything is unbelievably funny
Austria is the craziest comedy
I've ever come across

ME

The Austrians think
their fatherland is a tragedy
but it's really a comedy

PEYMANN

A comedy that's what Austria is
and what a comedy
an outrageous comedy
it's as though a reincarnation of Shakespeare had written it
In fact I often have the feeling these days Bernhard
that Austria is a comedy by Shakespeare
that you don't have to stage
it's already there
the one complete grand comedy the craziest comedy of all
is the Austrian comedy
Just think of the actors
they're already there
just think of the set
it's already there
just think of the score

it's already there
the craziest comedy of all time
that's Austria
no play in the world comes anywhere near it
and the Austrians themselves have staged this craziest comedy of all time
the complete people's comedy is Austria
the complete people's comedy
No writer not even you my dear Bernhard
could write this craziest of all comedies
no director not even me
could direct it
and this Austria as the set
is also the craziest one there's ever been
Probably this Austria is
the one and only total complete world comedy Bernhard
If there is theater
then Austria is it
if there are actors
then the Austrians are they
if there is a set
then Austria is it
Compared to this Austrian world comedy
you my dear Bernhard are nothing
and I myself am nothing compared to it
because you could never write something so monumental something so singular
something so outrageous
and I could never direct something so monumental and singular
and outrageous
and our friend Karl-Ernst Herrmann
could never build something so monumental
and something so singular and something so outrageous
compared to this we theater people are basically ridiculous little dwarves
You are a dwarf-writer Bernhard
I am a dwarf-director

Herrmann is a dwarf-stage-designer
compared to this Austria
Whenever someone asks me
so where is the best theater in the world
I always answer "Austria"
I say "Austria"
and then the people always ask "where in" Austria
and I answer "not in Austria Austria
Austria itself"
go to Austria I tell these people
and you'll show up in absolutely the best theater in the world
buy yourself a good ticket I tell all these people
get yourself a room at the Imperial or the Bristol
at the Sacher or the Ambassador
and enjoy the craziest theater in the world
I tell all these people
and of course they're taken aback
I thought say all these people
the craziest theater was
where you work Herr Peymann
and you do work starting now at the Burgtheater
so the Burgtheater starting now must really be
the best theater in the world
No I say nono it's not me
it's not the Burgtheater either
it's Austria
it's Austria that's the best theater in the world
that's how I take people aback Bernhard
that's how I make them uncertain
the people then think
I'm crazy
they factor in my megalomania
and discover
that I'm nothing but crazy
for saying that Austria
is the best theater in the world
My dear Bernhard

my whole life long I've led people
around by the nose
just like you your whole life long have led them around
by the nose
as the Director of the Burgtheater it's practically my duty
to lead people around by the nose
I thumb my nose at them
and lead them around by the nose
as the Director of the Burgtheater there's nothing else I can do
but lead people around by the nose
the thumbed nose
a Director of the Burgtheater is of course a great big
around-by-the-nose-leader
you know that Bernhard
you the great around-by-the-nose-leader
It makes me happy to think
that the two of us
you as a writer
and me as the Director of the Burgtheater
lead people around by the nose
what else is a Director of the Burgtheater there to do
but lead people around by the nose
by the Burgtheater nose
by this gigantic swollen Burgtheater nose
You should really write a play Bernhard
where you lead everyone around by the nose
that's the kind of play I wish you'd write
a real lead-around-by-the-nose play
you need to sit down Bernhard
and write a lead-around-by-the-nose play like that
Great theater Bernhard
all fatherland all scandal all megalomania
all criminal tasteless sordid
real Burgtheater theater
a real grand lead-around-by-the-nose comedy that destroys
    everything
put all your ruthlessness onstage for once
all your loathing of the world

not just half of your loathing of the world but all of your loathing
of the world Bernhard
write a play for the world theater
that will rip the Burgtheater to shreds
a real grandiose world joke Bernhard
that blows up the Burgtheater
that shakes the whole city of Vienna
you know what I mean
you know what I've always hoped for from you
this great big throw that overthrows the world
this comedy for everyone that really and truly takes the whole
world off its hinges
this comedic monster you know Bernhard
write something that puts everything else
in the shade
get all of world literature down on paper for once
just write it all down for once lock stock and barrel
pull yourself together Bernhard and write the world's head off
write a real worldbuster Bernhard

ME *who has followed Claus Peymann to the ring road and then back again on Kärtnerstrasse, without actually being able to keep up with him*
Are you sure you don't want
me to carry your old pants for you

PEYMANN
What are you trying to say Bernhard
you forget that I'm at the height of my powers
suddenly stopping short
You really have no idea Bernhard
how good I feel in this new pair of pants
A new Director of the Burgtheater
also needs a new pair of pants
don't you think Bernhard don't you think

ME
That is the truth that is the truth

PEYMANN

It's too bad that we can't go just like that
and buy ourselves a new head too Bernhard
right now at this moment I'd love to go into a shop with you
and buy myself a new head
our whole life long we run around
with a single outworn I want to say worn-out head
with a head that's gotten all shabby Bernhard
everyone's wearing a shabby head
every head we see is a worn-out head
me too of course I have a totally worn-out head
we hardly have a head at all
and already it's worn out
the world is full of nothing but worn-out heads Bernhard
Wouldn't that really be something Bernhard
if there were a store we could go into right now
and buy ourselves new heads
and you'd be wearing a new one
and I'd be carrying your old worn-out one in a plastic bag
and I'd be wearing a new one too
and you'd be carrying my old head in a plastic bag
and with new heads on our necks we'd go
have lunch at the Zauberflöte
and have our old heads in plastic bags
But sometimes it's enough
just to go buy yourself a new pair of pants Bernhard
it doesn't have to be a new head
or a new hat
and to carry your old hat in a plastic bag
Ah Bernhard
all the great things I expected from you as a playwright
But I haven't given up hope
I often say to myself when I wake up in the middle of the night
one day he'll write the play I'm waiting for
I haven't given up hope Bernhard
I've never given up hope

PEYMANN *walks into the Zauberflöte with me and we sit down, after he has looked at the menu and chosen something to eat and looked around in the Zauberflöte*
So who's that

ME
The Vice Chancellor
a Nazi

PEYMANN
And him

ME
The Minister of Agriculture
an old Nazi

PEYMANN
And him over there

ME
The Defense Minister
a Nazi

PEYMANN
And him

ME
The Foreign Minister
an old Nazi

PEYMANN
And him over there

ME
The head of the General Accounting Office
an old Nazi

PEYMANN

And him

ME

The Editor-in-Chief of the most prestigious newspaper in Vienna
an old Nazi

PEYMANN

And that guy there

ME

The Editor-in-Chief of the second most prestigious newspaper in Vienna
an old Nazi

PEYMANN

And him over there

ME

That's the Minister of Culture and Sport
an idiot a moron

PEYMANN

And that guy there

ME

That's the Chancellor
an idiot

PEYMANN

And him

ME

That's the newly elected President
an old Nazi

PEYMANN

And them over there

ME
  They're all Nazis

PEYMANN
  And those other guys

ME
  Those are all idiots and Nazis

PEYMANN
  And the waitress

ME
  She's a Catholic and knows everyone and doesn't know anything

PEYMANN
  All right then so we'll get beef soup

ME
  Yes of course

PEYMANN
  What else do you recommend Bernhard

ME
  Viennese boiled beef

PEYMANN
  Then we'll eat some Viennese boiled beef
to the waitress
  So we'll have beef soup with liver meatballs
  then boiled beef with horseradish bread
  and then some dessert
  how bout a sweet cream strudel with vanilla sauce
tucks the napkin into his collar
  Crazy city Bernhard
  crazy country Bernhard

Austria's something else Bernhard
stretches his legs before taking the first spoonful of soup and then,
as though in a sudden burst of happiness, cries out
Soon nothing at all will surprise me here Bernhard
not a thing not a thing
spoons his soup slowly at first, then very fast

Curtain

—Translated by Damion Searls

Bernhard's Heldenplatz, *the world-busting play Peymann implored him to write as they walked to lunch, premiered at the Burgtheater in 1988, fifty years after the Anschluss. The play, which sought to force Austrians to confront their past complicity with the Nazis, met with widespread protests. President Waldheim called it "an outrage against the Austrian people," many angry letters were written and threats of harm issued. An old woman on a bus attacked Bernhard with her umbrella. Nonetheless, the first performance concluded with a forty-five-minute ovation for writer and director. Bernhard died three months later.*

ELIZABETH HUEY, *RETRIEVE. RETRIEVE.*, 2008,
INK, PENCIL AND COLLAGE, COLOR, 8 X 10". COURTESY OF THE ARTIST.

THE FAMILY FRIEND

Ceridwen Dovey

HE WAS A FAMILY FRIEND; he had been at university with the girl's father, or scrummed on the same team, something like that. The girl had been asked to dinner out of common courtesy—she was starting her first job, alone in a strange city; he could offer her the companionship of a family kitchen, and anyway, she was a good tennis player and the court's lines had just been repainted and he always loved an opportunity to show off his prowess with a racquet, even at his age (especially at his age). He told her on the telephone that she should just let herself in when she arrived at the house and told her where they hid the key; he was always home later than he expected because of the pressures of his work, and his son usually had swimming or rugby or cricket after school and a bad habit of dawdling. She was grateful for the invitation to supper. Most nights since she'd arrived she had spent eating soup in her tiny flat with the radio on and she was beginning to wonder if she would be alright. The woman she worked for didn't like to speak much and whole days went by where the girl would realise that no words had passed her lips.

She found their house with some difficulty—it was in a suburb she had not been to before, hallowed and leafy as one would expect from the suburbs, and the house itself promised a weighted life of grace that her own lacked. She parked her car and, balancing the plum tart she'd made against one hip, tried the front gate, which gave to the pressure of her hand. The front garden overflowed its prim boundaries, threatening to consume the path she was following to the front door, a garden full of rosebushes left to track their own course in the world and hibiscus sticking out red tongues, and blue gums sucking up the lion's share of the water, and barely an indigenous shrub to be seen. She liked the garden. It had something oxymoronic about it, a cultivated wilderness of foreign plants allowed to go native. The house itself was large and open-faced, with bay windows and not a single burglar bar. Only the very wealthy, she thought, can afford not to have burglar bars. And the position of the hidden key—its edge visible from beneath the pansy pot beside the doormat—confirmed that this family had earned the carelessness that is the prerogative of the rich. She rang the doorbell, twice, just to make sure, then put the tart on the ground, slipped the key from beneath the pot and opened the front door. The hallway was scented with the spice of cut gardenias, which she found floating in a glass bowl of water, pruned of their glossy leaves; a woman's touch, she thought. The maid's? The daughter's? The girl left her handbag on an antique wooden chair beside the coat-rack and carried the tart through the living room (brocaded fabric and candle holders and claw-footed sofas) and into the cavernous kitchen, where she could tell immediately most of the living in the house was done. It was large, certainly, but unassuming, and the gingham curtains glowed and the hanging brass pots and pans gleamed with the rays of the dying sun. The days were beginning fractionally to lengthen.

She did not dare go upstairs to look around as it seemed beyond the boundaries that are set up between family and visitor, but she did wander about the downstairs sprawl of the house, mostly to look at photographs framed and hung on walls or propped on yellowwood chests. She had wondered before she'd arrived if there would be family photographs or if, by now, they would have taken them all down or turned them flat on their faces against the tabletops. But there were many of them, all a little dusty so she guessed that nobody had yet had the courage or the energy to contemplate taking them down, or even to take a photograph and streak away the dust with fingertips before putting it back in its place. Having never experienced grief herself, the girl wanted to know what it felt like. She knew it didn't always take the same form, that in another home she would have found the frames meticulously dusted or the photographs removed from sight, but she wanted to know the particularities of the emotion, what it felt like for just one family of four, now three.

And though she knew it should not matter—that grief was not partial to these things—it struck her that this family was more worthy of grieving because they were beautiful. Or at least she was beautiful, the mother, a woman who even in a photograph the girl could not take her eyes from, a curve of cheek and gloss of hair and wideness of mouth that made the girl ache inside—for seeing beauty is both pleasure and pain, even to someone who has a degree of it herself, and the girl would be described as such by somebody spotting her walking up the path holding her plum tart in her arms. There were a few pictures, in particular, that fascinated her. There was a photograph of the couple, perhaps taken before they were married, stalled on a tandem bicycle in high winds: her long, straight black hair streamed behind her into his face (she was sitting on the front seat), so he was barely recognisable, but through the strands you could see he was laughing, and making no attempt to move the hair from his eyes. He was probably, the girl thought, glad of a chance to have her so close to him, to have her hair in his eyes and mouth, to taste and smell her in ways that she perhaps would not have let him otherwise. In the photograph, she had both her bare feet up on the handlebar—slim, bony feet and slender ankles revealed by the wind tugging at her hems—and smiled her wide but beautifully aloof smile with her eyes closed and her face to the sun. Beside this was their wedding photograph, in black and white, with the lace of her dress all the way up to her throat and down to her wrists, and her hair pinned with pearls. He looked relieved in this photograph—relieved, the girl wondered, because he had finally claimed her as his and his only? For he was not what the girl would have thought of as conventionally attractive; yes, he was tall, and had a full head of lovely blonde hair, but he had unfortunate teeth which gave him the air of a rodent, and eyes that bulged ever so slightly. But women will give men the benefit of the doubt, and look past these things to other talents, of which, she had heard, he had many.

She was looking closely at another photograph, of the couple with their first child, a daughter, who was a few years older than herself, when she heard the gate open and saw through the bay window the family friend balancing his briefcase on his knee as she had balanced the plum tart. He was in his suit but with his tie loosened and his jacket slung over one shoulder and sleeves rolled up. She went to the front door to open it for him and he seemed glad to see her, and, once he had put down his briefcase and jacket in the hallway, gave her a hug and a kiss and held her at arm's length to take a good look at her.

'The last time I saw you,' he said musingly, 'was at your father's fortieth! And you must have been . . .' He paused.

'Fifteen,' she replied, 'and now I'm twenty-four.'

He smiled, and she regretted what she had said; guessed that he thought she was trying to impress on him that she had been a girl when last he saw her and now was something else. It was just that she knew she often came across as coltish, that people always assumed she was younger than she was. 'Did you not want to remove your coat?' he asked, solicitous but not fatherly. 'I can turn the heating on if you're cold.'

She let him take her coat, turning her back to him so that he could grip it around the lapel to slide it off her shoulders.

'Please, come through to the kitchen,' he said, 'have a glass of wine.'

She followed him obediently back through the living room and into the kitchen, now out of sun, and perched on a three-legged stool at the counter as he lit candles and lamps and began to take down pots and a cutting board from where they were displayed above the stove. He handed her a bottle of wine and a corkscrew, and busied himself setting water to boil and crushing garlic and opening tins of artichokes and plum tomatoes.

'Can I help?' she asked, gesturing to the cutting board and the unpeeled onions.

'No,' he said, 'just sit there and tell me about your life.'

She took two wine glasses down from the rack against one wall, poured the wine, and said, 'I'm not used to having to do that. Usually I'm the one asking questions.'

'Oh,' he said, 'but I'm a lawyer. Questions are my specialty.'

She sipped her wine. 'I'm working for a graphic designer, just a one-woman company, really, there's not that much for me to do.'

She stopped and he looked up. 'And you've found a place to live and all that?'

'A small flat,' she said. 'I live on my own.'

He nodded and threw the garlic into the pan of oil. 'It's not always easy,' he said. 'Before I married, I was obsessive about things: the cups had to be stacked in a certain way, and the dishtowel had to be washed every second day, and I couldn't bear having a pack of something—beer, juice—in the fridge with the plastic wrap still covering it.'

The garlic made the kitchen smell like home and the girl took another deep sip of her wine and laughed with the family friend but did not volunteer any of her own idiosyncrasies. There was a sound at the door then, and from the hallway came the clattering of a teenage boy returning from school and sports practice. They heard him approach over the wooden floors still in his pronged rugby boots, *clack, clack, clack* until he appeared at the entrance to the kitchen, grubby but fresh-faced.

'I don't know if you remember my son,' the family friend said. 'He would have been making a nuisance of himself at the party.'

The son was polite; charming for a 15-year-old, and he stepped forward to shake the girl's hand before he realised his own was caked in mud and retracted it. She laughed and took his hand anyway. He had about him the mystery of loss that made her feel as if she were the younger of the two. She looked closely at his face—his eyes, especially—trying, as she had with his father, to read the signs of his grief. There was nothing except a slight inwardness around his eyes, a drawing in, a pinching of something. She had not seen this on his father's face.

The son excused himself to shower, and when he returned, joined her at the counter, drawing up another stool across from his father at the stovetop. He smelled good, a soft boyish scent of changing rooms and fields, of chalk and soap. He took the glass of wine she had poured for him shyly, with a quick glance at his father's bent head.

'How did the game go, my boy?' his father asked as he poured a packet of pasta into the boiling water.

'We lost again.' He drained his wine glass while his father's back was still turned.

'Your team's not doing well?' she asked him.

'Horribly,' he said, 'we haven't won a match since . . .' He stopped. 'Since Mom died,' the son said quietly.

His father put down the spatula beside the frying pan. 'Oh my boy,' his father said, 'my poor son.'

The girl watched as a tear sloped down the tip of the son's nose and into his glass. She saw the veins on the father's hand, raised and green above his brown skin, as he squeezed his son's arm.

The family friend looked up directly at her. 'I want him to express his grief,' he said, 'whenever it comes over him. It's important. We have to grieve.'

° ° °

THE GIRL ASKED HER PARENTS when next they called if they had known the mother well. What she wanted to ask was whether she had been as beautiful as she looked in the photographs, but somehow that seemed a distasteful question.

Her mother hesitated over the telephone, said noncommittally, 'Fairly well,' then paused. 'She kept to herself,' she went on, 'it was hard to feel you really knew her.'

Her father said, 'We never really understood what she saw in him. I mean, he was always very clever and I suppose he was social too, but she was exquisite . . .' He changed the subject.

The family friend had asked her before she left his house after dinner to accompany him as his partner in a mixed doubles alumni tennis match the following Sunday, to be held at somebody's wine farm. She had agreed, although she'd warned him that she was a bit rusty, and on Sunday morning she stood outside her flat in tennis skirt and sneakers, her racquet slung across her back. It was a late winter's day, with sharp air and sharper colours, and she let the sun warm her back as she waited. The family friend arrived in a sleek car to fetch her and they drove out through the city.

'Thank you for dinner the other night,' she said as she settled into the seat.

'I'm glad you came,' he said. 'I'm just sorry it wasn't the most joyful affair.'

She let some time pass before she said, 'Do you mind if I ask how you met your wife?'

He rolled down his window, letting in the crisp air, and leaned his elbow on the edge. 'In a bus queue,' he said, 'of all places. She was ahead of me in the queue and I noticed she was reading the same book as I was, and, even more strange and wonderful, it was a book about coincidence that was quite popular at the time—I can't remember now who the author was.'

The girl fanned out her tennis skirt on the seat and tucked her hands beneath her thighs to keep them warm.

'And so,' he went on, 'I tapped her on the shoulder and showed her that I had the very same book in my bag, and she smiled the most beautiful smile at me—as guileless as a baby.' He paused to focus on exiting the highway. The scenery changed almost instantly, from rows of shacks to rows and rows of vines. 'Her name,' he said, 'was the most beautiful name I had ever heard.'

The girl looked at him sideways to see if he was crying, but he was wearing sunglasses and she could not tell.

He introduced her to the other players as the daughter of a dear old friend of his, and a stellar tennis player. She noticed (and wondered, did anyone else?) that he emphasised the fatherly nature of his relationship to her several times over the course of the afternoon, although when they were alone in the car she felt he treated her like an equal, like a stand-in for her father, a dear old friend and not a daughter. They played well together on the court, and came away with the alumni tennis challenge prize: a bottle of champagne that he promised to pop when next one of them had something to celebrate (she had never had real champagne).

On the way back through the city, he asked if she would mind if he stopped in at his office briefly, just to pick up some documents. 'Come inside if you like,' he said, 'have a look around.'

His offices were timelessly swank, wood-panelled and leather-upholstered and plush-floored, with elaborate chairs in enclaves within offices and fresh flowers delivered and arranged daily. His office was the biggest of them all, with a reception area and desks for two secretaries in the outer part, and his private library next door.

'It's an important case we're working on,' he said, lifting carefully prepared folders from his pigeon-hole.

'What's it about?' the girl asked.

'Somebody wanting to build a path through somebody else's land,' he said without the slightest hint of irony.

When he dropped her off outside her flat, he said, 'Please, you must treat our home like your home.'

'I did notice,' she said, 'that you have a grand piano.'

He looked at her in surprise. 'By all means, come and play our piano!' he said. 'You know where the key is now.'

So she did begin to visit them often, and sometimes they were there, and sometimes they weren't. She would bring her manila folder of photocopied Chopin, or Debussy, or Ravel, and play the grand piano in the living room, and if the family friend or his son came home to find her there, they would always ask her to stay for supper, and after supper, to stay for the night. She slept in the daughter's room (the daughter had moved out just a few months before) in the attic of the house, enjoying the coziness of the roof sloping down at angles above her head and the vastness of the bath tub in the ensuite bathroom where she would lie and soak before climbing under the daughter's duvet cover with a box of old family photographs that she'd found in the daughter's cupboard, and a felt-bound diary with the last entry dated quite recently. She stared at the mother's face in each photograph, many of which were taken of her gardening, in a sunhat and gardening gloves, and holding shears, and she looked with wonder and envy at the love on the family friend's face as he looked at his wife across a campfire, or on the shore of the sea, or beside her on a ferry. She read repeatedly an entry she found in the daughter's journal, dated soon after the mother's death:

Oh Mom. Do you remember when you were in the bath and I sat on the edge of the tub one night, and you were telling me how much you'd always loved Dad? And how your love for him had grown and grown with time?

One morning after the girl had spent the night, the family friend made brunch for her and his son. Afterwards, she washed the dishes and offered to take the dog for a walk at the park nearby.

'Want to come?' she asked the son.

'I can't,' he said. 'I have a test tomorrow.'

'And you?' she asked the family friend. 'It's not so cold today.'

He agreed, and they wrapped themselves in scarves and he found a woman's coat in the cupboard for the girl to wear. The dog pulled them tumbling towards the park, so that they were warmed-up and wind-swept when they sat down beside each other on a bench, keeping an eye on the dog as it stalked pigeons.

'How did she die?' she said, loosening the scarf from around her neck.

He rested his head against the back of the bench and knitted his fingers across his stomach. 'She had cancer for a long time,' he said. 'A tumour in her brain. We didn't know how long she had to live—the doctors said anything from two months to two years. She lived with it for three years.' He stopped and lifted his head and searched with his eyes for the dog. 'It was my son who found her,' he said. 'She had collapsed in our bedroom after a shower. He found her kneeling on the floor in her dressing gown, with her elbows propped on the bed. At first he thought she was praying. But she'd had a massive haemorrhage. There was nothing the medics could do when they arrived.'

From the coat came the barest scent of another woman's perfume.

THE GIRL HAD TO GO AWAY FOR WORK to the coast for two months. She missed her visits to the family friend's house, and carefully selected a gift for them a day before her return: a plastic packet full of hand-picked avocados the size and shape of giant gem squashes, and a bottle of raspberry vinaigrette. On the day she arrived back, she called and asked if she could pop around that evening for dinner. There was the faintest hint of hesitation, but then the family friend warmly agreed. The girl spent a long time selecting a dress to wear, and she knew that the bit of sun she had caught had freckled her nose and tinted her hair. She arrived at the house, carrying the packet of avocados, and rang the doorbell. When the family friend opened the door, the girl sensed immediately that something was different. He was sprightly and looked years younger. Impossible, she thought, it has only been two months! His grey hair was thicker, his teeth were whiter. Even the air in the house seemed to be charged with youthful energy.

'Have you been playing more tennis?' she asked tentatively.

'No, not really,' he said. 'Sorry my son's not here—he's at a party.'

At dinner he was as restless as a teenager, jiggling his leg beneath the table and clearing up as soon as she had finished eating.

'Have you been spending more time at the beach?' she tried again, hoping he would say that he'd been getting more sun now that summer had finally arrived.

Again, he said no. He didn't offer her coffee, as he normally would, and said nothing about her sleeping over in the daughter's room. He hardly asked her any questions.

Eventually, she said she would be going, hoping he would insist that she stay, perhaps play a bit of Bach for him before bed. But he ushered her out of the house almost gladly and down the path to the garden gate. He clicked it shut behind her.

She stopped and faced him across the gate. 'What is it?' she asked. 'You seem different—has something happened?'

He seemed surprised that she had noticed, then glad she had asked. 'Well, I wasn't going to tell you—we're trying to keep it to ourselves . . .

but I've met someone.' He looked at her as a puppy looks at its owner, expecting praise and excitement to match his own.

The girl tucked a strand of hair behind one ear. 'Who is she?' she said, trying to stay calm.

'Another lawyer,' he said eagerly. 'She's absolutely brilliant. And you know what she said to me?' He paused. 'That I'm the first man she's ever felt deserved her.'

The girl did not know what to say. She pretended to search in her handbag for the car keys.

The family friend leaned on the top of the gate with his elbows. 'The truth is,' he said in a low voice, 'I've realised that this is the first time in my life I've truly been in love.' He seemed to catch himself suddenly. He ran his hand through his hair, stole a glance at his wristwatch, and said, 'Come again sometime.'

The girl unlocked her car, put her handbag under the seat, and looked back towards the house. He had already gone inside. She climbed into the car and rolled down the window, briefly oblivious to the night's threats. The coral tree she had parked beneath was moulting. She sat in the dark, listening to the thuds of lucky beans dropping onto the roof of her car and wondering if she were imagining that she could smell the jasmine that wound itself around the tennis court fence. From an upstairs window of the house, from the room with the piano, light fell onto the thicket of mint thriving next to the garden tap. It was then that she saw it: the bottle of champagne, opened and empty beside the black bin, put onto the pavement for the council to collect early next morning. +

PATRICK O'DELL, *UNTITLED*, 2008,
COLOR PHOTOGRAPH. COURTESY OF THE ARTIST.

DRAWN AND QUARTERED ON THE INTERNET

Benjamin Kunkel

NO ONE WOULD DENY THAT THE INTERNET has altered the tenor, the feel, the style of public life. The web contains much of the record of that life, and in turn directs how that life is conducted.

The problem for description and analysis arises when you concede that the internet's effects on public life seem so contradictory. Everyone who looks (and the web sometimes makes you feel like a staring eyeball that can't blink) sees the same constellation of contradictions: more public shamelessness yet more public shaming; a threat to privacy side by side with a growth in anonymous communication; and more pure information together with an expanded circulation for baseless opinion. The temptation is to throw up your hands and just say that, thanks to the internet, the public sphere contains more of everything: more exposure, privacy, publicity, anonymity, truth, lies, opinion, information, pornography, culture, advertising—though probably not more art.

Still, it may be that if we can identify some *basic ways that the individual person relates to the public sphere*, we can begin to replace an online feeling of immersion with something more usefully aloof. One axis along which every individual relates to the public is that which runs from identification to anonymity. A police officer, named on his badge, chases a masked man down the street: one is identifiable, the other, for now, *publicly anonymous*. (This is different from sitting at home with the shades drawn.) But whether or not to reveal our identity in public—to disclose our face, name, or title—is hardly the end of our choices. Another axis runs from reticence to expressiveness. The police officer in pursuit, even if he shouts *Stop!* at the top of his lungs, is personally reticent and inexpressive: the uniform he wears is not of his design, and the laws he upholds are not of his authorship. Who knows what he thinks of them? The masked figure he's chasing, on the other hand, may be highly expressive even as he retains his anonymity and the opinions he expresses founder in banality: on some wall he has scrawled *Cops suck!* Of course the officer could at any moment shed his personal reticence and start declaiming to the assembled onlookers a print-out of the blog post he wrote the night before. The graffiti artist could likewise stop running and tear off his mask.

So there are four basic positions one can occupy in public, owing to the fact that at any given moment we can reveal or conceal both who we are (our physical and social container) and what we think and feel (our emotional and intellectual contents):

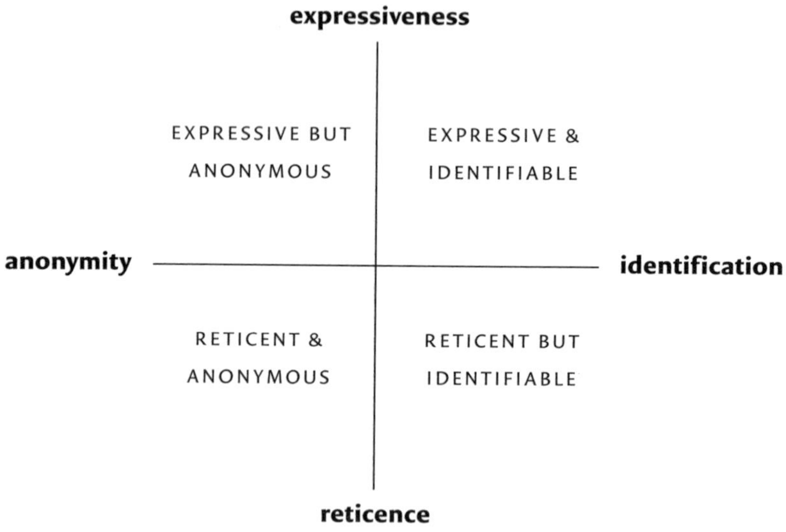

Each quadrant of the graph represents a potential way to relate to the public sphere—a terrific simplification, of course, but with luck a heuristic one. The result is four possible positions:

1. You can reveal both *who you are* (show your face, say your name) and *how you feel* (disclose your thoughts and desires, or some of them).
2. You can reveal *who you are* but NOT *how you feel.*
3. You can reveal *how you feel* but NOT *who you are.*
4. You can reveal neither.

What happens if we apply these four available positions to the internet—where, after all, so much of public life takes place these days? If the examples above of the police officer and graffiti artist seem antique and implausible, it is because the online world has so signally expanded the individual's capacity for virtual mask-wearing and virtual declaiming. The internet affords us unprecedented scope for appearing in public (even if only the atomized public of the internet). And if at first it seems hard to see how you could conceal who you are *and* how you feel and nevertheless publicly appear, it's necessary only to think of a site like Wikipedia, where anonymous individuals publicize facts about which they are not to disclose their own opinions.

Is it surprising that the four positions above seem to correspond strikingly well to four of the primary preoccupations of the World Wide Web?

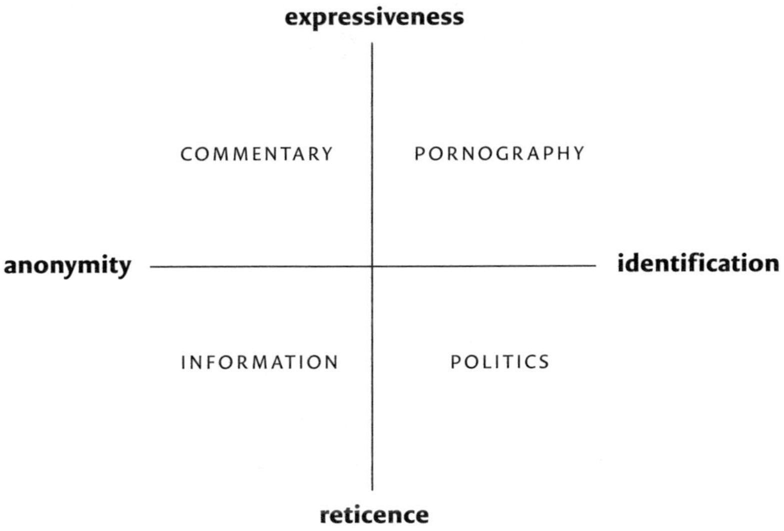

Pornography, politics, commentary, and *information* form a natural if antagonistic grouping, and we take them in that order.

∘ ∘ ∘

PORNOGRAPHY

EXHIBITIONISM ON THE INTERNET is hardly confined to pornography, but porn is where it flourishes most often, most popularly, and most purely. The internet has increased immeasurably the ease and privacy of accessing pornography at the same time that the porn industry can now cater to an incredible variety of sexual tastes (with a common basis in scopophilia). Much commentary has concerned the "pornification" of American mores: revealing dress, implants, oral sex as social skill. But in reality public behavior—except in various festival atmospheres like Spring Break, Mardi Gras, or Burning Man—goes on mostly as before the internet: no nudity or sex on the streets. The laws remain unchanged, and the 13-year-old girls openly masturbating in front of TV porn shows, as imagined in Anthony Burgess's novel *1985*, have not materialized. On the whole, porn has blossomed as a *cultural* phenomenon restricted to the private consumption of publicly available images, and not yet become much of a *social* phenomenon inducing nudism, orgies, and wildfire promiscuity.

The distinction is worth making since cultural expressions of every kind—and porn more obviously than most—consist largely of fantasies: not so much what a society does as what it wants and fears. The spread of porn surely counts as one of the significant cultural developments of the time, and nothing about porn in general is more striking than its utopian aspect: here is an imaginary world where, as in the Philip Larkin poem, to want is straightaway to be wanted.* More than that, porn is an imaginary world where in principle *shame is impossible.* The revelation of any strange appetite or unusual trait, according to porn's simple moral code, only prompts the appearance of a suitable fetishist, and no one is ever too ugly, smelly, or otherwise unappealing to want for a partner. Many of the classic arguments against porn may have been right, but the line of criticism that saw ordinary porn as so many rape fantasies inducing actual rape seems to have been mistaken. It is another item of the porn code (along with the impossibility of shame) that here rape can *not* take place.†

---

* See Nancy Bauer, "Pornutopia," *n+1* Issue Five.

† If in ordinary porn unsolicited advances and ostensibly degrading treatment turn out—"surprisingly" but consistently—to be welcomed by their objects, there must still exist porn that fantasizes outright coercion rather than consent. Even so, unless the film or photos record an illegal act and are therefore illegal themselves, consent of a kind necessarily exists: the performers have been willing to portray unwillingness.

In fact porn, with its strictures against violence and shame, represents the most robust form of utopianism in a time that otherwise considers utopia fatally infected with totalitarian ambitions. And what injects this fantasy with the necessary germ of reality is simply that the performers show their actual human faces to the world. They may perform anonymously or under *noms de porn*, but faces, more than names, constitute unique possessions—the performers have signed their work with their faces.

And yet this place of no-shame and exposure, so easily available to anyone with a computer, can only be entered, even now, discreetly and under penalty of public shaming. When Denver's city attorney, a Democrat, was accused in 2007 of stealing a laptop belonging to the state (which he claimed to have bought secondhand without knowing its provenance), the Republican district attorney not only trumpeted at a press conference the fact that the alleged thief had downloaded porn onto the computer, but made details of the downloads available in an unsealed affidavit. There was no suggestion that the pornography was of an illegal variety. The accused killed himself a few hours after a court hearing.

POLITICS

THE SPECIAL LIABILITY OF POLITICIANS to personal scandal is nothing new: Parnell in Ireland was brought down by adultery charges long before Gary Hart, whose own fall had nothing to do with the web. Still, in the internet age, the politician has become more than anything else a specially vivid instance of the unhappy celebrity we each risk becoming: a closely monitored individual with neither the glamour of the entertainment celebrity nor as many chances for public redemption in the aftermath of a scandal. And scandal—an impossibility in the fantasy world of porn—is dauntingly hard for even a minor politician to avoid. Audio and video clips of ill-judged words or gestures circulate endlessly online, and the likelihood of any politician's gaffe being recorded and disseminated has correspondingly increased. Any slip can also be discussed at length on blogs proper and in their comments sections.

The resulting atmosphere of heightened surveillance might in theory have led to a better and more tolerant understanding of the complexities and contradictions of even the most disciplined personality.

Instead, American public life has lately become more censorious and easily scandalized than ever. The intense digital invigilation of holders or seekers of public office naturally encourages politicians to exercise extreme care in their choice of words, gestures, and associates; they must live every moment as if crafting a social-networking profile. And yet the suppression of personality enforced by this media regime makes any slip or revelation seem only the more meaningful. If all one's best efforts can't conceal an impulse of sarcasm, snobbery, inconsistency, or lust, this must mean the given weakness, whichever it may be, offers the key to one's personality.

So while politics, like porn, supplies one of the main preoccupations of internet culture, the contrast between the two could hardly be more stark. Porn recognizes no taboo except coercion, and the event of *being found out* (cheating, peeping, et cetera) is always welcome for the increased chances for sexual fulfillment thereby afforded. Politics, on the other hand, mines the entire terrain of public life with taboo after taboo and makes discovery an occasion for dread. The political celebrity lives in constant fear of the exposure invariably welcomed by the porn figure.

If part of the burden of Foucault's work, against Freud, was to try to detach acts (of sex, madness, crime) from identity (e.g., that of the homosexual, the lunatic, the criminal), in politics no act is *not* a confession of the integral personality. (So are slips of the tongue, as in Freud's early work, windows onto the soul, along with other verbal inadvertencies.) Everything said and done must be "owned" or, with effort, "disowned," each facet of character being held to reflect every other facet. This idea imposes on the politician (or other suddenly publicized person) a terrible comprehensive responsibility to square his every known deed and statement with his every other one. So the task for even a minor politician or celebrity—or the celebrity *in potentio* with a social-networking profile set to public viewing—becomes a paradox, an impossibility: to make everyone know who you are without letting anyone know who you are.

° ° °

COMMENTARY

EVEN AS RECORDED INDISCRETIONS or mistakes by politicians, celebrities, and ordinary people come to light sooner and more reliably than ever before, the internet affords immense new scope for *anonymous* expression. Anonymous public messages often enough voice an anodyne enthusiasm, offer a helpful tip, contribute a relevant fact, or engage in civil discussion—but just as often these messages are scurrilous, abusive, or false.

The result is highly asymmetrical positions for the commenter and the commented-on. The commenter, because impossible to identify, can't be humiliated—while there remains something genuinely humiliating about the exposure of even the most cogent argument, beautiful face, or sincere statement to charges of stupidity, ugliness, or hypocrisy. In courtly society, an insult undermined the insulted person not necessarily because it was true but simply because it went unavenged—and still today the humiliation of the commented-on person comes not so much from what is said (we all know that nasty things are said behind our backs) as from the fact that it can be said *in public* without the commenter being challenged by name as someone also afflicted by stupidity, ugliness, and hypocrisy.

Yet for all the safety of his position the anonymous commenter also suffers in his own way—from anonymity. He is like the B-movie invisible man who can frighten, harass, and spy on the visible person but never be seen and recognized himself. The pain of anonymity supplies a possible explanation for the violence of the anonymous commentariat's rage against especially that category of person—the celebrity—who can suffer every mortal pain (injury, addiction, divorce, death, even bankruptcy) except for that of facelessness. The celebrity or politician's revenge comes about when an anonymous commenter unwarily leaves behind a crumb of circumstantial evidence establishing his identity. The moment the commenter is exposed as a sock-puppeting ranter—not only transparently incoherent, dishonest, hypocritical, and biased, but a real person exhibiting these defects, as well as the unforgivable liability of having a face and a past—the unfortunate figure crosses into the realm of politics, celebrity, scandal, shame.

INFORMATION

EARLY AND MID-NINETIES SPECULATION on the future on the internet worried about the promotion of a certain web-bound solipsism: the *New York Times* would give way to the hyper-parochial *Daily Me.* With the declining market share of "universal" sources of information and opinion—another obvious example was the evening news—and the corresponding proliferation of ideological niches, the population would fragment into so many mental cellules shielding their worldviews from inconvenient facts and incompatible views. This concern has been substantially realized. Ideological certainty can only become the more attractive in the face of a world (and World Wide Web) bristling with so much unsynthesizable *information.*

For the internet has made good on the early boosterish claim that it would democratize access to information.* It has streamed porn into every willing household, and made basically reliable historical, scientific, political, and biographical information available to all. If you want to look up a date or translate a foreign word, make a certain dish, diagnose an ailment, or compare real estate prices, the internet makes each of these tasks far easier than before. If we all passed our lives in small organic communities, we might simply ask our neighbors about these things—but as long as we're going to live the mobile, isolated lives of modernity, it's nice to have the internet to consult.

It would be a stretch to claim that informational abundance has made us more powerful as *citizens.* Campaigns for public office conducted by meticulously managed politicians unwilling to divulge their actual views on most subjects are clearly addressed not to citizens' burgeoning knowledge of the world but mainly to their unreasoning tastes, prejudices, and cultural associations. And "citizen journalism" is usually just a pretentious term invoked by professional gossips to dignify their work; only rarely does it refer to actual reporting by earnest amateurs. But the internet plainly makes people more powerful as *consumers,* as any doctor confronted by a patient well armed with information gleaned

* Think of the conclusion to Lyotard's *Postmodern Condition*: "[T]he computerization of society . . . could become the "dream" instrument for controlling and regulating the market system, extended to include knowledge itself. . . . But it could also aid groups discussing metaprescriptives by supplying them with the information they usually lack for making knowledgeable decisions. The line to follow for computerization to take the second of these two paths is, in principle, quite simple: give the public free access to the memory and data banks. Language games would then be games of perfect information at any given moment."

from the internet can tell you. And the internet not only lets you know when a movie starts and where the nearest retailer of a given product can be found, it also facilitates the founding of so-called knowledge blogs serving what might be called communities of concern, where geographically far-flung individuals with a shared problem (often a medical condition) or shared interest (e.g., petroleum depletion) can exchange views that, on the whole, probably move in the direction of the truth.

Much of the solid information collected online is gathered by salaried professionals: reporters and researchers. Sometimes these people receive credit for their work, but the wire service reporter and the uncredited researcher slip into anonymity, while the rest of the information online is published by people not only unknown but also unremunerated. These people contributing knowledge to the world in their spare time offer a heroic counterpoint to the villainy of many anonymous commentators.

The web's status as information clearing-house (along with its character as a pornographic commons) is another utopian dimension. And porn and information are curiously alike. In both cases, there is a striking and even touching *neutrality* to what is on offer: certain naked individuals contribute to the digital census of all sex acts and body types while certain *invisible* individuals contribute to the census of all facts. And just as in porn there is nothing wrong with any sex act as long as it stops short of illegality, all facts are equally innocent. A fact might refer to a terrible crime, but its publication can only count as a good deed. You can sometimes even feel moved that so many anonymous individuals have conspired to provision you with so much information for free. But the ant-like heroism of the anonymous information supplier crosses into something more like *informing* whenever a writer for a site like Wikipedia hides behind his anonymity and takes advantage of the stated neutrality of the site to seed the web with deliberate misinformation. Then the informationist became the worst kind of commenter.

PORNOGRAPHY, POLITICS, commentary, and information go together in the sense that each one, in its pure form, appears to illustrate a motto that is a variation on the mottos of the other three: *I will (or won't) tell you who I am while I do (or don't) say how I feel.*

Laid out schematically like this, the four roles we've isolated begin to look like four moral positions. Clearly the villains of internet-led public life are the politicians and commenters, not because of their actual flaws and shortcomings, but because they adopt public stances expressly designed to deny those flaws. The politician pretends to a perfect selfhood that no one could achieve; the commenter, sniping from behind a wall of anonymity, demands the same perfection from others. Each promotes an idea of the person as a knowable and integrated entity subject to being unlocked by a key gesture or word ("douchebag" comes to mind). And this idea of the person takes hold the more tenaciously the less anyone actually believes in it; the gaffe or slip-up theory of personality is a useful weapon against one's enemies but no tool of psychology. Anyone capable of introspection knows that his personality is either largely incoherent or possesses a coherence beyond his ken. As Freud said in rebuffing a would-be biographer, "Biographical truth does not exist . . . and in any case is not our Prince Hamlet right when he asks who would escape whipping if used after his just deserts?"

What is offensive about the politician and the commenter when they go on the attack is the combination of intense moralism with a total indifference to moral reality. Protected by, in the politician's case, a fraudulent public image of coherence and probity, and, in the commenter's case, a screen of anonymity, the politician and the commenter misconstrue, and extrapolate from, their enemies' words and gestures in a manner bound to violate any realistic sense of a person's complexity, contradictions, and final elusiveness. Their hope is not that, judged by the same standards, they would escape whipping; the hope is simply not to get whipped. That depends on not being found out. So the commenter and politician in their different ways become skulking, secretive creatures pushing their victims out into a light they do all they can to avoid. For both are potential victims of the theory of personality they lustily reinforce, one that makes hypocrisy at once especially inevitable *and* reprehensible.

In this atmosphere, the porn star and the informationist appear as heroes of a kind. Their tasks—which, because so many of them aren't paid for what they do, must often be pleasures—are neutral and unjudgmental in the extreme. Above all, their activities point to a sort of truth. The world truly *is* a collection of facts, if not only that; and adult humans really *are* lustful sexual beings, though they are other things besides.

The heroes, in other words, are the *a*moralists: the porn and information angels who add to the web's compendium of information and sex acts without attempting to place one sort of lust or one sort of fact above another. This person may prefer oral while disliking anal sex; and that person may be encyclopedic about submarine warfare while being ignorant of twelve-tone music. But no information or sexual desire is considered superior to other information or other desire. And proof of the simple acceptableness of sex and of fact is offered by the indifference to exposure enjoyed by both the porn person and the information angel: in porn, faces are already shown, while the unmasking of Wikipedia's main authority on the Cleveland Cavaliers or Yves Saint Laurent would presumably result in no particularly keen embarrassment.

The problem is that in life we can't ultimately sequester facts and sex from morality. There may be amoral activities—breathing, excreting, walking down the street: processes truly beyond, or beneath, good and evil—but sex is rarely one of these, and past early infancy there is no such thing as an amoral or value-neutral life. We ourselves (and other people) are facts and desires, but these facts and desires entail moral considerations whether we like it or not. That generally today we don't like it is evident in the overtones acquired by the verb *to judge*: "judging someone" sounds aggressive and unkind. And yet internet culture, outside of the neutral realms of porn and information, has encouraged us to make free with an array of insults containing strong implicit moral judgments: asshat, douchebag, jerk, et cetera. The moral pillorying of a politician, celebrity, or celebritized ordinary person provides one of the most regular of all internet spectacles. Sometimes the person's celebrity consists of nothing *but* his sudden shaming.

THIS SEPARATION OF PORNOGRAPHY, politics, commentary, and information is less a theoretical position than an observed tendency. The tendency isn't and will never be complete; the different modes can still overlap. But the porn performer's admission of lust, the politician's acceptance of responsibility, the commenter's avowal of an opinion, the informationist's presentation of facts—more and more these things take place separately, while at the same time we seem to observe a relative (though not necessarily an absolute) decline of what might be called holistic communication or self-presentation.

These activities in their isolation overwhelm the blending or combinatory operations visible in much art and argumentation, not to mention in any ordinary life. The result is a set of separate if not perfectly sealed chambers devoted to activities inhuman in their purity. In the pure lust of porn and the pure facticity of information there is something appealing; only neither realm can be inhabited by a real person. In the politician's total responsibility—his responsibility to a false idea of a thoroughly coherent self—there is something grotesque, as there is in the commenter's total irresponsibility. But once again, neither realm can be inhabited by you or me.

An atmosphere of moral unreality pervades the internet. That our profound though incomplete separation of different types of self-presentation is unworkable and unreal is revealed by the impression of shock and violence produced each time a door opens between the separate chambers. An upright politician turns out to be the prey of ungovernable desires, or we learn that a role-model celebrity has made an offensive remark. Or an outwardly decent person is discovered indulging in vile invective or self-serving commentary. Or what looked like neutral information turns out to be misinformation planted by an interested party. And the porn star, of course, would be encouraged to relearn the sense of shame she seems to have cast off if she attempted a public career of another kind.

Meanwhile the internet as we live it seems hostile to those varieties of communication that neither trade in the false and merely punitive and expedient morality of the commenter or politician, nor take refuge in the highly artificial amorality of porn or information. When we are online, or merely in a world that increasingly follows the internet's lead, morality alternates between being an embarrassment (and hence dropped) and a weapon (and hence picked up). Sometimes it is a faculty we decline to employ since, not wanting to judge, we wouldn't wish to spurn the abundance and diversity of what's online. We justify our choices and even our existence as being simply a matter of taste, tastes being something—unlike evaluations or judgments—that can differ without offense to anyone. At other times, we become violent moralists, and attempt not to counter our opponents' arguments or critique their behavior but to humiliate, insult, and destroy them. This is the mode of the commenter and the politician, but it is also increasingly the mode of the pundit (on his own blog or elsewhere) who signs his name to his work. Again, it's as if the choice were between the amorality of porn and information and the moralism of politics and commentary. The space on the internet and in our public life for moral reflection or "nuance" seems remarkably small, in spite of the breadth of the World Wide Web.

Answering the question of how this came about looks daunting, and is certainly impossible here. American morality, as it enters into public life, is split most prominently between a certain bankrupt Christianism and a certain pale relativism. The Christianism's inability to reckon honestly with sexuality, its bafflement before the aggression on which it obviously thrives, and its low exegetical standards are only some of its failings. The relativism most of the rest of us profess has, for its part, few powers beyond the descriptive; it can say what we do, but not why. Still, this schism, however freshly exploited by the culture wars, began to open up in the eighteenth century, and by Nietzsche's time had become fully articulate on both sides. And if, in the twentieth century, psychoanalysis sometimes tried to accommodate moral life to the insuperable reality of individual desire, this tradition had already badly faltered by 1981, when Alistair McIntyre's *After Virtue* proclaimed modern Western morality a hopeless jumble of fragments and—less persuasively—proposed a neo-Aristotelian communitarianism as the remedy. The moral incoherence of a civilization is hardly the fault of the internet; the web has merely exacerbated it by expanding the opportunities for mere descriptivism, on the one hand, and stark hypocrisy on the other.

Still, moral realism (whatever that might turn out to be) would need patience and some tolerance for subtlety to flourish, and these delicate moods are exactly those the techno-determinists tell us the internet can never support. They may be right. Though one can spend hours online, the sensation of being there is usually one of impatience, and each of the segregated public realms we've discussed notably appeals to impatience. The immediate gratification to lust and curiosity offered respectively by online porn and online encyclopedias is easy enough to understand. But what in us is gratified by the punitive hypocrisies of politics and commentary? Why, when we are online, do we so often prefer expressing or seeing expressed contempt (and sometimes adulation) instead of moral judgments of more complexity, not to say reality? It must owe something to the immediacy of these varieties of moralistic satisfaction. It's a pleasure to hate and to adore, to insult or to flatter, and a pleasure you can come by fairly quickly. The satisfactions of respect, understanding, and explication need more time.

It is also gratifying to feel as if you know what you think and how you feel, particularly when you don't. The internet has this twin character: its contents are overwhelming and disorienting, and its denizens regularly affect a furious certainty as to their ideas and opinions. So the vastness of the internet, as of our world and culture generally, and the speed at which new "content" pops up—the freshly discovered curiosity—promotes a self-protective attitude in which everything is known and judged in advance. Internet-led culture has encouraged us to be impatient with efforts at thinking out loud; the preferred style is a certain glib knowingness. It's worth asking whether the attraction of glibness—glib contempt especially—doesn't consist in being able to apply a steady and reliable attitude to an online public world otherwise overmastering in its breadth, diversity, and novelty, a world of which we have, by now, a lot of experience, but still very little knowledge. +

PHILIPP C. JAHN, *HOTEL UZBEKISTAN*, 2007,
B/W PHOTOGRAPH. COURTESY OF THE ARTIST.

SUMMER IN SAMARKAND

Elif Batuman

WHEN I TRY TO REMEMBER how I ended up in Samarkand, I am reminded of an anecdote about the folk hero Nasreddin Hoca. Walking along a deserted road one night, the story goes, Nasreddin Hoca noticed a troop of horsemen riding toward him. Filled with terror that they might rob him or conscript him into the army, Nasreddin leaped over a nearby wall and found himself in a graveyard. The horsemen, who were in fact ordinary travelers, were interested by this behavior, so they rode up to the wall and looked over to see Hoca lying motionless on the ground.

"Can we help you?" the travelers asked. "What are you doing here?"

"Well," Nasreddin Hoca replied, "it's more complicated than you think. You see, *I'm* here because of *you*; and *you're* here because of *me*."

I can vividly imagine Nasreddin Hoca's experience: the road at nightfall, a dog doubtless barking somewhere, the panicked leap and heavy fall, the smell of damp soil, the sound of approaching horsemen, and finally the faces peering over the wall, concerned and mildly astonished. And what I like about the story is how perfectly it encapsulates the riddle of free will in human history: a realm where, as Friedrich Engels observed, free wills are constantly obstructing one another so that, inevitably, "what emerges is something that no one willed." Nobody, least of all Nasreddin Hoca, willed for Nasreddin Hoca to end up lying in the graveyard that night; nobody forced him there, either—and yet there he was.

THE CHAIN OF EVENTS WAS SET into motion by my decision to study Russian literature: in itself an impulsive decision, not unlike jumping over a wall and ending up in a graveyard, although things eventually, on the whole, worked out well for me. Still, learning Russian takes a long time, and time passes so slowly in college. After two years of what felt like endless study, I still couldn't pick up a Russian book and read it. I couldn't understand a Russian movie without subtitles. If I tried to talk to Russian people, they stared at me like I was retarded. I decided that the only solution was to actually go to Russia.

In the spring of my sophomore year, I applied for a grant, for a study-abroad program in Moscow, and I applied for two jobs: one as a personal secretary to a frozen-foods exporter from Peru who was negotiating with a Moscow-based supermarket chain, and the other as a researcher for the *Let's Go* travel guides in Russia. The outcome of these applications wasn't exactly bad, but it wasn't anything I had willed, either. I got a travel grant—for half the amount I asked, not enough for the study abroad. The Peruvian entrepreneur said I could be his secretary—pending submission of a "recent full-body photograph." *Let's Go* offered me a job—in Turkey, because they said my Russian wasn't good enough for travel in Russia. My Turkish, by contrast, was good enough for travel in Turkey. The previous year, *Let's Go* had sent a young man who spoke no Turkish at all and who had consequently, as the result of a never fully explained "misunderstanding," gotten beaten up by a pimp in Konya, after which he actually had some kind of nervous breakdown, which was even somehow minutely documented in *Rolling Stone* magazine as part of an exposé.

I patched up things as best I could. I wrote a polite refusal to the Peruvian, I used the grant money to arrange a two-week stay in Moscow with some destitute academics, and for the rest of the summer I took the job in Turkey.

TURKEY

THE POSHEST OF THE TURKISH ITINERARIES—Istanbul and the Aegean coast—was assigned to a Turkish archaeology graduate student called Erhan, who was actually kidnapped somewhere near Fethiye, only it then turned out that he hadn't been kidnapped at all but had gotten married; nonetheless, he never came back to Boston, and never sent in any copy either. My family was in an uproar—not about Erhan of course, because we didn't know about that at the time, but because I had been given such a deadbeat itinerary: the disputed territory of Northern Cyprus; the Mediterranean coast, where the Eurotrash discos only end when you approach the Syrian border and have to start looking out for the PKK; and the backwaters of Central Anatolia, where my mother claimed never to have heard of half the cities on the list.

One city was called Tokat, which literally means: a slap in the face. This is also the title of a famous manifesto by the Russian surrealists: "A Slap in the Face of Public Taste"—or, as it is known in Turkish: "Toplumsal zevke bir *tokat*." I might add that, if you visit YouTube and search for "Osmanli tokad (Osmanlı tokadı)—"the Ottoman slap," referring to the technique developed in the Ottoman army, where punching was considered to be bad form—you will see hundreds of videos of Turkish people getting slapped in the face, mostly by other Turkish people, although also, in one case, by a monkey. My mother had particularly bad feelings about my going to Tokat.

When I got to Ankara, where I stayed at my grandmother's apartment, I gradually realized that my mother had taken steps to ensure my safety. She somehow convinced my aunt Arzu, an officer in the Turkish National Intelligence Organization, to have me followed after sundown: not by an actual intelligence officer, but by one of their chauffeurs. I met my pursuer one night in Gaziosmanpaşa, where all the foreign embassies and five-star hotels are. I was wandering around an enormous, depressing nightclub called No Parking, trying to determine the price of an Efes Pilsner, when a man in a suit tapped my shoulder and informed me that my car had arrived.

"But I didn't call a car," I said.

Nonetheless, explained the man in the suit, the car was there. It had perhaps been sent by a distinguished lady, possibly some kind of a relative. "She gave a very detailed description of you," he said, looking directly at me. "A very detailed description."

I followed him outside. Another man in a suit was standing beside a parked car. When I understood who he was, and why he was there, I felt so beleaguered that I burst into tears.

"Please don't upset yourself, miss," the driver said. He opened the door to the backseat.

I climbed into the car and we drove back through Gaziosmanpaşa, past the bulletproof glass cubicles in which soldiers were reading newspapers and smoking cigarettes, back to Kavaklıdere where my grandmother lived. The driver addressed me only once, at the big intersection outside Swan Park. In Swan Park, vendors sell bags of almond crackers, which you can eat yourself, or feed to the swans. As a child I was fascinated by these crackers, which do not contain almonds, but are shaped like almonds. This was my first lesson in metaphor versus metonymy. Here, stopped at a red light, the driver half turned to face me.

"Would you like an apple?" he asked.

"No thanks," I said.

"I picked these apples myself," he said. "With my own hands, from my own garden."

From a plastic bag on the passenger seat, he produced a small apple.

The apple was hard, green, and misshapen, like the answer to some pointless riddle.

I LEFT ANKARA EARLY in the morning, before my grandmother woke up. I left a note telling her not to worry, that I would call her soon. I did not specify my destination. Nonetheless, when I got off the bus in Tokat, I was personally greeted by the municipal water inspector. A melancholy bureaucrat with a mustache, he spoke of my aunt Arzu with great respect, and took me to visit the waterworks.

I was to discover, over the next weeks, that my aunt Arzu had mobilized a diverse group of contacts to look out for my welfare. One evening in Kayseri, the Turkish pastrami capital, I was collected from my hostel by a sergeant in the army. The sergeant drove me to a military kebab restaurant on top of an extinct volcano called Mount Erciyes. Skiing Turks, who I believe are not numerous, go there in the winter.

At this time of year there was no snow on Erciyes. Outside the windows of the military restaurant, the sun was setting on some grazing sheep, dyeing them pink, like big dense clouds of cotton candy. It was strange to eat lamb while actually watching these pink fluffy sheep.

The sergeant asked about my studies. When I said that I studied literature, he asked whether I was reading the works of Yaşar Kemal (a famous Turkish novelist who wrote his first short story during his military service in Kayseri). I was not reading the works of Yaşar Kemal.

"What author are you reading? What author are you concentrating on?" he asked.

"I don't know yet," I said. "Maybe Pushkin."

"Pushkin? Who is that, an American?"

"Well, more of a Russian, actually."

This information clearly made no sense at all to the sergeant. He blinked once or twice and told me how lucky I was to study at such a famous American university, how many Turkish boys and girls—and not only boys and girls—would give their ears to have such an opportunity. "An opportunity for what?" he demanded rhetorically, leaning toward me over the table.

"An opportunity for what?" I echoed.

"An opportunity for having their voices heard! For telling people the truth about Turkey, and not the nonsense propagated by Europeans!"

It was dark when we drove down to the city, past Kayseri's third claim to fame, after pastrami and skiing: a hulking fifteen-hundred-year-old citadel, hewn from black volcanic rock. Lit by spotlights, it resembled a diabolical cauldron.

Looking back, I am surprised by how much I took to heart the words of people like this sergeant. I didn't actually feel a responsibility to tell Americans the truth about Turkey, but I did feel it was somehow wasteful of me to study Russian literature instead of Turkish literature. One was constantly being told, in those days, that all languages were universally complex, to a biologically determined degree. Didn't that mean all languages were, objectively speaking, equally interesting? And I already *knew* Turkish; it had happened without any work, like a gift, and here I was tossing it away to break my head on a bunch of declensions that came effortlessly to anyone who happened to grow up in Russia.

Today, this strikes me as terrible reasoning. Today I understand that love is a rare and valuable thing, and you don't get to choose its object. You just go around getting hung up on all the least convenient things—and if the only obstacle in your way is a little extra work, well, cheer up and buckle down, because *that's* the wonderful gift right there.

But I was younger and dumber then, and demoralized by the state of the Turkish novel. The thing that immediately struck one about the Turkish novel was that nobody read it, not even Turkish people. I often noticed this when I was in Turkey. Most people just weren't into novels at all. They liked funny short stories, funny fables, serious fables, essays, letters, short poems, long poems, newspapers, crossword puzzles—they liked practically any kind of print matter better than novels. Even in

1997, of course, there was already Orhan Pamuk, already writing novels . . . and you could see how miserable he was about it. I bought *The Black Book* that summer. It was about a guy looking for a woman called "Dream." This guy was walking around in the streets of Istanbul calling: "Dream! Dream!" I remember reading this on a bus in Turkey and feeling deeply, viscerally bored. I spent the rest of the bus ride looking out the window. I was interested by the names of towns. I remember the sign for a town called Şereflikoçhisar, literally, Fortress of the Honorable Ram.

As a less strenuous concession to the idea of "local color," I started reading Pushkin's Turkish travelogue, *Journey to Arzrum*. It was much more entertaining than *The Black Book*. I was already entertained by the very premise that Pushkin had ever set foot in Turkey. This was fully as entertaining to me as the premise of Jesus Christ having set foot in England is to English people. For example, to William Blake: "And did those feet in ancient time / Walk upon England's mountains green?" Interestingly, one of Pushkin's most famous lyrics is an elegy to feet: "Ah, little feet, little feet! where are you now? . . . Cosseted in Oriental languor, you left no tracks on the sad northern snow." Pushkin is not here referring, of course, to his own feet. Nonetheless, I saw a pair of Pushkin's boots once in a museum, and they were very small.

As the summer rushed on, I took night buses from one unknown city to another, visiting caves where Christians had hidden from Romans, and Greek amphitheaters which had been converted into caravanserais by the Seljuks; drifting in and out of sleep, I looked out the bus windows for Pushkin's tracks. They could be anywhere! Truly, Pushkin's cartoonish omnipresence is one of the wonderful things about Russian literary culture. Daniil Kharms wrote a play about it, called *Pushkin and Gogol*, in which Pushkin and Gogol keep tripping over each other:

> GOGOL, *getting up*. This is mockery, through and through! *(walks, trips on Pushkin and falls)*. Pushkin again!

That's how it is: Pushkin is everywhere. To this day, "Pushkin" is used interchangeably with the phrase "someone's uncle," in Russian expressions such as: "And who will foot the bill—Pushkin?"

This is my favorite part about *Journey to Arzrum*: Pushkin himself keeps stumbling over a nobleman called . . . Count Pushkin. Pushkin and Count Pushkin decide to travel together, but argue and part company.

Pushkin will have no part in Count Pushkin's plan to cross a snowy mountain pass in a britzka pulled by eighteen emaciated Ossetian bulls, and their courses diverge . . . but they meet again in Tiflis. They can't escape each other.

In Turkey, I was reminded of Count Pushkin every time my path crossed that of another Elif, a thing I wasn't used to, growing up in the States. I went into all the stores called "Elif Clothing." I bought something from every "Elif Grocery." Once I gave a dollar to a Gypsy woman. "My daughter's name is Elif!" she exclaimed. Then she added: "Isn't that right?" and I was startled to realize that the daughter was actually standing beside her: a skinny child, 5 or 6 years old. The Gypsy looked at my palm and told me to beware of a woman called Mary.

The further I read in Pushkin's *Journey*, the more I identified with his experience. As Pushkin was in hiding from the secret police, so was I hiding from my aunt Arzu. As Pushkin was mistaken in his travels for a Frenchman and a dervish, so was I mistaken for a Spaniard and a pilgrim. As Pushkin happened in his travels upon a soiled copy of his own earlier Caucasian poem, "Prisoner of the Caucasus"—the very text he was supposed to be updating with his new Eastern impressions—so was I constantly stumbling, in teahouses and gardens, upon earlier editions of *Let's Go*. Finally, as Pushkin, a Russian, was ambiguously positioned between the "Orient" and the 17th-century Anglo-French tradition of travelogue, so was I ambiguously positioned between Turkey and the exasperating 20th-century discourse of "shoestring travel": the quest for an idyll where, for three US dollars, Mustafa would serve you a home-cooked meal and tell you about his hair collection. The worst part of this discourse was its specious left-wing rhetoric, as if it were a form of "sticking it to the man" to reject a chain motel in favor of a cold-water pension completely filled with owls.

I stayed in all the novelty hotels—tree-house hotels perched on stilts, troglodyte hotels carved from dolomites—and everywhere I found the same atmosphere of distrust. The travelers lived in terror of getting ripped off, or missing an "authentic" experience. The locals were terrified lest they miss some "opportunity" afforded by their foreign visitors. Of course I met many kind and reasonable people among both groups, but it was the importune ones who specially sought me out: the tourists cadging insider tips, the locals demanding that I lure rich foreigners to their establishments. A Turkish schoolteacher turned hotelier gave me a typed report he had written debunking the Armenian genocide, for me to give to the American government. A tour-bus operator wanted me to help his uncle get a kidney transplant "in Houston." "And who will pay for that," I reflected gloomily. "Pushkin?"

THE RUSSIAN EAST

I SPENT THE LAST TWO WEEKS of the summer living in Moscow with two very kind but depressed Russian academics: a mathematician from the Academy of Sciences, and his wife, a biologist who had recently been fired from the Academy of Sciences and who spent all night in the kitchen playing Super Mario Brothers on a Nintendo Game Boy. They were renting me the bedroom of their daughter, who had been banished to somebody's dacha. Back at school that year I managed to get a somewhat larger grant, and to enroll for the spring semester in a study-abroad program. This program was operated by two Russian entrepreneurs, both named Igor, and had a distant affiliation with a liberal arts college in Kansas.

Moscow in 1998 was like Paris during the Restoration. The Caspian oil pipeline had drawn the largest foreign investment in Russian history. The city was overrun by speculators. Mayor Luzhkov resurrected Peter the Great's Table of Ranks, and plotted the construction of an underground city in the suburbs. The state had stopped funding the maintenance of Lenin's corpse in Red Square, and the vast reserves of unemployed master embalmers were hired to restore the victims of Mafia car bombings, and to mummify the nouveau riche in marble mausoleums.

In Moscow, for the first and last time in my life, I dated bankers. Things didn't work out with the first banker, but I still remember the second banker fondly. His name was Rustem, he had remarkable yellowish brown eyes, and he had until recently been an engineer at an explosives factory in Yekaterinburg, designing bombs that were named after flowers. Now he was working for Bank Menatep, which the oligarch Mikhail Khodorkovsky used to manage the state funds for Chernobyl victims, and to buy the majority of shares in Yukos oil, and also to commit alleged embezzlement and tax frauds for which he is currently in prison. Rustem was saving up money to pay for parachuting lessons.

Rustem often traveled to Uzbekistan: his sister had married an Uzbek magnate and now lived in Tashkent, which Rustem said resembled the American west of cowboy movies. He could count to ten in Uzbek, and I was amazed to realize that the numbers were almost the same as in Turkish. I had been told that Uzbek was related to Turkish, but I hadn't believed it. The fact hadn't been presented in a convincing way. A distant uncle of mine had married an Uzbek beauty called Lola, who never talked to anyone or even opened her mouth (although she smiled often, showing beautiful dimples). Only two years after their marriage did it become known that Lola had three gold teeth. Everyone would always ask my uncle: "How do you live with someone you can't communicate with?" And my uncle always shouted: "Uzbek Turkish is very close to our Turkish language!"

I hadn't believed my uncle, partly because he was crazy—he spent his later years in a gardening shed in New Jersey, writing a book about string theory and spiders—and partly because, in my experience, Turkish people thought that *every* language was close to our Turkish language. Many times I had been told that Hungarian was related to Turkish, that the Hungarians and Turks descended from the same Altaic peoples, that Attila the Hun was Turkish, and so on. Later I went to Hungary and discovered that Hungarians do not share these beliefs at all. "Of course we have some Turkish words in our language," they would say, "but that's because you occupied our country for four hundred years."

But Rustem had some Uzbek money in his apartment, and it was so strange to see the familiar Turkish words in Cyrillic letters, above stern, Asiatic portraits of Central Asian bards and geographers. I was greatly struck to discover that there was a physical location in the world where Turkish and Russian somehow overlapped, and generated some other thing, with its own language, that you could study and learn about.

Several years later, while writing my dissertation (which was about European novels), I formulated a theory of the novel: the novel form is "about" the protagonist's struggle to transform his arbitrary, fragmented, given experience into a narrative as meaningful as his favorite books. Looking back, this is how I understand my interest in Central Asia: there was an actual place you could visit, with a language you could learn, that linked my favorite books, *Anna Karenina* and *Eugene Onegin*, with one of the more arbitrary and "given" aspects of my life: being Turkish.

Once I learned about the existence of Tashkent, too, it kept turning up. Anna Akhmatova was evacuated to Tashkent from Leningrad during the siege. So was Bulgakov's widow: that's where she hid the manuscript of *Master and Margarita*. Solzhenitsyn's stomach tumor was miraculously cured at a Tashkent hospital, which became the setting of *Cancer Ward*. At the end of *Anna Karenina*, Tolstoy sends Vronsky to Tashkent with a toothache.

I decided to visit Tashkent for spring break. Rustem wanted to come with me, but he couldn't leave the bank. The nation's bankers were working long hours in those days. I wasn't following the escalating financial malaise, which Rustem rarely mentioned; as for Raisa, the elderly pensioner with whom I was living, she only turned on the news when it was about the Lewinsky scandal. "I don't watch our news—it's so dark. It leaves you feeling bad."

"Monica Lewinsky leaves me feeling bad, too," I said.

Raisa shrugged. "For you in America, it's a big drama, but for us, it's just funny. Your Clinton is a young, healthy, good-looking man! Where's the misfortune? Look at our half-dead Yeltsin . . . if we found out Boris Nikolaevich was sleeping with a young girl, we would declare a national holiday."

Meanwhile at the university, the smaller of the two Igors turned out to be a friend of Anatoly Chubais, the privatization czar who was at that point in charge of the entire economy, which was collapsing, and even got him to come and give a speech to the advanced Russian class. "You know who must have a lot of free time," I remarked to Rustem later, "is this guy Chubais. He's going around to universities, talking to foreign students."

It took several minutes to convince Rustem that I wasn't joking. "She's seen Chubais!" he marveled. "And what did he say?"

Unfortunately I couldn't remember anything he had said, except that he had used a lot of past participles.

I ended up going to Uzbekistan in the company of one of my classmates from the university, a Taiwanese mathematician called Alex. We got to Tashkent in the pouring rain and started to walk from the bus station to our hostel, making our way through a maze of courtyards, ignoring all the dogs that were barking at us from behind chain-link fences, crossing a huge puddle on a bridge made from a rotting plank.

"Tashkent is the Venice of the East," Alex announced, in his weird monotonal voice.

My recollections from this trip are scattered but vivid. We lived on some kind of chocolate spread, which we ate from a jar using a souvenir Uzbek scimitar. We constantly had to bribe people. At one point we spent twenty minutes wandering through a pool hall near a bus station, trying to identify the guy we were supposed to bribe. I had to do all the talking, because nobody could understand anything Alex said. To my dismay, I also had to do all the financial calculations.

"Aren't you the math major?" I asked Alex once, in the middle of trying to sort out who owed what for a Kirghiz visa.

"I only deal with numbers on a theoretical level," Alex intoned.

We spent three days each in Uzbekistan, Kirghizstan, and Kazakhstan. We spent a lot of time in bus stations, where Alex made us do calisthenics, "like the Germans." "We are wasting minutes!" he would shout, attempting a German accent. Sometimes, the buses turned out to have been requisitioned by soldiers—there was a war in Kirghizstan—and then, even if there were empty seats left, we had to wait for the next bus.

"Couldn't we take this bus, too?" I asked once.

"What—with the soldiers?" exclaimed the station attendant. "Ha! Ha! Ha!"

In Bukhara we visited the emir's palace, which was overrun by peacocks. Some of the rooms had been filled with cement. "That used to be the conservatory but the Soviets objected to grand pianos." In the Kirghiz mountains, we visited a thermal bath, where we sat in wooden cubicles, immersed in sulfurous water. The sulfur blended with the sickly sweet smell of horsemeat, which someone was boiling outside over an open fire. In Bishkek we rode a Ferris wheel that marked the place where Tamerlane had allegedly once expressed the wish to be buried. He hadn't been buried there. The Ferris wheel stood in an otherwise empty plaza, where a little boy with several gold teeth was riding a bicycle in circles; another little boy, dressed in a gray suit, was shooting at a lone shrub with a toy machine gun.

But the city that left the strongest impression on me was Samarkand, with its abandoned Soviet department store, and the astronomical observatory where, in the fifteenth century, Ulughbek had mapped the coordinates of 1,018 stars, and the deserted medieval university. The Lion Medrese's mosaic lions—half tiger, half clock—were clearly the work of someone who had never seen a lion. Samarkand is where

Tamerlane was actually buried, under a six-foot slab of jade taken from a temple in China. It crossed my mind that I might like to come back someday, when I was less tired, dirty, and confused.

SHORTLY AFTER I RETURNED TO THE US that summer, the Russian ruble crashed. Many of the banks, including Menatep, collapsed overnight. Rustem liquidated his rubles by buying fax machines; he occasionally sent me faxes at my miserable summer job, in the copyediting department of a big New York publishing house. Eventually the faxes stopped, the summer came to an end.

Back at school that fall, I started studying the "Russian Orient": I read Soviet Realist stories by Uzbek and Kirghiz writers, Pan-Slavic treatises by Soviet linguists, Pan-Turkic treatises by Kemalist Turks, "Caucasian" poems by Russian poets. I signed up for a beginning Uzbek class, which was taught by a graduate student, a Samarkand native called Gulnora, and I was fascinated by the language, which was like a harsher, more naïve, more Russian version of Turkish. Where Kemalist Turks had borrowed French words (for things like trains, and ham), the Soviet Uzbeks borrowed Russian ones.

At that time I was greatly struck by a book about Pushkin by Monika Greenleaf, a professor at Stanford. There was a chapter about *Journey to Arzrum*. According to Greenleaf, the trip to Arzrum was a substitute for a journey to France. All his life, Pushkin had dreamed of Paris—"In a week I'll definitely be in Paris!" begins an unfinished play—but he was refused permission. By 1829, Pushkin wasn't allowed to leave the country at all, but it was easier to slip across the Turkish border, so that's where he went. The Orient, which was supposed to stand for "the open spaces of adventure and personal reminiscence," actually stood for the opposite of freedom: banishment from Paris, the center of the world, to the most meaningless peripheries.

CALIFORNIA

A YEAR LATER, I GRADUATED COLLEGE and wanted to write a novel. This in fact is why I had been doing all these difficult and uncomfortable things and reading the most outlandish books I could find: I was trying to understand the human condition, so I could write a book about it. But writing a book takes time, and time is expensive. I ended up in the comp lit department at Stanford. I thought I would spend a year or two there at most—much as, in *The Magic Mountain*, Hans Castorp thought he was visiting that tuberculosis sanatorium for three weeks.

My best friend in the Stanford department, Luba, was a Russian-Jewish émigré who had grown up in, of all places, Tashkent. In between sessions of our graduate seminar on an obscure school of 1920s Russian filmmakers, known for their "eccentric" use of circus paraphernalia and human-size rubber mannequins, Luba and I would take long walks around the graduate-student housing complex, united by the mystical bond of the "motherland." Invariably, on the course of these walks, we would get lost, or wander into some kind of a ditch, dissolving into hysterical laughter. Like Castorp in his first weeks at Davos I thought: *This can't last much longer.*

After one year at graduate school, I filed for a leave of absence, moved to San Francisco, and tried to write a novel. In between working odd jobs, I wrote a great deal. Nonetheless, the result somehow wasn't a novel. It didn't have a beginning or an end. It didn't seem to be telling any particular story. I was sure I had enough "material," and I wasn't having trouble with the actual process of writing; so this production of a non-novel was difficult for me to understand.

I was contemplating this mystery on the evening of September 13, 2001, while running to the Golden Gate Bridge, when I tripped over some kind of plastic barrier—erected, I later learned, with the intention of protecting the bridge from terrorists. Some other joggers helped me to my feet. My arm felt very strange. I walked to the nearest hospital and spent some hours in the waiting room, where a television mounted to the ceiling showed endless footage of bodies being dragged from the World Trade Center. Eventually I was admitted to the emergency room, where doctors removed the bloody gravel from my knees, x-rayed my arm, informed me that my elbow was broken, and outfitted me with a cast and sling. The bill came to $1,700. This experience caused me to take a cold, hard look at the direction my life was headed in. What was I doing, running around this world—a place about which I clearly understood nothing—with no health insurance and no real job, writing an endless novel about God knows what? A week later, the head of the Stanford comp lit department called and asked if I wanted to come back that winter. I said yes.

BACK AT STANFORD, I had to start taking a Russian language pedagogy class, to prepare for my mandatory year of teaching Russian to undergraduates. The class was taught in Russian by a Soviet-trained linguist called Alla who advised us, among other things, to treat our more stupid students with sympathy, "as if they had cancer."

While I was still in pedagogy training, a scandal erupted around one of my classmates, Janine, a nonnative Russian speaker who was teaching first-year Russian. Alla had monitored one of Janine's classes and seen her, before his eyes, write on the blackboard the phrase *vasha imia* ("your name")—which would have been fine if *imia* ("name") were feminine, but in fact it is an irregular neuter, so the correct form is *vash*e *imia*. Janine's class was immediately reassigned to another graduate student (who now had a double teaching load); for the rest of the year, all Janine was allowed to do was grade homework papers, using an answer key.

I thought a long time about Janine's situation. Granted, "name" is a pretty common word in first-year language classes, so the teacher should probably know what gender it is. On the other hand, what we were really talking about here was a one-letter spelling mistake on an irregular noun. Who among us was safe from such a misstep?

As I was having these thoughts, nearby Berkeley announced a search for an Uzbek language instructor. This seemed like a gesture from the "invisible hand." I had had only one year of Uzbek language instruction, but the Berkeley department chair—Irina Paperno, the author of a famous semiotic study of suicide—said that if I took an intensive all-summer course in Uzbekistan, I could have the job. The director of the Stanford special languages program also said I might be able to teach Uzbek at Stanford: either the Berkeley or the Stanford Uzbek class would count for my language-teaching requirement. This seemed like a great idea to me, because who was going to refute my spelling of Uzbek words on the board? Nobody.

The only US-accredited intensive immersion program in Uzbek language was run by ACTR-ACCELS and cost $7,000. "I wonder why it's so expensive," I remember remarking to Irina Paperno. "Airfare is a thousand dollars . . . but after that, you'd think the overhead in Uzbekistan would be pretty low." And Paperno counted off on three fingers: "One thousand for instruction, one thousand for room and board, and four thousand for the body bag to send you home."

Well, I got the $7,000, most of it from Stanford and the rest from the US Department of State, but then came a new development. It suddenly turned out that the salary for the Berkeley job was paid by a government grant for which only native Uzbek speakers were eligible. Bizarrely, it also turned out that the director of the Stanford special-languages program had told the grant-awarding committee that I had *fabricated the entire conversation and email exchange* in which she told me there was a possibility of my teaching Uzbek at Stanford. I still have the email to this day. It says: "I would be delighted to have you teach Uzbek in the Special Languages Program." "I never told that woman anything," the special-languages director apparently told the grants committee.

I didn't take the news too badly. Maybe, I reasoned, it was all for the best that I wasn't being encouraged to run away to Uzbekistan with a $4,000 body bag, just because I was afraid of being caught by Alla in a spelling mistake. I made an appointment with the administrator in charge of NIS-region grants, to explain that I wanted to return the money. As I told her my story, the administrator's face grew stony and blank.

"This doesn't look good," she said. "You're backing out of your research proposal just because you aren't eligible for this particular job at Berkeley, this particular year?" She shook her head. "It doesn't look good. I like you, Elif, and I want you to succeed. That's why I'm telling you that, if you back out of your proposal now, the likelihood of this committee ever awarding you a grant again will be very small."

Of all the circumstances that contributed to my ending up in Samarkand, this ultimatum was the most unexpected. Go to Uzbekistan now . . . or you will never get departmental funding ever again? My first instinct was to tell them all exactly what they could do with their departmental funding. But three things changed my mind. First, departmental funding and departmental goodwill are really, in the cold light of reason, nothing to sneeze at. Second, I was at that time greatly under the sway of *The Portrait of a Lady*, a book in which one finds the following line: "Afterwards, however, she always remembered that one should never regret a generous error." As a result I was constantly rethinking all my conservative decisions and amending them in favor of "generous errors," a category which surely included going to Samarkand to learn the great Uzbek language. Third, I was unhappy in love and wanted to get away.

The plan backfired somewhat because one of the people I wanted to get away from, my college boyfriend Adam, insisted on coming with me, for his own set of reasons (concern for my safety; his belief—accurate, as it turned out—that it would give us things to talk about later; and some kind of obscure geopolitical ambitions which entailed a quest for total world knowledge). Despite myself, I was moved. I was also impressed by how easy it was, once you had paid your $7,000, to bring your "significant other" along with you to the former socialist republics: just a couple of hundred dollars added another person to your homestay arrangement, and even to your accidental death and dismemberment policy, which I received in the mail a few weeks later:

LIFE:	$25,000
TWO OR MORE MEMBERS:	$25,000
ONE MEMBER:	$25,000
THUMB AND INDEX FINGER:	$6,250

COMBINED MAXIMUM OF $50,000 FOR EMERGENCY OR MEDICAL REPATRIATION, OR REPATRIATION OF REMAINS.

REPATRIATION OF REMAINS: COVERED SERVICES INCLUDE, BUT ARE NOT LIMITED TO, EXPENSES FOR EMBALMING, CREMATION, MINIMALLY NECESSARY CASKET FOR TRANSPORT AND TRANSPORTATION.

SAMARKAND

THEY SENT YOU TO WASHINGTON, DC, first, for "orientation" at a mid-range hotel decorated completely in mauve. There were thirty-five students in the Russian Language and Area Studies program, thirty-three of them going to Russia.

At the orientation dinner, we were presented with some truly awful linguini while we listened to an address by a professor from Middlebury who had invented a system of rating second-language proficiency. The genius of this system rested on the concept of rating second-language proficiency on a scale from one to four.

It occurred to me that there was nobody *making* me stay in this room. Surely it would be more constructive to go buy a sun hat, because I have black hair and Uzbekistan is very sunny. Along with Liechtenstein, Uzbekistan is one of only two double-landlocked countries in the entire world! The speaker either affected not to notice or did not notice my departure from the hall. In the lobby I asked the concierge, whose name tag said "Albrecht," where I could buy a sun hat. Albrecht suggested that I might like to look for a hat in nearby Georgetown. "So we're *here* . . ." he said, poising his hotel pen over a map. But the pen just hovered there, like a helicopter. Albrecht couldn't locate our hotel on the map. "This is very embarrassing," he said. His sincerity left a strong impression on me.

In the humid evening, fireflies hovered at eye level over little brick streets. Somehow I ended up in an Urban Outfitters. All around me, girls were buying absolutely unwearable-looking clothes: sheer dresses with V-necks down to the navel; jeans measuring literally two inches from waist to crotch; rhinestone-encrusted G-strings with *no elasticity whatsoever.* I found a hideous white ill-fitting sun hat, bought it, and fled to the Barnes & Noble.

There was one other student in the program going to Uzbekistan: Dan, a Tashkent-bound political science major who was indescribably average in both appearance and demeanor, like a kind of composite sketch. We were on the same flight to Tashkent, with a stopover in Frankfurt. On the plane, Dan managed to befriend a group of twelve Uzbek and Ukrainian exchange students and now, in Frankfurt, we all sat in two rows of seats in a waiting area, looking at a photo album belonging to a young Uzbek called Muratbek. Muratbek was very tan, with bleached hair and a fixed grin. To his every utterance in every language, he appended the exclamation: "Awesome!" "*Turkcha gapirasizmi?*" he asked me. "Do you speak Turkish? Awesome!"

Having extinguished two hours of my youth in this way, I went to meet Adam, who had skipped the orientation and was flying to Frankfurt directly from San Francisco. His plane arrived in another, larger terminal. A BMW sedan, the grand prize for something, was parked in the middle of a vast atrium. On the other side of a glass panel, an open cart piled high with suitcases glided majestically along the runway, against the mauve early-morning sky. A wall-size television screen was broadcasting a World Cup match: Turkey versus Japan. A small group of Turkish janitors were gathered in front of the screen. At tense moments, they would drop their mop handles and grip one another's arms, shouting at the players in German.

Adam came out of the plane wearing a white T-shirt and a backpack, looking, with his gentle blinking Chinese eyes, as philosophical and good-humored as Snoopy. Because Adam belonged to the US Naval Intelligence Reserves (part of his geopolitical ambitions), we ended up in some kind of a military lounge. It had free internet and bran muffins, and a tiny television broadcasting the Japan-Turkey game. Turkey won, 1–0. Awesome.

IT WAS LATE AT NIGHT when we got to Tashkent. The baggage claim area felt like a room in a dream, a room in someone's house. A breeze was blowing through an open window.

We passed through customs and filed into a parking lot, where Dan's Tashkent host family came to pick him up: three teenage boys with hangdog expressions, and their mother Marjuda, an overweight woman with gold teeth and a bright red dress. Marjuda was very kind to me; she wrote her phone number on a piece of paper and told me and Adam to visit her in Tashkent. Then she gestured to Dan to come to their car. Dan turned to me. "So you're going to stay with us tonight, right?" he said urgently, as though I were his closest friend.

"Ah, no, in a hotel," I said. They were sending a driver to take us to Samarkand the next day.

"But she just invited you!" I still remember his expression of alarm.

In a haze of sleep, Adam and I got into the car of an ACTR officer, who was taking us to our hotel. Propaganda slogans were printed in enormous letters on walls and billboards—I could recognize HALQIM, "my people," and VATANIM, "my country"—signed "Islom Karimov," the president of Uzbekistan since the fall of the Iron Curtain. His last reelection had been in 2000, when he won 91.9 percent of the votes from his sole opponent: a professor of Marxist philosophy, who later admitted that he himself had voted for Karimov.

The next morning, a tiny Korean car, buzzing with the vibrations of a poor-quality stereo, picked us up at a street corner. The driver, an inscrutable Tajik, turned off the stereo when we got into the car. Once we reached the main road, the sun blazed down and it was unbearably hot. The driver periodically made tiny adjustments to the temperature. He turned the air conditioner between "lo" and "off"; opened and closed the vents; rolled down the window a crack, then closed it again. No matter what he did, it was unbearably hot.

After an hour of silence, the driver turned to me and said, in Russian: "So you didn't bring any cassette tapes with you?"

We hadn't, I said, but maybe we could listen to some of his tapes.

The driver remained silent for a moment. "What if you don't like my music?" he asked finally.

"Oh, I'm sure we'll like it," I said.

The driver looked genuinely confused. "How can you say that?" he asked. "You don't even know what kind of music I have."

Thirty kilometers of the highway from Tashkent to Samarkand passes through Kazakhstan. The moment we cleared the police checkpoint, the landscape looked completely different. Patchy, grayish fields stretched as far as the eye could see. There were no trees at all, no human figures. Here and there stood a few melancholy, skeletal horses, with drooping prehistoric heads.

Twenty minutes later, trees reappeared, leafy trees, on both sides of the road, with the trunks painted white; Uzbek police were guarding a roadblock.

"So we're back in Uzbekistan?" I asked the driver.

"Yes, this is Uzbekistan. Trees, you see."

"They, um, don't have trees in Kazakhstan?"

He shook his head, frowning. "Don't like them."

"The Kazakhs don't like . . . trees?"

The driver shook his head more emphatically. "No way."

We pulled up in front of the Asadulloyev residence late that afternoon. Two massive wooden doors were set in a pink plaster wall; one of them swung out slowly and Gulchekhra, our "host mother"—they really called her that, as if we were tapeworms—came outside. Peculiarly familiar music drifted toward us. Gulchekhra smiled graciously at me and Adam, and less graciously at the driver, whom she addressed in Tajik: she was apparently trying to dismiss him, while he shuffled his feet and looked at the ground, with the appearance of somebody waiting to be paid. It was not, as we later learned, a deceptive appearance. The driver was a sort of relative, in the broadest sense, so one tried to be kind to him, Gulchekhra explained; but it was the Americans in Tashkent who had his money; they hadn't given it to her.

We walked through a covered passage, to a stone courtyard with a square pool, its water green and cloudy with vegetable life. The hot, shimmering air throbbed with the music of Enrique Iglesias. Next to a large boom box, a boy with a weedy adolescent mustache was washing a Daewoo sedan with a garden hose.

Adam and I were given an entire wing of the house, consisting of three rooms: a bedroom, a little sitting room with a television, and a dining room with a long table that could seat twenty. (The malfunctioning toilet was in a different wing.) Gulchekhra told us to call her Gulya, and announced her intention to call me "Emma," because my real name was so complicated. A former Communist apparatchik, she now worked as a travel agent and had been to "every country in the world, except America, Africa, and Japan." She had two children: Inom, the teenager with the car, and Shirin, a 3-year-old girl. Inom and Shirin's father had, Gulya explained, "become a Yogi" and moved to California two years ago.

THAT AFTERNOON Inom drove me to the university, where I met Vice-Rector Safarov, a personage whose refrigerator-like build, rubbery face, and heavy eyelids brought to my mind some anthropomorphic piece of furniture in a Disney movie. Reclining in a leather chair in his office, Vice-Rector Safarov gave me a speech in Russian about the importance of comparative literary and cultural study.

"We can study symbols and how they are used in different cultures," he announced, "or we can study systems of folklore, or we can study how different languages structure people's perceptions of the world." He leaned back in his chair with his arms folded. "What kind of language do you wish to study here, in the principal aspect?"

"The Uzbek language," I ventured cautiously. Did he already know that I was supposed to teach Russian next year?

Taking out a notebook, Safarov proceeded to sketch my program of study. I would have four hours of class every day: two hours of "spoken speech," and two hours of "written speech": a.k.a., the great Uzbek literary language. I was the sole student in these classes. Safarov opened the door to his office with a flourish, revealing a lanky young man in a button-down shirt. "Here is your language teacher," Safarov said. "His name is Muzaffar." Muzaffar, a philosophy graduate student, had pale skin, pale almond-shaped eyes, high cheekbones, and a floppy, sad, puppetlike comportment. He bowed, lifting one hand to his chest. Despite his exotic appearance and foreign gestures, his general air of malaise was familiar to me from previous observations of philosophy graduate students.

Muzaffar had been instructed to accompany me back to Gulya's house, which I found somehow irritating. At one point during our walk, we passed some Russian girls smoking cigarettes. "I have to apologize to you, Elif," Muzaffar said in English, softly and in what seemed to me an insinuating tone. "Our girls, Uzbek girls, of course do not smoke in street, but Russian girls, they do this."

"That's fine," I said. I tried twice to invite him to go home and let me walk the rest of the way alone, but it was no use; man or God had impressed him with too strong a sense of responsibility for my welfare.

We turned onto Gulya's street. "I will see you tomorrow," Muzaffar said. "We will work very hard."

"Great," I said.

"At our age," he observed, "we must work and study a lot, while we still have the strength."

This remark for the first time began to dispose me kindly toward Muzaffar. I laughed, and a glint of amusement appeared in his pale eyes. "While we still have time," he clarified. "Already time is running out, but soon we won't have strength left, either."

By now we were a few yards away from the massive wooden doors; I could already hear Enrique Iglesias. Muzaffar said that it was time to say good-bye, and that he would now stand behind a tree until I was safely inside the house.

"Oh, OK," I said. "Good-bye."

"Good-bye. You go into the house now. Don't worry. I will be here." He pointed at an emaciated tree.

I knocked on the door, glancing over my shoulder where Muzaffar, faithfully stationed behind the tree, raised one limp arm. I returned this gesture. Inside the courtyard, the music was very loud. Inom was washing his car again.

"Was there a man hiding behind that tree?" Gulya asked, suspiciously.

"I didn't see anyone," I said.

CONTINUED IN ISSUE 8

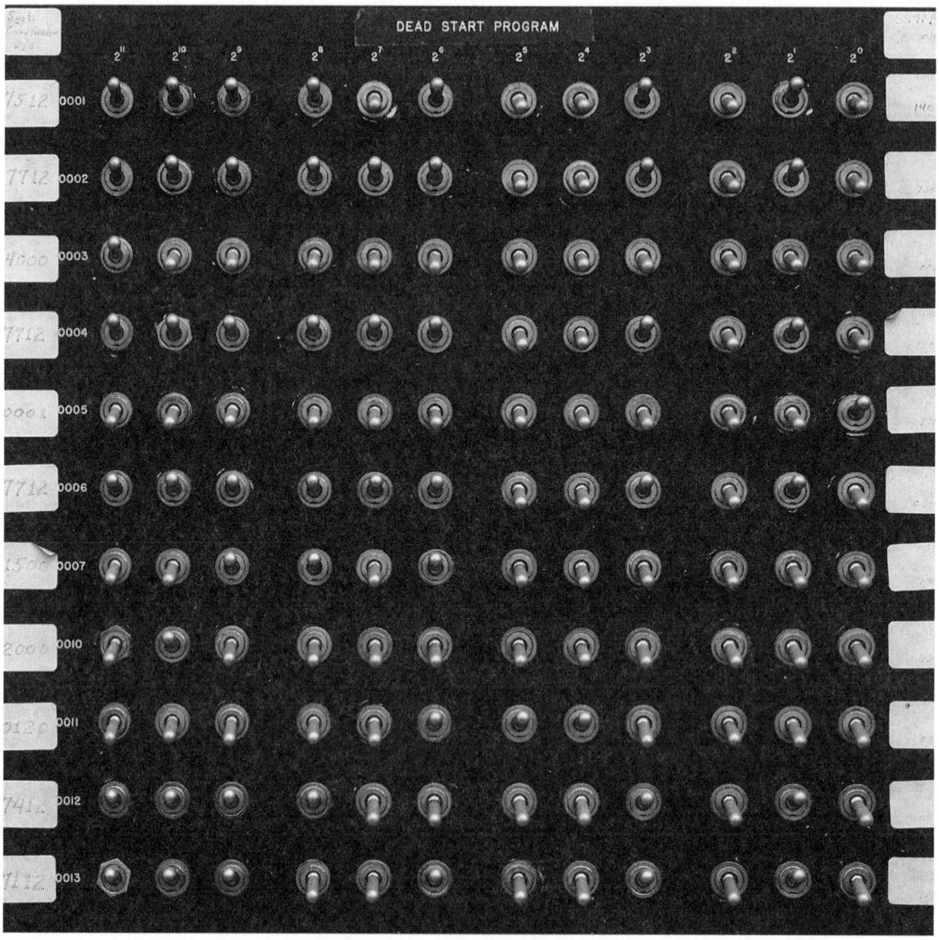

MARK RICHARDS, *CONTROL DATA CORP 6660*, 2007,
FROM *CORE MEMORY: A VISUAL SURVEY OF VINTAGE COMPUTERS*, BY JOHN ALDERMAN & MARK RICHARDS, CHRONICLE BOOKS.
COLOR PHOTOGRAPH. COURTESY OF THE ARTIST.

CONFESSIONS OF A DJ

Jace Clayton

I'VE DJED IN MORE THAN TWO DOZEN COUNTRIES. What I do isn't remotely popular in any of them.

It's hard to reach North Cyprus—the Turkish portion of the island that seceded after a war with Greece in 1974—not least because only one country, Turkey, officially recognizes it. Yet there we were, whizzing through arid country past pastel bunker-mansions, the architectural embodiment of militarized paranoia and extreme wealth, en route to an empty four-star hotel. We were going to rest for a day and then play music in the ruins of a crusader castle. It was the year 2000. I was the turntablist for an acid jazz group from New York City. The band didn't really need a DJ, but it did need someone to signify "hip-hop," and that was me. There were six of us—our saxophonist leader, Ilhan Irsahim; a singer, Norah Jones, before she was known for anything besides being Ravi Shankar's daughter; a bassist, a drummer, and a Haitian sampler-player. There were four attendants in the hotel casino, bored behind the gaming tables, and only two other paying guests—British pensioners, holdovers from remembered pre-1974 days when Cyprus was undivided.

I sat beside the pool talking to our host, trying to figure out why we were there. Down the coast, thirty miles away in the haze, a tall cluster of glass-and-steel buildings hugged the shore. "What's that city?" I asked. It looked like Miami. "Varosha," she said. Completely evacuated in the 1974 conflict. A ghost town on the dividing line between North and South Cyprus. The only people there were UN patrol units and kids from either side who entered the prohibited zone to live out a J. G. Ballard fantasy of decadent parties in abandoned seaside resorts.

If North Cyprus represented the forgotten side of a fault line of global conflict, how were we getting paid? Who owned those scattered mansions that we saw on the way from the airport? Was our trip bankrolled with narco-dollars, to please the criminals hiding out in an empty landscape, or with Turkish state funding, to win tourists back? I never found out. I bought a laptop with my earnings, quit the band, and moved from New York to Barcelona.

DJed music develops in the great centers: London, New York, Paris. But the artists make much of their living in forays to the periphery. To state culture bureaus, our music sounds like art and the "avant-garde," a means of prestige. To kids coming of age in a world of technology and unhinged capitalism, our music seems to sound the way global capital is—liquid, international, porous, and sped-up.

Yet our sounds are also a vocabulary for those who detest the walled-off concentrations of wealth, and steal property back: the collectives that build their own sound systems, stage free parties, and invite DJs to perform. The international DJ becomes emblematic of global capitalism's complicated cultural dimension. On flights and at the free Continental breakfasts in hotels, often the same soul-destroying hotel chains in each city, we get stuck chatting with our fellow Americans and Western Europeans, the executives eager to find compatriots. We make small talk with these consultants and deal-makers in the descending elevators in the evening—then go out to the city's dead-end and unowned spaces or its luxury venues to soundtrack the night of the region's youth, hungry for something new. DJ music is now the common art form of squatters and the nouveau riche; it is the soundtrack both for capital and for its opposition.

As a process, DJing is inevitable and necessary for our times, an elegant way to deal with data overload. As a performance, it's what the kids are grooving to the world over. As a product, it's largely illegal.

In 2001 I recorded a three-turntable, sixty-minute mix called *Gold Teeth Thief.* I put it on the internet so my friends could listen. Who else would? One magazine reviewed it, then another, and soon a lot of magazines, leading to hundreds of thousands of downloads. Meanwhile, I was in Madrid without regular internet access. I didn't know what was up. A few months after it went online, I got a phone call from a large European independent label. I'd used one of their songs on the mix. They loved it! It was the best DJ session they'd heard in ages! They wanted to license the mix, assuming they could pay the various labels a fee of $1,000 per track. (There were eighteen tracks on the run list.) "That'd be fantastic," I said, "but pretty expensive. I use forty-four different songs on it. Some of those are major pop tunes, and a bunch are unlicensable bootlegs. It'd be a nightmare to do legally." They insisted that I send a complete track list so that their legal department could decide. Result: "Impossible. Our lawyers laughed at us."

If I were a band, and *Gold Teeth Thief* an album, not a mix, that would have been my big break. A powerful label, big advance fees, well-connected publicists, a coordinated tour. But it's more common for even a popular DJ to receive a cease-and-desist order than to get a mix-album deal with a large label.

It's hard to care. Viral culture doesn't play well with intellectual property laws. I knew *Gold Teeth Thief* couldn't enter the commercial world when I did it. I didn't need it to. Word-of-mouth buzz and bootleg mixes are the DJ's symbolic currency; gigs provide the cash. I've toured well in countries where my music wasn't available for purchase—people had heard it. On his first visit to Moscow, a rapper friend named Sole found his own music bootlegged in a black-market mall. In fact, the place is called the Black Market Mall. He was thrilled, and with good reason—that night's audience sang along word for word. He was able to tour. Metaphors of the "underground" and codifications of the "commercial" mean less and less with MySpace.

Economics favor the DJ. A club can make an event out of one big-name DJ plus local support, and pay just the headliner. (And DJing can make for a long night of drinks-buying: in a rare example, eight hours of nonstop entertainment from a particularly famous Chilean-German drugged-up minimal techno superstar.) A popular indie band would have to be paid vastly more for each member to walk away with similar earnings. Plus it's only one plane ticket for the DJ; the band needs to drive, needs roadies, et cetera. Even in cheapskate America—a country notoriously apathetic toward DJ culture (which it created!)—upper-echelon techno DJs have received, say, $18,000 for a three-hour club performance in Manhattan. That's $100 a minute. But only a few dozen DJs worldwide can command those fees. The much more common scenario is that of the DJ who plays for free drinks and cab fare, never earning more than he spends on records.

° ° °

At the other end of the spectrum from the official luxury clubs lie the squatted venues, the microcommunities. These anarchic spaces are best understood as alternative social centers, especially in Western Europe where property laws offer squatters a modicum of legal protection. A thousand people came to the last party that my friend Filastine and I threw in La Makabra. La Makabra sprawled across *media manzana* (half a city block) in the Barcelona district called *Poble Nou*—"new city," in Catalan. The squat had a gymnasium, library, nursery, skate park, two concert halls, and space for at least thirty people to live. They had a lawyer. We met Swiss gallerists and homeless kids, all dancing. Six months later the cops evicted the residents (illegally) and bulldozed the place within hours. But Makabras exist all over Europe: in Milan, Paris, Ljubljana.

Between the rich and spiritually vacant venues and the poor and illegally occupied ones are all manner of places to perform, from crazy artist-run clubs like Hamburg's infamous Golden Pudel to countryside festivals with temporary populations the size of a small town (including the teknivals staged by "travelers," a European hybrid of ravers, anarcho-punks, and off-the-grid nomads). Not to mention middle-range loopholes where economic rules are suspended. Government money for cutting-edge parties? It happens. Impossible things become possible. Dead of winter, somewhere in Austria: we're playing outside—well, technically we're playing *inside* a subzero meat locker in a parking lot near a cleaned-up industrial canal. We, the performers, are in one meat locker, and the speakers are in two adjacent meat lockers for the audience, where the thermostats are set as low as they can go. I can't remember if the hot cider was free or not. I can't imagine why it wouldn't have been: everything else was funded by Austrian taxpayers. Arts funding in Europe is like magic dust.

When you're back home, a different kind of magic accompanies the DJ's aura: the easy money of remixes, corporate events, advertising. Twice I've been scheduled to play a gig with a really well-known DJ. Twice he's canceled to do a corporate event. Global brands fly him around the world to entertain their private parties. Since these events pay so well and are so fundamentally uncool, there are DJs whose corporate earnings far exceed that from their public gigs—but they'll never admit it. A couple of years ago a magazine even flew me across an ocean to play for forty-five minutes. Naked girls on pedestals got their bodies painted and everybody else shouted at each other over mouthfuls of free sushi.

I do receive plenty of remix offers, courtesy of everyone from an Algerian raï singer to a Spanish girl group asking me to "improve" their number one hit. You can't improve a number one hit by making it better—not in these people's world. When people request remixes, what they really want is to attach a DJ's name to theirs. Aura is contagious, aura rubs off. The music tends to be secondary. And so the more money a label offers me to remix, the less time I spend on it. For remix offers of $1,000 and up, my time limit is eight hours of work, start to finish. If I spend any longer, the track will inevitably get more personal and the label people will be less likely to accept it. Besides, eight hours is a lot of time to spend on something that you won't necessarily get paid for. If a label rejects your remix, you can't release it elsewhere, since the label owns the music.

On tour, life becomes simplified. Travel, wait, play, sleep, repeat. Countries blur. Languages splinter; all you need is English. Few musicians bother to learn about the countries they perform in. We're the opposite of tourists. All cities look the same when you arrive at night, get driven to the venue and leave the next morning. But DJs understand rooms as few others do. You can walk into an empty venue and instantly envision how that night's crowd will react to the architecture of that space.

Both DJing and electronic music production are learned in an artisanal way. One is generally either self-taught or apprenticed. The mechanics of DJing are simple to demonstrate. All you need to do it right are years of practice and the sensitivity of real listening. For the DJ, the actual performance is never just about the musical selection and mixing, something you can work out in advance. There's the dynamics of the sound system to contend with, and how the bodies are reacting to what comes out of it, and what you then have to do about it. When I DJ, I almost never pick out individuals in the dancing crowd. At a good party, the temperature will noticeably heat up when you put on a song that makes people move. You can feel it on your skin even if you don't look up from your decks.

You have to be watchful for the pieces of musical culture that don't translate, even when they come from the places you're playing in. A few months ago I performed in Dubai. I'd mix in a big Arabic tune, but blend it with other rhythms, so that people would hear my mix style cutting up and overlaying the Middle Eastern source records. I'd do a dancehall reggae riddim underneath Egyptian cabdriver chaabi. A stuttering breakbeat pulse bulwarking Rachid Taha's remake of Dahmane el-Harrachi's exile anthem "Ya Rayah." The Lebanese contingent went wild. But a concerned Arab came up to the booth. "Could you play less Arabic music?" He pointed to two blonde Western girls he was getting down with. Arabic language alienated them, whereas the "niggas" and "bitches" of my rap a cappellas made them want to party. I changed course. Later in the evening the Scottish club manager came over with the same request. "Too much Arabic music. Do you mind ending with something in English?" "It's not Arabic," I said, "it's Berber. From North Africa—Morocco." He shrugged. He later told me that nobody had ever played Middle Eastern music on his night. He'd be able to spin the whole thing into a noble example of his ecumenical curatorial slant.

Near the beginning of my career, I wound up doing a DJ set at the Montreux Jazz Festival. Up in the mountains of Switzerland. For me it was crazy. I was DJing in front of a thousand people for the first time, and it was working, they were following me. I was doing what I would do at home, no holds barred. It's a predominantly white, European crowd, and I'm a black DJ. (The festival program said I was a woman of Egyptian-Italian descent, but we all make mistakes.) There's lots of security up front, and I see this one other black guy, trying to reach me.

"Hey!" he's yelling. "Hey DJ!"

I didn't look up. Ten minutes later he's still there, still gesturing.

I asked the security to let him get close so I could hear. "'Back That Azz Up'!" he shouted. "Play 'Back That Azz Up'!"

Ten years later, it's no longer a Juvenile song, but a song by a kid from Juvenile's crew—Lil Wayne—that somebody will still shout for, every night, anywhere in the world.

BANDS PERFORM SONGS, DJs perform records. With the old techniques, scratching, cutting, beat-matching, and blending, DJs synchronize two records around a common tempo, using a mixer to blend the songs together. The how-to developed in the hip-hop scene of the South Bronx in the 1970s and has changed little since. The workhorse turntable, standard in clubs the world over, is still the Technics 1200.

The design of this twenty-six-pound behemoth hasn't changed since its 1978 debut. I purchased my 1200s, secondhand, over ten years ago. They work as good as they did the day I bought 'em.

I use three turntables, which makes things more delicate. One slip will send the pattern from harmony into "trainwreck," so called because the arrhythmic clatter of beats will derail the dance floor. But if you mix right, you can get a single "new" totality, whose individual elements can still be heard clearly if you know what you're listening for. A fan who's been watching comes over and says, "I really like that song. What is it?" I can only ask, "Which one?" The DJ's job is to make disparate records sound like a whole, and the more successful you are at it, the less likely the novice onlooker is to know it. DJs have to work to avoid silence and make things appear seamless. You build things up. One of the paradoxes central to the DJ's art is that some of the most demanding, virtuoso work is the hardest to recognize.

Live electronics performers, streaming their own recorded music from laptops, work differently. They follow the basic template given to us by dub reggae. Take a preexisting song, add effects, momentarily remove ("dub out") parts. Live electronica performers basically mess up their own music, which is prebuilt and then disassembled. The more "active" they appear, the more the original piece is being interrupted.

Just as there's a limited number of computer programs that let you make beat-based electronic music, only a few let you perform it. In the past half dozen years, nearly all have been supplanted by a popular upstart—Ableton Live. The majority of "live" dance music acts now use Ableton, won over by its performance-optimized stability. I grind my teeth when I recognize Ableton's built-in FX. *That ping-pong filter-delay algorithm is so obvious! It's like pouring ketchup on everything!* My friends tell me to relax.

Which program you use can affect the product and sometimes nearly determine your genre. With Ableton, it's as if the software's Berlin-based programmers wanted everyone to play techno. Max/MSP tends to produce tone-clouds of granulated noise. FruityLoops favors the stiff drum programming found in reggaeton. The most popular music software in the favelas of Rio de Janiero and their villa counterparts across Latin America is Acid (what I started on, and my favorite program to date, truth be told), a simple application for making sample-based music—perfect for folks without much musical training.

Nearly all of us DJs try our hands at making original electronic music at some point. It's a tricky proposition. Good DJs must have great taste, but great live DJ mixes are exciting in precisely the way that great original albums aren't—they're heterogeneous, unanticipatible, improvisatory.

In 2005, I made an original album, *Special Gunpowder*. I'm not sure I'll ever make another. Why? I'm lazy. I was trying to push too many different kinds of sounds instead of one marketable line. The album-as-major-statement seems less viable nowadays, anyway. (Watch out, novel!) Between the shuffle function on portable MP3 players and the single-song downloads of iTunes and audioblogs, the album's heyday as a sequentially ordered object of contemplation is ending.

It'd be easier to dispense with the notion of albums (and album sales) if Americans were more hip to DJ culture. Unless you're playing weddings, this is a bad country in which to be a DJ. The fees tend to be lower than in Europe, and the treatment by venues is almost always worse, not to mention the ubiquity of rock sound systems ill-equipped for dance music. It's not uncommon for DJs and electronic musicians who can draw a substantial crowd in middle-size European towns to face half-empty rooms in US cities.

Why hasn't DJ culture taken off here like elsewhere? I'm not sure. Americans do love a spectacle. One of the most talked about electronica groups of recent years, Justice, perform their Parisian electro-disco with a stack of iconic Marshall amplifiers, unplugged, onstage. Without the rock facade (and Daft Punk's manager steering their career) they'd be another faceless techno act.

American audiences like to see the artist expressing inner joy or channeling demons (or at least dressing up and dancing). The connection between a guitar and its player is physical: each action corresponds to a sound. The same thing is true of a DJ using vinyl, but the correspondences are more difficult to see. As for musicians and DJs using laptops, for all you know they could be onstage checking their email.

I RECENTLY MOVED TO NEW YORK CITY after seven years in Spain. My "quality of life" ratcheted down several notches; my living expenses doubled. I no longer live next door to an active bullfighting ring with views of the Mediterranean, Gaudí's Sagrada Família, and the mountains. (At the start of my time in New York, I lived in a room in a shared loft. Rent on that Brooklyn room cost approximately as much as that of a family-size apartment in Barcelona.) Staring at my bank account, a strange fact hits home: as an international DJ, the scale of my income is completely uncoupled from the costs of wherever I happen to live. It's inadvisable to live in one of the world's most expensive cities when your workplace is global. Money burns faster here.

DJs are improvisers, however. We adapt. As for me, I take a lot more transatlantic flights than I'd like. I do more concentrated touring now.

Media attention cycles continue to shorten. Trends in dance music accelerate, with each new flavor yielding a clutch of DJs and producers offering free material online, their sheer numbers slowly pulling entry-level booking fees downward. Hot DJs spend less and less time in demand, especially ones coupled to a particular style. Dubstep, a genre splintered from UK garage, is only two or three years old, yet it has become codified, arthritic. The genre's pioneers distance themselves from the name as satellite scenes outside of Britain trudge on in disbelief—*"How can this be dying down if it hasn't really started here?"* MP3 revenue doesn't compensate for plummeting CD sales, which prompts record labels to make highly conservative decisions when signing artists. And let's face it: even if you can survive all this to scrape out a living, do you really want to be playing raves when you're 40?

I'm not saddened by the state of things. I was inspired to become a DJ by nights spent in an after-hours club in Boston where you couldn't see the DJ performing. The DJ wasn't an icon of cool there, he or she was a faceless person surfing the restless slipstream of musical pleasure. Now is the best time ever to be a music fan. The overall movement is toward more ways to share music (and ideas) with like-minded individuals, whether online or face-to-face, body-to-body. What DJ is not first and foremost a music fan?

Between tours I've been tapping into the enormous amount of unreleased music I receive. In addition to releasing other people's music on my homemade label, Soot, I've gotten involved in another start-up—Dutty Artz. We're producing an album by Jahdan Blakkamoore, a Guyanese reggae vocalist who sneaked into America, alone, when he was 8 years old. Our business model would be incomprensible to an old-time record exec. We're releasing music commercially, giving away more pieces for free, pumping internet TV episodes into YouTube (interviews, street fashion, cooking shows, party footage), and, on rare occasions, deliberately inserting our official releases into the bootleg CD gray-market economy. (One man's piracy is another's distribution network.) A trio of Africans runs the NYC bootleg market. If you hand them your original, they give you a flat fee of $250, and then make as many copies as they like, selling them for $5 apiece. Of course the $250 is really a courtesy since they bootleg whatever they want anyway and usually don't pay a dime.

When you tally up the work we put into them, the records we release don't make money—they push sound into the world. Business model be damned. In 2008 you need to believe in music or money, not both. And what I do with all the artists is try to tell them the truth about what's happening. Since the official music industry is a kind of pathetic vivid nightmare, run by greedy people, dilettantes, and folks who don't like music, it's surprising how helpful honesty can be. +

REVIEWS

GAME THEORY

Neil Strauss. *The Game: Penetrating the Secret Society of Pickup Artists.* Regan Books. September 2005.
Neil Strauss. *Rules of the Game.* Harper. December 2007.
The Pickup Artist. 3Ball Productions, VH1. August 2007.

THE "SEDUCTION COMMUNITY"—MOST insidious of oxymorons—grew up on message boards and newsgroups when the internet was still a place of social exile. The early adopters were people prepared to start life anew—that is, losers. As in recovery movements, acknowledging the problem was the first step.

These were hard-up men perplexed by women and determined to figure them out, as they had figured out the algorithms of the computer programs they wrote, or the patterns and strategies they mastered to make it through the video games they played. They were nerds who had been pushed around by jocks and made envious of cool guys all their lives. There were things that cool guys did, innocently, as a function of their social programming, that made them cool. The losers were going to study their behavior, and they were going to start replicating it. And once they were done with the process of breaking down what the successful behaviors were and why they worked, and once they were done rewiring their own brains (which are far more plastic, the neurologists tell us, than we have ever imagined), they would find they could react in new ways to the old, scary stimuli they got from women—ways even more effective than those of their persecutors. In fact, because they were taking a methodical approach to what others did only by instinct, and because they had an analytic understanding of what others did in an unpremeditated way, they were going to be better at being cool guys than any truly cool guy could ever be.

They renamed each other, taking on talismanic handles, each of which declared a secret hope. Mystery. Extramask. Juggler. Playboy. Sin. Lovedrop. Matador. At sites like alt.fast.seduction.com, men from around the world posted detailed narrative accounts of their dates, soliciting, offering, and receiving critical dissection of every statement and gesture. The men volunteered their experiences as data in a vast scientific trial that no responsible researcher would ever attempt. You could even say that these men were engaged in a strange parody of the activities of the men of the Enlightenment, who used the printing press to diffuse a new attitude toward life that broke with the inherited traditions and dogmas of the past. It was a free and open exchange of ideas across international borders in which men distilled the chaos of experience into universal principles. Together they created a body of knowledge that was rational, pragmatic, purposive, and—above all—subject to the test of experiment.

By means of the collective efforts of hundreds of recovering AFCs (average frustrated chumps, in the literature) and aspiring PUAs (pickup artists), they were able to observe, tag, categorize, and devise a winning response to every twitch, flutter, or hesitation that a woman might offer in the progress, as their eventual leader Mystery would flatly put it, "from meet—to sex." If a subject looked back at all his successful sexual encounters, he would see that each and every one of them passed through a sequence of three stages. Mystery defined these as attraction, building comfort, and seduction. By detaching oneself from the welter of passions that afflict us in our everyday behaviors, one could arrive at a method to move through those stages, consciously and with maximum efficiency.

All of us who have tried and failed to break through to the opposite sex think about what works and what doesn't when it comes to the entirely unnatural sociability one must learn to master in a city full of strangers. The internet created a new space to transform that blind empirical groping into what would become, in the hands of its most gifted practitioners, a positivistic system of human relations.

WE HAVE A RECORD, of sorts, of what the world of the pickup arts used to be like. Tom Cruise is the medium, in the role of Frank T. J. Mackey in *Magnolia*. Mackey opens his class by slowly flexing his biceps beneath a brightening spotlight on a darkened stage of a rented hotel conference room. Richard Strauss's *Also sprach Zarathustra* blasts through the speakers.

"*Respect* the cock!" Cruise shouts, to the answering cries and bellows, hoots and chanting of his audience, "and"—with this he launches himself to the lip of the stage, revealing his chiseled face to the camera, kneeling with his arm outstretched in a gesture of embattled striving—"*tame* the cunt!"

His students are beefy rage-filled mooks in pleated Dockers. They work themselves into a frenzy at every cue, including the moment in Cruise's presentation when he feigns the act of intercourse—intercourse from behind—onstage. They learn how to, as the overhead projections tell them, "Fake Like You Are a Nice and Caring Guy." They are instructed to "Form a Tragedy," as a technique for earning sympathy, all in service of turning "Your 'Friend' into a 'Sperm Receptacle.'"

Cruise's portrayal was a cartoon that nonetheless captured something about the state of the pickup artists in their early days. The pioneering figure of the online seduction community was a man named Ross Jeffries; the music writer Neil Strauss, in his immersive account of the PUA world titled *The Game*, describes him as a "tall, skinny, porous-faced self-proclaimed nerd." Jeffries's early e-books, which relied on a pseudo-hypnotic technique called neuro-linguistic programming (which instructs its would-be practitioners to "seed" conversation with subtly hidden commands that will act on the subconscious of the recipient), were crudely written and full of sarcasm, resentment, and rage. They were distinguished by the typographical quirkiness, tonal crudeness, and brash salesmanship common to the work of autodidactic experts. In their desperate insistence and at least partial honesty, they are also strangely touching.

"There's no such '*thing*' as love. There's no such '*thing*' as passion. There's no such *'thing'* as attraction, or chemistry, or lust," Jeffries wrote in one of his early manuals.

> I know, I know, you're saying. That's the problem . . . for most of you, most of the time, there's no such thing. There's just boredom, frustration, and playing with Mr. Winky. But that's not what I'm talking about, so pay close attention.
>
> I'm not saying that people don't experience *states* of 'attraction' or 'chemistry' or 'lust'. What I am saying is that these states are processes that take place inside the human mind and body. Which means that they are states that . . .
>
> *CAN BE SUMMONED FORTH AND DIRECTED AT WILL!!!*

NEIL STRAUSS LEARNED about this community just as it was beginning to make its transition from being the obsession of a few isolated weirdos to a flourishing commercial venture for many weirdos. He was handed a copy of one of the first "Layguides" and ventured onto the message boards as a reporter researching a story. It didn't take long for him to lose his reportorial detachment. Soon he was stuffing $500 cash into an envelope addressed to Mystery, a legendary figure on the message boards who had coined many of the terms in the PUA lexicon. Strauss overcomes the reader's skepticism with the same élan with which he learned to "blast last-minute resistance," conceding, with disarming candor, that it is "no easy feat to sign up for a workshop dedicated to picking up women. To do so is to acknowledge defeat, inferiority and inadequacy. It is to finally admit to yourself that after all these years of being sexually active (or at least sexually cognizant) you have not grown up and figured it out."

By the time Strauss arrived on the scene, the pickup artists had already begun to clean up their act. The documents they wrote were becoming more professional in their style and presentation, the theoretical framework had grown more sophisticated. The experts had begun to scrub away the resentment and raw misogyny adhering to the community's rhetoric. Accordingly, a new kind of student entered the scene: good-looking, successful, and competent men who were looking to make their sex lives less like gambling and more like shopping. These men had other aspects of their lives working; now they wanted to "solve" the woman problem.

Strauss was present at the first seminar, run by Mystery, at which students actually left the classroom to go "in field." Mystery began by explaining the basic structure of seduction—FMAC, for find, meet, attract, and close. He explained the power of the mysterious "neg," one of the great innovations of the seduction community. Strauss describes it thus:

> Neither compliment nor insult, a neg is something in between—an accidental insult or backhanded compliment. The purpose of the neg is to lower a woman's self-esteem while actively displaying a lack of interest in her—by telling her she has lipstick on her teeth, for example, or offering her a piece of gum after she speaks.

"I don't alienate ugly girls," Mystery explains. "I don't alienate guys. I only alienate the girls I want to fuck."

It was 2002. Armies of outlandishly dressed men (done up in accordance with "peacock theory") began appearing in bars around the country. "Did you see those two girls fighting outside?" they would ask their targets, delivering the same canned material time and time again. They would come in with their bodies at an angle and give the appearance of being ready to leave at any moment. "I can't stay long—I've got to get back to my friends," they would say, delivering the "false time constraint" that preempts any social discomfort their entrance into the "set" would generate. With their first entrance, they'd "buy the next thirty seconds," and with the story they told, they'd buy the next two minutes, while "demonstrating higher value" through precisely calibrated routines. "I need a quick female opinion on something," they'd begin, and then launch into a story. "Would you let your boyfriend keep a box of photos of his ex-girlfriend? Because my buddy . . ." They'd talk to the "obstacles" (the ugly girls surrounding the target) and the men in the set, conspicuously ignoring the target. When she began to clamor for their attention, they'd throw out a neg. "I like your nails. Are they real?" Strauss carried around, in his seduction kit, a large ball of lint that he would pick off a girl's sweater. (Strauss eventually received historical confirmation of the value of the neg when he learned that Warren Beatty would blow his nose and hand the crumpled tissue to a woman.) Then the men would reverse course, give the target an opportunity to demonstrate her higher value, and play push-pull, like dancing a string around for a cat to chase. Once you have reached the "hook point," when she stops wondering when you're going to leave and begins looking for ways to make you stay, then it's time to propose an "instant date"—"bounce" to another club, party, or diner, to embed the impression of familiarity. "Every location that you move with her in which she doesn't wind up raped and murdered by you," Mystery observes, "builds comfort." And when it comes down to last-minute resistance—which is a perfectly natural feature of her primal cognitive programming—she'll ask herself "Do I know this guy?" and have a panorama of images of you in different settings to refer to.

With the rise of "in field" training on the Mystery model, the emphasis on esoteric techniques for controlling the behavior of women fell away. The new pickup artist was fun and positive. He had empathy with a woman's feminine needs, and was willing to remake himself into the kind of man able to fulfill those needs. Not the things she says she wants, or even the things she thinks she wants, in accordance with the cant espoused by our Rousseauist-egalitarian upbringing, but the primal needs designed into her neural circuitry forty thousand years ago, when people developed their social instincts while living, as Mystery puts it, "in a fifty-person society" with an alpha male at its head.

Evolutionary psychology and computer science, combined with behavioral economics' study of the systematic irrationality that is intrinsic to human cognition—that is to say, machine engineering combined with those growth areas in social scientific research that elaborate the materialistic, calculating, and hedonistic view of human nature that dominates "ideas" in the mainstream—all contributed to the pickup artist's vocabulary. "We backwards engineer the way the brain works, to figure out why she does what she does," says Mystery, who was living with his parents in Toronto and trying to make it as a magician while becoming known as the most eloquent of the message board experts. According to Mystery, we are all "biological machines" programmed to do just two things: survive and replicate. And we go through life looking to align with people who will increase our likelihood to survive and replicate.

By offering a method and a pseudoscientific rhetoric to accompany it, the pickup artists offered hope to men who had lost hope. By giving students canned material to repeat, they overcame the single most intense social anxiety of any man in a club—that he will have nothing to say. By encouraging the men to see the activity of approaching women "as a video game," they provided emotional prophylaxis to men who were terrified of rejection. By assuming an authoritative role as paid experts, the lead pickup artists were able to tell men things they needed to hear: Lose the sweater. Shave your head. Get contacts. Get a tan. By introducing their students to the concept of sub-communication—body language, vocal intonation, and rhythm—they equipped them to begin the most important self-reappraisal they would ever do. The most valuable things the pickup artists told men were things that others had told them before, but that no one had ever directly linked to sex. Things like, for instance—"Smile." "Don't be the guy trying to look all serious and deep," the pickup artist Lovedrop told his students, with a wicked impression of a brooding face perched over a beer at a party. *"Mr. Serious Deep Guy."*

MYSTERY TAUGHT EIGHT MEN the rudiments of his art in the VH1 reality television series *The Pickup Artist*. It was a spectacle that managed to make Mystery's ruthlessly Darwinian method into the basis of heartwarming television. It was an exemplary product of our culture industries, on the cutting edge of the drive to combine uplift, self-help, and sociopathy into an appealing entertainment package.

The men were introduced—ordinary, slightly nerdy men—already "in field," failing to meet women at a bar. At the end of the night, they returned home without a single phone number in their pockets. Then Mystery appeared. "Who you are today," he said—slowly, clearly enunciating, maintaining eye contact with his audience, dramatically pausing—"dies here."

And we saw, right away, who his students were: a 43-year-old virgin, a fat guy, an Indian guy, an Asian guy, two computer nerds, and, a bit incongruously, a buff, good-looking Hispanic guy who was also a boxer. With the exception of this last, they were the sort of people who appear in the media only as comic figures. They remained so here—they could not sustain any other role—but there was no derision in the feelings they evoked; they were the protagonists on a quest for their manhood, and we watched them grow and change. They had been carefully vetted—they were awkward, they were abashed by their predicament, but not a single note of resentment toward women escaped them. One of the first rules that a pickup artist learns is that it's never her fault. "She's not a bitch," as Mystery put it. "She's just being a bitch to you." Because a beautiful woman, you see, has been hit on thousands of times in her life, and she has developed strategies for screening out the "bucketful of bore" that men want to impose on her. "Hi. My name's Charlie. What do you do?"

And thus the principle, "It's never her fault. It's always yours," reinforced the assumption that the game, properly played, could never fail. If at any point she shrugged you off, it was because you failed to do something essential in an earlier stage of seduction. This was, at one and the same time, a way of overcoming the ugly resentment that afflicts some AFCs, the ultimate form of self-protection, and, of course, a descent into total solipsism. Early on in *The Game*, after Strauss had his first "fool's mate" (the term for scoring with a woman just as eager as you to get laid on a given night, who does not require any game) and after he had "number-closed" a woman in a video store who turned out to be Dalene Kurtis, the Playmate of the Year (he's too frightened to call), he begins to notice it:

> It was then that I realized the downside to this whole venture. A gulf was opening between men and women in my mind. I was beginning to see women solely as measuring instruments to give me feedback on how I was progressing as a pickup artist. They were my crash-test dummies, identifiable only by hair colors and numbers—a blonde 7, a brunette 10. Even when I was having a deep conversation, learning a woman's dreams and point of view, in my mind I was just ticking off a box in my routine marked rapport. In bonding with men, I was developing an unhealthy attitude toward the opposite sex. And the most troubling thing about this new mind-set was that it seemed to be making me more successful with women.

BUT THIS OBVIOUS OBJECTION came later in the progression through the Game than any of the AFCs on the first few episodes of *The Pickup Artist* had yet reached. They had baby fat, they had smooth skin, they hadn't done a day of honest labor in their lives. They possessed that wide-eyed look—at once mentally slack, physically languid, and emotionally frightened—that you find when you meet those cosseted children of American suburbia who have remained mired in that shapeless setting. The Asian guy, when asked what sort of man he would like to be, responded, without missing a beat, "James Bond." The viewer cringed, a little, and squirmed, a little—a painful little ecstasy. Later on the fat guy, who managed to last until the later episodes, broke down in tears of appreciation, not just of his new skills, but of the new male friends he'd made. We learned that in real life he lived in his parents' basement, that there wasn't a door on his room. We learned that his only friends were friends he had made playing World of Warcraft. When, on a show that used his pain as a diversion from the emptiness of the lives of bored gawkers, whose diverted, emptied consciousness VH1 in turn sold to advertisers, he told his housemates that they were the coolest guys he had ever met, and the best friends he had ever known, with his face reddening and his eyes brimming over with tears, we knew that he meant it. This was good TV.

It was also a series-length infomercial. On the show, we watched pickup artistry slough off its vestiges of Ross Jeffries–style cynicism and pick up a new kind of cynicism: that of professional self-help. Mystery went from a dark seducer to a figure oozing that commercially factitious "caring" of our major corporations. These were some of the most helpless and emotionally immiserated men in America—and while it was true that Mystery had gotten rich off them, maybe he had done more for them than most therapists could. Admittedly, it was the two handsome guys who were there in the end, the handsome blonde guy who made out with a stripper in the backseat of a limo, and the handsome and gregarious Hispanic guy who was ultimately selected by Mystery to complete his training as a master pickup artist. And, admittedly, the first guy off the show was the sweet Asian guy (as I predicted), and the second guy off the show was the 43-year-old virgin.

THE PICKUP ARTISTS were once good cinema because they were far outside the mainstream of American life and mores. The pickup artists became good television by embedding their practice within a familiar rhetoric of change and growth. In December 2007, Neil Strauss released a sequel, *Rules of the Game*—a slender, two-volume guidebook that promised to help its readers "master the Game in thirty days." In fact the book does not attempt to come close to delivering on that claim. A true PUA defines mastery according to Mystery's immortal formula: "five for five." That is—the true master has the skills to walk into a party, open five sets, and turn them into five girlfriends. The reader of *Rules of the Game* aims to get one date in thirty days. It is pitched at the most benighted of way-below-average frustrated chumps, consisting of bite-size assignments to complete each day (first assignment: say hello to a single stranger), interspersed with nuggets of wisdom fished from self-improvement books. The devious "neg" appears now as the more benign "disqualification." The wicked gleam in the eye of a man putting one over on the world has been carefully suppressed. A new earnestness brings the whole enterprise closer to the mainstream than it has ever been before.

The book's chastened tone makes this sequel feel like an act of expiation. "I didn't want to write this book," Strauss writes in the very first line. "I am as embarrassed to write this as you may be to pick it up." Strauss presents the book as his gift to the world. "Even though I had no such intentions when I wrote *The Game*, I started doing a few things in my spare time to help the many guys who reached out to me after its publications with emails, calls, and letters full of heart-wrenching stories. I coached frustrated teenagers, thirty-year-old virgins, recently divorced businessmen, even rock stars and billionaires." He observes that women have entire industries "to help cope with the challenges that come with being a woman in the world." He contrasts this to the cultural landscape of men. "Everywhere they turn, men are shown images of women they are supposed to desire. Yet there is little advice of substance available to help them learn to attract these women, to figure out who they are, to help them improve their lifestyle and social skills."

As pickup artistry became a business and changed the face it showed to the world, it lost the utopian, collaborative dimension of its earlier internet days, when men produced knowledge together for free. Now Mystery competes for the dollars of men who pay up to $5,000 for a weekend spent in field. The website TheMysteryMethod.com is no longer affiliated with Mystery the man, who is suing and being sued by its current owners. Even while his show makes him the most visible face of the pickup-artist world, as Strauss is its best known scribe, rivals and challengers in seduction lairs around the internet announce technical breakthroughs in the science of pickup that claim to put Mystery's primitive techniques to shame.

BUT WE SHOULD HAVE KNOWN where it was heading all along. About two-thirds of the way into *The Game*, Strauss is dating ten women at once. "They were what PUAs call MLTRs—multiple long-term relationships. Unlike AFCs, I never lied to these girls. They all knew I was seeing other people. And, to my surprise, even if it didn't make all of them happy, none of them left me." Strauss had become what Freud called the primal father, though on the free market model—he didn't mind if his women were having other relationships too, just as long as they responded when he called, and as long as he didn't owe them anything, by way of protection or otherwise, beyond offering enough value to keep them around in exchange for the value they offered him. It was a rational, realistic arrangement that everyone went into with eyes open, assented to voluntarily, was free to back out of at any time. Not backing out meant implicit consent, and implicit consent meant they remained because they calculated that they were better off by remaining. Everybody wins, right?

Early on, we watched as Strauss transformed himself into the man he has since become. He studied hypnotism, voice training, the Alexander Technique, and the secrets of a sexual shaman named Steve P., who gave him a method of stacking orgasms to make any woman squirt. Once he mastered the Game, this lovable loser who used to constantly find himself in LJBF ("Let's just be friends") Land could walk into every encounter in a bar with an HB (Hot Babe) *knowing* that he would be able to "kiss-close" her within half an hour.

By this time, Strauss was living with Mystery and a handful of other PUAs in Dean Martin's old mansion in the Hollywood Hills, a headquarters they named, in a reference to *Fight Club*, Project Hollywood. Men flew in from around the world to take classes with them. Soon Strauss would successfully run Game on Britney Spears. Courtney Love moved into the house. Strauss was about to stumble across a more or less foolproof technique for getting women to engage in a threesome.

And yet the whole endeavor had already begun its descent into hell. Strauss opens the book with a scene in which he drives a suicidal Mystery to a psychological clinic. Throughout the book he builds a portrait of a profoundly damaged person with "a gaping hole in his soul." Mystery's goal in the Game was "a blonde 10 and an Asian 10, who will love each other as much as they love me." His goal in life was "for people to be envious of me, for women to want me and men to want to be me."

"'You never got much love as a child, did you?' [Strauss] asked him.

'No,' he replied sheepishly."

They were living with two other pickup artists known by the handles Papa—a rich Asian boy—and Tyler Durden—the name of the new identity hallucinated into life by *Fight Club*'s psychotic narrator. Papa's immediate claim to fame was number-closing Paris Hilton at a taco stand (she never did come to a party at the mansion), but his obsession was building up the pickup school business he was running with Tyler. Leading and profiting off men, rather than meeting women, becomes their dream. Tyler and Papa represented a new breed of pickup artist—preternaturally obsessed with observing and modeling the best PUAs, incapable of talking about anything else. These younger PUAs came to the Game before they developed autonomous personalities. They were nothing more than the sum of their programming.

Strauss began to see that the Game had turned many of these men into what he calls "social robots." He produced a long post for the online group discussion board called, "Are You a Social Robot?"; the answer for most of them was clearly yes. And from there on out, Strauss started to tally up all the costs the PUAs had absorbed in exchange for their conquests, and the costs they imposed on others.

So while the first half of the book induces an irresistible high as we watch Strauss's brazen ascent, the second half of the book is a long, painful withdrawal from the inflated hopes placed on a handful of rather threadbare routines. Cruelty enters Strauss's behavior. Misogyny insinuates its way into the others'. They manipulate people and then despise them for their susceptibility.

Given an opportunity to fuck a coked-up porn star in a bathroom, Strauss can't get it up.

THE GAME SAYS, LET WHOEVER can attain transcendence attain it, whoever wants to pine for it, pine for it. As for us pickup artists, we serve the world as it is. We give it what it wants, and what it would ask for, if only it could bear the reality of its own desires.

The attitude of these men followed a sorrowful trajectory—from resentment toward women for their intractability to contempt for the same women upon their capitulation—though along the way, there were all the excitements that come with mastering a skill, as well as the incidental sexual gratification that one encounters in one's homosocial quest for self-empowerment. The men gleefully pursued an antinomian goal, and grew powerful because of their disregard for limits that other less desperate and disenchanted men still obeyed—the illusions that give love whatever meaning it still sustains in a world that has systematically converted every transcendent value into a mere advertising slogan, except for the one illusion whose sanctity we cannot yet extinguish, advertising slogan though it may be—that two souls might meet and assuage each other's loneliness.

The players of the Game made explicit the workings of a new sexual economy, one that was always implicit in the old, but was mediated by illusions that, it turns out, did more than merely obscure. We had disaggregated community, love, sex, and the family to allow a new protocol of maximum efficiency to establish itself. The Game players applied the logic of bourgeois productivity to slash open the myth of bourgeois romance. The mystery of romance yielded all its secrets to a method, ruthlessly deployed, which set its practitioners free from a fate that was never going to include them in its hoped-for happy endings anyway. Without explicitly criticizing it, they disclosed with unusual clarity the nature of the larger game we all play: one in which each player gives what he must and takes what he can. In this ordinary game, you judge your own value dispassionately, and cultivate the art of presenting it in the best light. Inasmuch as the purpose of the Game was to recalibrate a man's own programming to make him a better kind of biological machine, it was also a form of self-discovery, because every step along the way brought a new discovery of how much his own programming, and the world's, already consisted of self-maximizing behaviors that he simply hadn't mastered properly: You neither offer nor expect loyalty; in place of this premodern virtue, you offer honesty, transparency, and efficiency. If you find a better deal, you are free to go. If both members of a pair rationally calculate that they aren't likely to do better on the open marketplace than they are with each other, they commit, though they know that commitments are always reversible. They may search for stable foundations, but they should preserve flexibility for the day—its arrival is inevitable—when conditions change.

And so our individual quest to render ourselves invulnerable to the storms of fortune makes universal vulnerability the rule from which none of us can opt out. Inequality is built into the structure of this game, as nature assigns its endowments, and fortune doles out favorable circumstances in an unequal way. So the woman who does not have it all will not get it all: maybe she talks a little too loudly; maybe she weighs a little too much; and the man she wants will take what she offers without giving her what she seeks in return, and will not feel obliged to. So the man who has it all will get it all, and the man who has none will get none, and they all will be grateful for the little they get, or grow sickened on the excess of all they can have, or consume themselves with bitterness knowing they are stuck with nothing, and be given commercial substitutes for what they cannot get on their own—pornography that traffics in revenge fantasies, online dating sites that reinforce the world's hierarchies.

The Game exposed that system by taking it apart piece by piece and showing us how it worked. But it also shored it up. It told us that through dogged effort and the application of science, anyone could transform himself from pauper to prince. Helena Rubinstein, the cosmetics magnate, once said that there were no ugly women, only lazy ones. The promise of magical self-transformation offered by the marketplace is at the same time a pitiless injunction suggesting that women born without the favor of beauty deserve the neglect they experience from the opposite sex. And what good does our pity do them anyway, if pity alone is all we are willing to give to them? Better to give them the knowledge and techniques they need to remake themselves as the world will have them. Once informed, the responsibility for continued failure to rise above genetic inheritance is theirs alone. So too, now, for the men who didn't acquire Game.

Strauss's dark cautionary tale has a happy ending. The contrast is as glaring as in one of those Hollywood endings from the 1950s, the kind that spiteful directors would tack on at the behest of the studios, deliberately playing up the mechanical artifice to expose its falsity. In Strauss's case, however, you feel that he is personally invested. He wants to tell us that after extending his capability to such inhuman lengths by such inhuman means, he's still human after all; he's preserved that fragile part of himself that in the social robots has gone callous and cold. He wants us to know—and he wants himself to believe, you feel—that he's still capable of love. And so, he finally meets a woman who is impervious to the tactics of the Game. She is beautiful, she is smart, she is unflappable, and she can't be manipulated. "Lisa was neg-proof. Next to her, other girls seemed like incomplete human beings." And so on. She becomes his case of "one-itis"—and though he does go on the sex rampage that is the preferred PUA cure for the syndrome, he can't get her out of his mind. We are meant to diagnose this not as thwarted ego, or the Gamer Gamed, but as the stirrings of true love. When they finally fuck, he stays hard for four or five sessions in a row, and without the aid of Viagra. This must be the real thing.

At the end of the book, Strauss turns his back on the Game. It's a nice ending, but just because you leave the practice of the Game, you don't escape the world for which it is a useful guide. A year later, Wikipedia reports, Strauss's one true love left him for the British pop star Robbie Williams.

—Wesley Yang

SWEDISH DETECTIVES

Åke Edwardson. *Frozen Tracks.* Viking Adult. August 2007. (2001.)
Kjell Eriksson. *The Demon of Dakar.* St. Martin's Minotaur. February 2008. (2005.)
Helene Tursten. *The Torso.* Soho Crime. April 2007. (2000.)

THE DETECTIVE PLOT, LIKE THE MARRIAGE plot to which it bears so many resemblances, is a conservative structure: beginning with antisocial confusion, it moves through a process of discovery and self-knowledge to reach recognition and, finally, arrive at social re-order. So it's not surprising that the golden ages of detective plots in whatever medium have all come during periods of turmoil, when the rule of law was a soothing fantasy: 1930s Britain, 1970s America, and, most recently, Sweden in the 1990s and early 2000s.

In this last period, an economic downturn brought into sharp relief the effects of fifty years of Europe's most liberal immigration policy. Sweden spent the postwar years proving its "moral superpower" status (and expiating the guilt from its collusion with Germany during the war) by accepting all kinds of oppressed people, from Ugandan Asians exiled by Idi Amin to Chileans fleeing after the coup against Allende. Unlike in the rest of Europe, where migrants from poorer countries came for a bit to work, and then, generally, left, these refugees entered Sweden and stayed. Without resources or connections, frequently the traumatized victims of war and torture, rarely familiar with Swedish (unlike people from the former French or British colonies who migrated to countries that spoke their language of education), they were in a much different situation from the guest workers on the continent.

They found themselves in a country that viewed itself to an astonishing degree as a racially discrete unit. It was a country that had a functioning, government-approved eugenics program, based at the Institute for Race Biology at Uppsala University, from the 1920s until 1975. Official Swedish policy was to integrate rather than to assimilate the ethnically foreign refugees; a sensitive approach, perhaps, but one with the unfortunate side effect of creating ethnic enclaves in the affordable-housing projects that ringed Sweden's major cities. And when that first round of unassimilated migrants started having children, and those children grew up speaking fluent Swedish and being in all respects Swedish except for their race and their poverty and cultural disenfranchisement, it created confusion for ethnic Swedes. Allan Pred's 2000 book on Swedish racism, *Even in Sweden*, quotes the center-right paper *Svenska Dagbladet*, editorializing in 1993: "The Swedish people no longer recognize their country. Sweden's ethnic identity has been changed, and another Sweden, consisting of a growing underclass and a cultural and economic proletariat with different skin and hair color, is in the process of developing." Even now, it's possible to walk around downtown Stockholm for days without spotting any people who deviate from the Scandinavian norm, although 13 percent of Swedes are foreign born.

Throughout the 1980s and into the 1990s, first the Iran-Iraq war and then the breakup of the Soviet Union produced unprecedented numbers of refugees, and this—alongside a major recession that led to a 10 percent rise in unemployment—put unprecedented pressure on the welfare state (or *Folkhemmet*, "the People's Home," as it's called). Violent crime rose precipitously over this period, causing many Swedes to doubt the foundations of the society they had believed in so strongly for so much of the 20th century. And this became particularly true after the assassination of Prime Minister Olaf Palme in 1986—a crime that remains unsolved.

Nineteen ninety-one was the crucial year, both for Swedish immigration policy and for the birth of the modern Swedish detective novel. In September, a center-right coalition led by Carl Bildt's Moderate Party, running in part on greater restrictions for refugees, ended a Social Democrat reign that had persisted with only one interruption since 1932. In the same election, a right-wing party founded just six months before, the New Democrats, won almost 7 percent of the national vote on an anti-immigration platform. Meanwhile, over the course of six months starting that August, a neo-Nazi named John Ausonius, known as the Laser Man, shot eleven dark-skinned immigrants with a laser-sighted rifle and a revolver, killing one. The son of German and Swiss immigrants who changed his name and dyed his dark hair blond to seem more Swedish, Ausonius became a symbol of the sick racist id of Swedish society. The government's response to the killings struck many as maladroit, exemplified by the unfortunate attempt by the culture minister, Birgit Friggebo, to force an angry, frightened group of immigrants at a press conference to sing "We Shall Overcome."

It was in 1991 also that Henning Mankell published his first Kurt Wallander novel, *Faceless Killers*. An old couple is brutally slaughtered, and the wife dies with one word on her lips: "foreign." The police detective on the case, Wallander, is a grumpy, volatile middle-aged man coping with his own demons—an estranged wife and daughter, an eccentric aging father, and soft-core fantasies of anonymous sex with black women. He tries to keep the victim's last words a secret, afraid of fueling conflict between the Skanian natives (he lives in the southern town of Ystad, close to the ports through which most refugees enter) and a local refugee camp. But word leaks out, and nativist groups begin placing harassing calls to the police station, finally setting off a bomb in the camp and shooting a Somali refugee.

Yet it is the Swedish welfare state rather than Swedish racism that is the villain of *Faceless Killers*. Toward the end of the book, Wallander ruminates about the new violence of Swedish culture and how the welfare state fails to protect its own citizens: "How long would the principle of the generous refugee policy be able to hold without leading to chaos? Was there any upward limit?" The Swedish couple's murderer does turn out to be a foreigner, though not a racial outsider: he's a Czech who convinces immigration officials that he's a Gypsy, a persecuted minority, to gain refugee status. Sweden's open-door policy, then, carries the responsibility for the first two deaths—and its tendency to cluster refugees in port-city camps while they await reassignment is implicitly given some responsibility for the third.

CRITIQUES OF THE WELFARE STATE have held a place of honor in Swedish literary fiction since the 1960s. Jan Myrdal's 1968 *Confessions of a Disloyal European*, a meandering journey through the author's many sexual experiences that closes with a denunciation of the modern European intelligentsia as the "whores of reason," marks a watershed because Myrdal's parents, Gunnar and Alva Myrdal, were also essentially the parents of the Swedish welfare state. Both Nobel Prize winners (Alva in 1982, Gunnar sharing it with his rival Friedrich Hayek in 1974), the Myrdals represented the best and worst of the welfare state at its birth. They were humane scholars, Alva of social welfare and Gunnar of social economics. (Gunnar was the author of the 1944 study *An American Dilemma: The Negro Problem and Modern Democracy*, a major source for the 1954 *Brown v. Board of Education* Supreme Court decision.) At the same time, husband and wife both considered themselves Malthusians and argued for the sterilization of the "mentally deficient."

Jan's very public split from his parents (played out in the pages of several excoriating childhood memoirs as well as *Confessions*) augured the beginning of a generalized if subdued revolt against the *Folkhemmet* politics of the past generation. The welfare state was now figured as Kafkaesque, a mind-numbingly impersonal machine, bankrupt in its promises of humanity and justice. P. C. Jersild's "bureaucracy" novels are typical of this period. In *House of Babel*, published in 1978, he satirizes the dehumanizing inefficiencies of a massive Stockholm hospital, calling it a medical "cathedral . . . meant to lull people into faith and security."

More recently, a boom in first- and second-generation immigrant fiction has taken place in Sweden, just as in Britain and the US. But much literary writing by native Swedes has become locked in a sterile postmodernism that doesn't concern itself very closely with

The Kitchen Club
open 7 days a week
for lunch and dinner
30 Prince Street 212-274-0025

politics. For the majority of Swedes—and the vast majority of non-Swedes—questions of race and immigration over the last fifteen years have largely been left up to writers of detective novels.

OF THE MORE RECENT major Swedish crime novelists to have benefited from Mankell's success by having their books translated into English, three of them—Helene Tursten, Åke Edwardson, and Kjell Eriksson—are intimately concerned with the same political problems as Mankell and, very generally, share his sense of crime as a social problem, not an individual one. Another, Håkan Nesser, sets his novels in a fictional but vaguely Dutch-sounding nation where immigrant-related crime is just something to occasionally boast about having suppressed; perhaps as a result, he is frequently compared to Georges Simenon rather than Mankell—unlike the first three, who are forced to put Mankell's name on their every book jacket.

Still Tursten, Edwardson, and Eriksson, for all they owe to Mankell, seem different from him—more optimistic. No one ever wonders, as Wallander does at the end of 1997's *One Step Behind*, "if a complete collapse of the Swedish state was a real possibility." Instead, they probe the same issues but pull back from Wallander's gloom; perhaps they put their faith in a bright Communist future, as Eriksson seems to, or they think, as Tursten's heroine, Detective Inspector Irene Huss, does in her first novel, "You become jaded and cynical in this profession . . . But she didn't want to become either jaded or cynical! You had to go on, keep moving forward. You couldn't stop and dig yourself a hole."

It's true that Sweden has stabilized, in many ways, since the traumas of the mid-'90s. The main result of the recession was that the Social Democrats—voted back into power in 1994—embraced neoliberalism, backing off somewhat on social welfare and tightening the borders. But there is still plenty of material for writers of noirish *policiers*. Although some restrictions (not all of them entirely abided by) have been placed on the influx of immigrants, Sweden has continued to handle large numbers of refugees from former Yugoslavian countries, while the numbers of Middle Eastern and North African immigrants have also been on the rise. Like France, Sweden has struggled to uphold its much-vaunted reputation for tolerance and liberalism over the basic xenophobia that exists on an everyday level; at the same time, while Sweden hasn't been prone to the level of violence among its Muslim youth that Britain and continental Europe have, many Swedes feel it's just a matter of time, and radical Islamic groups have been tracked in the prisons and some mosques.

The police force has changed too. It's not surprising that a large number of the new fictional detectives are women (including Wallander's daughter Linda in Mankell's most recent books), given that the Swedish police force is now one-third female and Stockholm has had a woman police commissioner since 2003. The new detectives tend to be more modern in their living arrangements, too—instead of grumpy divorced middle-aged men, they are single women, unmarried couples, parents of out-of-wedlock children, and so forth. They use DNA testing and new computer systems; they argue about September 11 and the Iraq war.

And the crimes are different. Despite the new specter of Islamic violence in European society, the events tend to be isolated, based on personal rather than antisocial rage. The scope of the novels is smaller, less international; the newer novelists often focus on a single family and its conflicts. Racial problems in these novels tend to be personalized, and peripheral to the plot: a detective struggles with his or her own prejudices or an interracial couple jokes about having a black Saint Lucia; '90s-style political correctness is mocked or defended; suspects are automatically tagged as foreign or "as Swedish as they come."

IN HELENE TURSTEN'S NOVELS, Irene Huss is about as far from the grim, stolid Wallander as it gets. She is sparkly, athletic (a national champion at judo), and charming in a slightly ditzy, Nancy Drew–ish way. Unlike the perennially lonesome (and poorly fed) Wallander, Huss is happily married to a chef who works part time so he can take care of their twin daughters while Huss races about solving crimes.

In Tursten's first novel, *Detective Inspector Huss,* Huss is working to catch the murderer of a wealthy financier, Richard von Knecht, pushed from a balcony just as his estranged weakling son Henrik and his manic wife Sylvia pull up to the building in their Mercedes. Soon after, von Knecht's office buildings explode, and Irene Huss gets drawn into a nest of Swedish Hell's Angels and the complicated dynamics of the warped von Knecht family. The Angels' actual connection to the crime remains fairly obscure, but they do provide a fantastic scene in which Huss, beaten senseless, tied up, and urinated on by the bikers, still musters the strength—she's a former handball goalie—to chuck a grenade back out the window of the shack where she and a colleague have been left to die.

Now if this were a Mankell murder, it would have turned out that von Knecht was selling drugs to Latvian crime lords, or funding a white supremacist movement in an African country; instead, after many arcane twists and turns, it turns out to have been Knecht's foxy daughter-in-law—and lover—who kicked him off the balcony because he dumped her when she became pregnant with his child: in other words, it was a strictly family affair. But Huss's own family affairs serve as a counter-arc that gives the novel its political framework. *Detective Inspector Huss i*ncludes one of the only sequences in the major Swedish detective novels to explore the motivations of young neo-Nazis. Huss's daughter Jenny comes home one day with a shaved head: she's fallen in love with a white supremacist. Huss tells her fellow detective Tommy Persson what's happened, and he launches into a Wallanderesque speech against a formally generous but emotionally alienating social-democratic system: "How do you think these young criminal immigrants are supposed to have any feeling of solidarity with Swedish society?" he asks. "They're consistently locked out of everything! . . . Our kids don't feel any sense of belonging in Swedish society either; they just cling to ready-made, cheap solutions."

It's another example of the Swedish degeneration argument—less focused in its accusations than Wallander's, but with a similar denunciation of the social forces that misshape individuals. Still, it's resolved: Tommy has a man-to-man talk with Jenny, in which he reveals that he's the son of a Holocaust survivor; then Jenny's neo-Nazi dumps her for another girl and she decides she's not a skinhead anymore; and the family gathers together to watch *Schindler's List.*

The whole Huss series is larded with this sort of well-meaning, politically correct, *Sesame Street*–level sensitivity training. In *The Torso,* the Swedish police discover the eponymous dismembered part washed up on a beach (quite misleadingly, the cover illustration shows an attractive, naked, fully membered female torso—*caveat lecher!*). At the same time, Irene is asked to help track down a former neighbor's daughter, who may be working as a prostitute in Copenhagen—which happens, coincidentally, to be the location of a store whose sign matches a mysterious "Asian" tattoo on the torso's skin. The store, a gay sex shop run by a Japanese former sumo wrestler, at first appalls Huss (who had, one thought, learned that gay people were Just Like Us when she befriended Richard van Knecht's illegitimate son, a gay man dying of AIDS, in the first novel). "No!" she exclaims, when her Copenhagen host tries to calm her down, saying the sex toys are "just for fun." "It cannot be fun to have that huge rubber dick shoved in! It must hurt terribly!" However, when she meets Tom Tanaka, the former sumo wrestler ("To Irene's relief, he was not wearing the diaperlike pants in which sumo wrestlers compete") and current sex shop owner, she is impressed by his kindness, and they talk about martial arts together.

The murderer in *The Torso* turns out to be a member of Irene's own team, a gay autopsy technician with necrophiliac tendencies who chops up his victims while videotaping them and then paints their disembodied heads. But before Huss can apprehend him, Tom Tanaka, described by a witness as "a huge and amazingly fat Chinese man," gets there first, killing the killer in revenge for the death of his lover. Tursten bends over backward to avoid equating necrophilia with homosexuality; nonetheless, all the dangerous characters in *The Torso* are gay or Asian, or both.

You may think it possible that I'm demanding too much of poor Helene Tursten, who is after all a writer of popular genre fiction and not, say, Jürgen Habermas. But the experience of reading the much more sophisticated authors coming out of Sweden at the moment renders that objection moot. The best of the bunch on a technical level is easily Åke Edwardson, who frequently betters Mankell as a writer and constructor of plots, if not in the psychological complexity of his detective, Erik Winter, who is dashing and clever but lacks the comfortingly real bulk of old Wallander. Edwardson's crimes are often committed by characters who have been around, unsuspected, since the beginning.

In 2001's *Frozen Tracks*, a series of attacks have been made on Gothenburg's college students with a weapon that may or may not be a branding iron. While the police are still scrounging around fruitlessly for the culprit, toddlers are being abducted, but just as quickly returned, by a man with a toy parrot in his car. As the brutal student attacks taper off, the child snatcher becomes more brazen and more violent. The earlier two Edwardson novels, *Sun and Shadow* and *Never End*, revolved around crimes against the family—specifically Winter's family (his girlfriend, Angela, gets abducted toward the end of her pregnancy in *Sun and Shadow*), but also families in general. And *Frozen Tracks* culminates this pattern. Not only are the preschool victims the age of Winter's daughter, Elsa (and evidence is eventually found that she was a target), but the two sets of crimes are linked to an original sin, the abuse of a foster child forty years before. Family dramas proliferate at varying levels of perversion, including allegations of child abuse against Winter's closest friend on the force, and Winter's own anxieties about fatherhood and his relationship with Angela, whom he has not yet married.

The family in Edwardson's novels sometimes takes on the role that the welfare state has in Mankell's: unstable, vulnerable, capable of producing horrific offspring. Following

the resolution of *Never End*, for example, a novel about a series of rapes that ends up being linked to a victim's father, a policeman remarks to Winter that "There are a lot of villains in this story." Winter replies: "And victims. . . . Most of them are victims." The quote recalls Mankell's notion of collective societal blame for the murders in *Faceless Killers*, although Winter's problem isn't with the "nanny" state, but with actual families. Since the Winter novels also describe happy families, particularly Winter's own, there's some sense (absent in Mankell) that other models are possible; that bad blood can be bred out, that a collective unit can produce good results as well as evil ones.

CONSERVATISM IN DETECTIVE plots works on two levels: the structural movement from anarchy to unity, and the related, more literal movement from individual power (the criminal) to collective state power (the law). When the state and the detective are in conflict, the intellectual triumph of the latter (Sherlock Holmes running circles around Scotland Yard) supposedly represents the victory of the individual. But even then, the detective himself just becomes the emblem of a smarter kind of order: he is saving the state from itself, but he is still a tool by which the state consolidates its power.

In the Swedish novels, the old opposition shifts: instead of private investigator versus bumbling police force, it is police detectives versus bumbling state, with its unrealistic approaches to law enforcement and immigration. At the same time, the police detectives do work for the police, and their victories over the criminals they track represent a victory for the state.

Novelists like Mankell, Tursten, and Edwardson, whose politics are fairly moderate—at least on the Swedish spectrum; in the US they'd be raving in *Z Magazine*—can use their detectives as vehicles for critiquing the state and society and then turn around and rescue that state without much sense of contradiction. With Kjell Eriksson, however, the compunction to rescue Social Democrats from themselves becomes weaker. A member of the Swedish Communist Party, Eriksson is politically the most radical Swedish crime novelist since the team of Maj Sjöwall and Per Wahlöö, who had a detective say in *The Laughing Policeman* (1970) that "the police are a necessary evil." Eriksson occasionally subtracts that "necessary." Feeling little obligation to resolve his stories in favor of the ordered state, Eriksson lets his detective plots implode.

This is less the case in his earlier novels, which adhere more closely to the Mankell model of critique and eventual resolution. *The Princess of Burundi* (2002) has two killers: one a vicious racist psycho, Vincent Hahn, who seems loosely based on John Ausonius; the other a more mundane fellow who stabs to death a small-time crook nicknamed Little John over money. In both cases, either environmental or psychological factors are shown to be entirely responsible for the murders. The Uppsala-based detectives (Ann Lindell is nominally the hero, but the whole squad functions as a central character) focus mostly on Little John's background and his failed attempts to get out of the poor neighborhood he grew up in and find a job. Berglund, the respected older cop who provides a moral center for the group, spells out this idea in one conversation: "There is a kind of culturedness that exists apart from the kind transmitted by schools and universities. . . . Once upon a time I think this kind of culture flourished in the neighborhood where Little John grew up, and it helped to stem the flow of today's lawlessness. Of course, there were scum in the fifties and sixties, but there was also

a social resistance that is lacking today." When Riis, another cop, tries to blame this change on the influx of immigrants, Berglund takes passionate exception, blaming instead the Social Democrats: "[B]oth Little John and Vincent Hahn are products of Swedish social democratic policy, our so-called People's Home."

But this point of view raises an intriguing problem for detective fiction, something that even Mankell has never quite plumbed: If the state is to blame for everything, why should we be punishing individuals? Eriksson's most recently translated novel, *The Demon of Dakar*, bursts the limits of the detective plot in a decisive way. The murderer in *Dakar* is an immigrant, Manuel, a Mexican who comes to Sweden to find his brother Patricio in jail for drug smuggling. To get the money owed to Patricio (and to avenge his brother, Angel, who died on another run), Manuel tracks down the two drug dealers who employed his brothers, kills one of them, and takes a job in the other's Uppsala restaurant, Dakar, as a dishwasher. The kitchen at Dakar is a mini UN: other employees are from Portugal, Spain, Finland, and the US. "And we are all gathered here," says one of them, in case we missed the point. "In Dakar's kitchen." The group becomes tightly bonded, and Manuel even begins a flirtation with Eva, the Swedish waitress.

Although Manuel comes plotting revenge, Dakar becomes a place where he manages to regain his humanity among other outsiders. In the end, after Patricio is sprung from jail almost by accident, the two brothers slip through Ann Lindell's fingers to return to their village in Oaxaca.

In that sense, *The Demon of Dakar* is a police novel turned almost entirely upside down—the logical conclusion of the process that begins with Mankell's doubts about society's responsibility for crime. Though Lindell and the other detectives remain sympathetic characters, the author is clearly rooting against them. The people who aid Lindell in the manhunt for the two brothers are generally racist: one speaks of "a dark-skinned man of suspicious appearance." A certain justice is carried out when the drug dealers (foreign but white), who are presented as the actual bad guys, are punished, one shot by Manuel and one finally imprisoned by the police for drug possession. But the murderer at the center of the novel (and the focus of the detectives' exertions) takes no legal responsibility for his actions—and the detection plot becomes a sinister tool of white oppression. There are higher laws, *The Demon of Dakar* suggests, than our little bourgeois schemes of crime and punishment.

—Britt Peterson

KICKSTART MY HEART

Shire Pharmaceuticals. Adderall. 1996.

AMONG CHILDREN BORN IN AMERICA IN THE late 1980s, my classmates at the San Francisco Day School must have been the happiest, healthiest, most unthinkingest cluster of them all. Our parents raised us to give thoughtful Bar Mitzvah gifts, walk or jog daily, recognize Kwanzaa. If the community was not quite anti-intellectual, it was certainly not a culture of quiet indoor pursuits. The weather was too nice, for one thing. And our parents, who hadn't attended Ivy League schools and didn't read literature, had yet done well enough to afford beach houses up the coast and a rainbow flock of Polar Fleeces. Among us, their offspring, there was no such thing as academic rivalry. We worked together if we worked at all.

This changed when I began my first year at the Ivy League university from which I recently graduated. There I met freshmen who had taken the SATs more than twice, who spoke three Asian languages, who began drinking coffee in middle school. "Things are different on the East Coast," I told my mother on a cell phone from the campus Starbucks, where I was conspicuously reading the *New Yorker* and hoping to make friends. The kids of the East Coast intellectual guard had a whole culture of rituals and objectives by which to define themselves: anticipation of the LSATs, the *New Criterion*, cocaine.

It was this New York and Boston–bred clique that taught me what I know about Adderall—or showed me, rather, since the drug is less talked about than exhibited. It is not hard to tell if someone has taken a lot of Adderall. His mouth will be tensed, his shoulders stiff, his gaze unwavering. Everyone looks the same after ten or so hours of untrammeled focus. During freshman year I got mine from Bronson, a sloth of a boy from Brooklyn whom I hooked up with at a party. Bronson was prescribed the drug for his ADD but it had a somewhat deadening effect on him, and he made extra cash by selling what he didn't use or want. Once a month I would visit him to sit on his dorm bed while he counted out pills from an organizer. There was a *Scarface* poster on the wall and on the mini-fridge, a jar of weed which Bronson would uncap and wave under my nose, as though it were single-malt scotch or chloroform. He refused to sell me his 20-milligram pills because he thought I might have a heart attack, so I took 10s.

ADDERALL COMES IN TWO FORMS: fast-acting and extended release. Fast-acting looks like aspirin and has a sweetish taste. In theory it can be crushed and snorted, though I've never seen anyone cut a line of Adderall purely for recreation. Bronson sold me the extended release version, marketed as Adderall XR, which resembles something that Neely would have chased with vodka in *Valley of the Dolls*. It is the Las Vegas of pills, an object that conforms so gleefully to every pill cliché that taking it feels cinematic. The drug comes in a gleaming capsule, blue or tangerine colored, and it can be swallowed or sprinkled over cafeteria applesauce. It is made of equal portions of four amphetamines, all of which the body metabolizes at different rates, and which are packaged in tiny rotund beads that dissolve at varied speeds, so the effect is consistent. A 10-milligram capsule lasts about six hours and a 20-milligram capsule doubles the duration.

It is difficult to know whether it is a drug itself or a drug culture that attracts certain people to certain substances. In the case of Adderall, I came for the culture and stayed for the drug. Nothing had ever tempted me before. As an adolescent girl, alcohol was closely allied with promiscuity, and I was a prude. Weed suggested foolishness and snacking, and I was foolish and hungry enough as it was. But then came college, and with it, Adderall—a drug associated with writing, thinking, and joyful, hermetic reading. Adderall Me and Ideal Me were nearly the same person, and I saw no reason not to dabble in my best self.

ADDERALL HAS BEEN on the market since 1996. It is produced by the British drug maker Shire Pharmaceuticals and is currently the 125th most popular clinical drug in America. The Shire website offers some vague information about ADHD, the disorder for which Adderall is prescribed, and warns that the consequences of untreated ADHD can include relationship problems, drug abuse, and frequent job changes. There is a link for people who are already taking Adderall. "Congratulations!" it reads. "By taking ADDERALL XR, you're showing your commitment to reaching your potential in all aspects of your life—and to being the person you were meant to be."

Once or twice a week during my first three years of college I'd dip into my supply of pills (I kept them in a turquoise Tiffany's case, to avoid crushing), gather a bundle of work, and incubate myself in the common room of the French House, where I lived. I had to be careful not to take the drug in my dorm room, because if I did, I might spend hours plucking my eyebrows or digitally altering photographs. The common room was a ballroom-sized space with a fireplace, wood paneling, velvet chairs, and a desk. It was a popular place among my housemates, but I liked to work alone in my Adderall outfit (a T-shirt with the armpits stained corncob-yellow from amphetamine sweat), so I would push all the furniture except one chair into an adjacent room and shut the doors. There were water fountains nearby and nobody bothered me.

The feeling begins about twenty minutes after you take the pill: a mental tightening, as though someone had refined your scope of vision into a narrow and penetrating line. All peripheral distractions disappear (you would make a very poor hunter or soccer player). There is a slight fluttering of the heart, and gentle, persistent waves of warmth that are not distracting unless it is hot outside. This is how I experienced Adderall; some people have panic attacks and others feel nothing at all.

Any actual amount of time spent under the influence is hard to describe, because time passes very quickly. It's a euphoric drug, but also an alienating one. If I took a pill with my morning coffee, it would wear off by early evening. All of my work for the coming week would be finished, and I could take an aspirin, shower, and go to bed. Having missed the transition from day to night as well as all three meals, my dreams would be hysterical, but I always woke the next day feeling chipper and accomplished.

FAKING ADHD IS A CAKEWALK, but the testing process is expensive. It is easier to buy the drug from those who already have it, for $2 a pill, or $3, or $5 if you are dim enough to make your purchase during finals period. The summer after sophomore year, stranded without Bronson and determined to write a novel, I found an online foreign pharmacy that sent encrypted catalogs of drugs to my Gmail account. Rohypnol, Valium, Oxycodone, Prozac, and Ritalin were all in stock—no Adderall, but Ritalin would do in a pinch. (Ritalin is the Salieri to Adderall's Mozart.)

I bought thirty tabs of generic Ritalin with a moneygram. It cost $50, but I was living at home that summer, and also, I reasoned, I'd save money on all the food I wouldn't eat.

"Who do you know in Panama City?" my mom asked when the package arrived. Inside was a folder wrapped in black sandpaper and a 'Smints container full of pills. The Ritalin lasted all summer, and in September I traded the leftovers for Adderall. When I ran out and couldn't locate any more at school (Bronson was abroad), I called a friend at Sarah Lawrence, who sent me envelopes of pills wrapped in tissue paper.

Like so many things at my school, Adderall consumption has a lot to do with money. One senses that the students who blow $100 a month on extended release capsules are the same ones buying prosciutto sandwiches for lunch instead of eating in the cafeteria. But unlike other drugs, Adderall doesn't lend itself to group consumption, so it is hard to tell who does it and how often. Adderall has no Kurt Cobain, no Snoop Dogg or Bret Easton Ellis. It's not as glamorous as heroin nor as benign as weed, and it is not a status symbol like cocaine. Adderall, after all, is a drug prescribed to kids who drop their pants in the schoolyard instead of playing hopscotch.

It is probably surprising that the drug backfired only once, when I stayed up on Adderall for seventy-two hours before a philosophy final. My appearance in the testing hall the next day was so tangled and shaky that the professor removed me from the room. I was sent away with permission to return later and finish the exam in his office. Instead, I slept. In the end it didn't matter that I failed the exam, because a semester of A+ Adderall papers had left me with a decent grade in the class. If the proof is in the transcript, then Adderall is hardly a self-punishing habit. Sometimes I think about how Marion Jones has to return all the prize money she earned while taking steroids, and I wonder whether I should be stripped of all the A's I received for papers written on Adderall. This is a haunting or a comical thought, depending on my mood.

Of course, I could have studied in college without Adderall, just like I did in high school—I just couldn't have studied with such ecstasy. Theoretical texts, in particular, were transformed into exercises as conquerable as a Tuesday crossword. I could work out in the gym with a Xeroxed packet of Gayatri Spivak perched on the elliptical machine in front of me, reading and burning calories at the same time. The efficacy of the multitasking was exhilarating. On Adderall, the densest writing became penetrable. I had an illusion of mastery, at least, that lasted long enough to write the necessary papers and presentations. I could never remember what I had written the next day, but I justified this forgetfulness as an accelerated version of what would happen anyway after I graduated.

More than anything, Adderall simulated the enthusiasm that a good teacher naturally stokes. For three years my brain, normally so recalcitrant, became my will's devoted vehicle. But there's a downside to a drug that makes everything interesting. By the end of junior year, I still had no idea what I liked or was good at. This past fall, when my senior year started, I took a break from the drug—at first because I couldn't find any, and then because I refused it. It took these four abstinent months to realize that I was not supposed to be electrified by everything I learned in school; that some of it had a vaccinating purpose, so that by trying a little now and reacting badly, I could fend it off later.

Finals period without Adderall passed slowly and pleasantly. It turned out that the feverish moral imperative to work was an effect of the drug, not a cause. I lingered over my reading and drank coffee to stay awake. There were no more ecstatic Joan-of-Arc-in-the-library experiences, no more imagined channeling of dead literary critics—but this, I suppose, is appropriate when what's at stake is only a fifteen-page essay on Jane Austen, double spaced. I turned in my last exam on a snowy Saturday morning and flew home the same day. It was twenty-seven degrees in Boston when I left and sixty in San Francisco when I landed, warm enough to jog without a Polar Fleece.

—Molly Young

OUR CONTRIBUTORS

Elif Batuman is a Senior Writer at *n+1*.

Thomas Bernhard was a novelist and playwright. He died in 1989.

Roberto Bolaño died in 2003. His posthumous novel, *2666*, is published by FSG.

Jace Clayton is DJ /Rupture.

Ceridwen Dovey is the author of *Blood Kin*, a novel.

A. S. Hamrah is the film critic for *n+1*.

Britt Peterson is on staff at the *New Republic*.

Damion Searls's *What We Were Doing and Where We Were Going*, a book of stories, will be published by Dalkey Archive Press in spring 2009.

Frederick Seidel's most recent volume of poetry is *Ooga-Booga* (FSG).

Wesley Yang's essay "The Face of Seung-Hui Cho" appeared in *n+1* Issue Six.

Molly Young is a writer living in New York.

n+1 *would also like to thank: Atossa Abrahamian, Will Augerot, Caroline Bankoff, Silje Bekeng, Joshua Cohen, Avi Davis, Morgan Frank, Molly Fischer, Elizabeth Huey, Hal Parker, Claire Pauley, Meriah Schultz, Liza St. James, and J. Kyle Sturgeon.*

LETTERS

WHAT THE MIRROR DOES

Hello Wesley,

Thanks for sending me that ["The Face of Seung-Hui Cho"]. I was mesmerized by it. It's a scarily good piece of writing. Can't think of when I read a piece about a mass murderer that was about identifying with him. You DO have a bad personality (so do I ((so do I (((ha ha)))))). In fact, funnily, I actually wrote that ("I had a bad personality") in the section of my autobio-in-progress that was recently published in the *Brooklyn Rail.*

I mean I identified with your piece in a way that was almost creepy, and was creeped out by it! There's also a passage in my novel *GO NOW* about identifying with an unnamed serial killer (it was Ted Bundy). Forgive me for so crassly responding to your piece by finding myself in it. But somehow I feel invited to! I don't mean to be flippant. It really is a great piece of writing, even if it left me with this strange emptiness inside. I can't help myself!!! Somebody stop me!

—*Richard Hell*

APOCALYPSE THEN

Dear Editors,

I have read none of the novels Chad Harbach reviews in "The End," and am now happy not to need to be planning to. They interest him because of their content, because of the ways their imagined future is or isn't plausible or like the past; Cormac McCarthy's *The Road* is "the best" of them not because of its "novelistic means" but because those means are "in line with its vision of a radically impoverished world." At the end of "The End" he asks, rhetorically, "Why bother dreaming up a devastated world when you live in one?"

It's a good question, but one that cannot be addressed or even asked within the range of Harbach's article. To say that "the bulky, unmemorizable novel" is "an oil-dependent technology" which requires the geopolitical system in which the present-day American economy is embedded is true only with an extraordinarily narrow definition of "the novel." Cervantes wrote novels, as did ancient Greeks; novels are shorter than the *Iliad* memorized by Greek bards or the inordinately longer Tibetan Gesar epic still memorized today. Mary Shelley's *The Last Man* of 1826 is not the first "post-catastrophic novel"—nor is Charles Brockden Brown's *Arthur Mervyn* (1798–1800, about the yellow fever epidemic in Philadelphia), nor *Robinson Crusoe,* nor even *The Decameron,* in which "Florentines fell ill daily in their thousands, and since they had no one to assist them or attend to their needs, they inevitably perished almost without exception. . . . In the face of so much affliction and misery, all respect for the laws of God and man had virtually broken down and been extinguished in our city . . . everyone was free to behave as he pleased."

No, post-catastrophe goes much farther back: we have Ragnarok in Snorri Sturluson; we have the Book of Jeremiah; in Aeschylus, *The Seven Against Thebes,* the chorus describes an apocalypse from which it turns out they will be spared, but which so many others have undergone. In Stephen Sandy's translation:

> do not annihilate our city
> and raze our homes to hearth- and
> foundation-stones
> One drags another off, butchers him,
> then torches the scene, all the whole city
> soiled
> with smoke and the god of war, raving
> trampler
> Man cuts down man; the wails of mothers
> meet
> the little cries of nursing infants drenched
> in blood. People fleeing take to pillage,
> your own kin join in rapine and robbery.
> Can words describe what all of this will
> mean?

The grudging argument that these scenarios are local, not global—that natural disasters or holocausts of war which leave a village or nation with no survivors, women and children burned alive, salt sown into the ground: that this "doesn't count"—is specious. When our geographical knowledge and range was smaller, there was less to be destroyed to constitute the destruction of our world. In other words, the apocalyptic imagination has been with us for centuries, for millennia, for as long, I am sure, as we have had imagination.

I don't mean this to be a quietist argument—"People have imagined the apocalypse forever, and the world hasn't ended yet, so environmentalists today are alarmist as well." I think they were wrong in the past, when they thought the world was coming to an end, and we, with our advanced, unparalleled systems of knowledge, are right; granted, every other generation before us thought exactly the same thing, but (like them) I think my generation is different. We are right. We know. The analogies with the past don't weaken my certainty of impending disaster; if anything, I know we are right because they were right too—Cherokee and Cathar and Carthaginian. Their apocalypse did come, as will ours.

So it may well be that the thoughtful, historically aware novelist can no longer console him- or herself with the dream of a possible posterity, as Harbach says. But writers have not "always" been able to do so—that security, that consolation, is the recent exception, not the timeless rule. It lasted a century or so, this justified faith in the power and importance of books. The fact that we, or some of the people we know, are old enough to remember this golden age makes its demise harder to take. But whether for reasons of technology, taste, or environmental apocalypse, it seems to be definitively over.

Taking a wider view, the way novelists—or imaginative writers generally—have mostly hoped to "matter" is religiously: the monk spending his life transcribing holy texts, or writing the scriptures on a grain of rice as a spiritual task. This was secularized by the Romantics into following one's Genius or indwelling Creativity; secularized further (but re-Judaized) by Kafka; and taken the final step by Borges (who still smuggled in Gnostic and cabalistic systems to do so). One's work matters not because of any dialogue with the future, but because of its immersion in the voices of the past, because you have synthesized something within your inner privacy and laid that synthesis at the feet of an abstract higher power, whether or not you call it the Throne of God.

That is the crucial missing piece of Harbach's "The End": he leaves out the beginning and the middle. His tone of entrapment and despair, this feeling of thrashing about in a vacuum—arguably like many of the tones of *n+1*, with its No Dead Writers policy—stems from isolation from the consoling and suggestive imaginations that have come before us (and have come true too). With no future, the obvious place we should look for community and significance, for our writing to "matter," is the past—we can write not for posterity but for the tradition, for and to and about the writers and thinkers we have read. Most writers do this anyway, outside the US at least.

If we are indeed at the end, let us make our work a fitting coda to what came before us. That is as worthy a goal as any we writers have left, and one we can't aim at with our sights set forward.

—*Damion Searls*

POLITICAL TERROR

To the editors:

Never mind that capitalism is to blame for the overwhelming share of violence in this era—and how much more so if you factor in the everyday brutality of exploitation? In "The Spirit of Revival," *n+1* joins in the reflexive violence-baiting of that system's revolutionary opponents.

Trotsky and Robespierre part of a "blood-drenched" tradition? No one but a psychopath likes to see blood spilled for its own sake. But this is a world where a lot of it gets spilled quite needlessly all the time, and those who are seeking to change that can't just shrink from the sight of it all. They must ask on which side it is being shed in what Marx called the only just war in history: that of the slaves against their masters.

And if that war ever had a general, it was Leon Trotsky leading the Petrograd workers in insurrection, and later at the head of the Red Army. Robespierre, of course, helped lead the most pivotal previous campaign in this same struggle. More people were killed on a daily basis in any of Napoleon's major battles than during the whole of the Paris Terror, but it's the latter that the exploiters remember as "blood-drenched"—because it was their blood.

—*Alan Horn*

FLEX WORKERS, FLEX!

Dear Editors,

Thanks to Nikil Saval ["Birth of the Office"] for his inquiry into the history of the architectures of the modern office, both physical and mental. Since his essay begins and ends with a call to collective organization, I thought it might be worthwhile to point toward some examples of what that might look like.

Many of the phenomena Saval discusses have been grouped together as the condition of "precarity" by theorists like Michael Hardt and Antonio Negri. Neoliberalism and the "Empire" of multinational capital prioritize the "flexible," "fluid," "free" movement of workers, which means removing restrictions on relocations, restructuring, and firing—and using the World Bank, the IMF, the WEF, and all those other acronyms we learned after Seattle '99 to force global acceptance of those standards of labor. Negri and Hardt also described the theoretical ability of capital to overcome and appropriate the freedom-seeking antiauthoritarian

(a few books that failed to make the world other than what it since has become)

24 TIMES, EXACTLY, AS MANY LETTER-SPACES AS WOMEN PHOTOGRAPHED

My days are given over to writing you letters. Nothing gives me more pleasure and never again shall I make complaint about the dearth of your correspondence. To date I have received a whole flock of letters from you none of which have I properly answered.

This is a swell day on Grand Lake. Having ~~nothi~~ little to do there is much time to think about the pleasant things that have happened in the past weeks. I like to look over the old lake when I get in these sappy moods so I just repaired to aplace where I could look around and contemplate the scene of our last year's adventures. The water is calm the sun bright and there seems more peace and contentment in the world today than I have known since I returned. Time's healing process. If it were not so much trouble and I had not to go to Deer Lake on Wednesday I would have launched myz boat and gone for a cruise-probably to Hind's Brook. Now if you were here I would not think it any trouble at all to do that. But alone it is not so interesting.

Green just telephoned to say that he had a case of pneumonia for me,two mat. cases just ready to bust and that Mrs. Green had baked a host of mince pies for my specia delight. That's what I call good news. With the excellent warm day this warms me. The prospect of more comfortable quarters, better food and the chance to see a few more peoplex bucks me up. This place seemed pretty flat when I got back. I had never realized the lousy conditions under which I have been living, the meagre diet and what a total lack of agreeable human companionship can do for one. I do think that you saved from a life like this. I was fast slipping into a final acceptance of this life as my lot.

ONE OF OVER ONE HUNDRED LETTERS SENT IN THE MID-'30s FROM NEWFOUNDLAND TO A WOMAN WITH A CLOSE FRIEND WHO WOULD BECOME THE LAST SURVIVING SURVIVOR OF THE GENERAL SLOCUM DISASTER

SEARCH FOR TO READ MORE

WHATEVER HAPPENS

MEANS THAT THE WORLD WAS ALWAYS STRUCTURED SUCH THAT IT COULD HAPPEN

IMPLIES A COSMIC GROUND OR MATRIX ALWAYS HAVING HAD THE PROPERTY OF THAT HAPPENING AS A POTENTIAL

THE COSMOS[1] IS ALIVE[2]

1. Itself. The whole thing. 2. Literally. With Earth a part of it, in what sense could it NOT be?

THE PRECISE THEN THAT LED TO THIS NOW

"As long as man continues to be the ruthless destroyer of lower living beings he will never know health or peace. For as long as men massacre animals, they will kill each other. Indeed, he who sows the seed of murder and pain cannot reap joy and love." - attributed by Ovid to Pythagoras

Mrs. Green had baked a host of mince pies

movements of '68 and to adopt their discursive structure. The current trend toward "microfinance" is arguably just a continuation of those terms—promoting a capitalism of individual autonomous workers without social networks, each working only for his or her individual profit.

In post-industrial countries like France, Germany, and the UK, precarious office workers, many of whom are young and work as "temps" or "flex workers," began several years ago to organize May Day protests against their working conditions. In 2003 or '04, the anti-precarity movement coalesced around San Precario, the patron saint of temp workers in Italy, where protests against precarious working conditions often take the form of carnivalesque processions down city streets. In 2004 Serpica Naro, a fictitious fashion designer whose name was an anagram of San Precario, was entered into Milan Fashion Week to draw attention to the movement. French youth held massive protests in 2006 against laws that would make it easier for them to be fired and ultimately defeated them. Of course, then Sarkozy was elected and Berlusconi re-elected.

Meanwhile in America, all news of these organizing potentials has been subsumed, first by the War on Terror and now by the Race to the White House. The only way to remove the cubicle that they've put in our head is to stop prairie-dogging and start standing together.

—Ethan Heitner

GERMAN CANDY BOMBERS

Dear Editors,

I thought that you would be pleased to hear: an old friend of mine who is working at Heidelberg University told me he'd just read a note in *Zeitliteratur*—the literature section of *Die Zeit*, which I think is easily the best paper in Germany—referring to *n+1* as *ein Rosinenbomber voller originalen Gedanken*—"a candy-bomber full of original ideas." Congratulations.

—Moira Weigel